Dedication

To my beloved Earth

~ and ~

To all those rare souls
who have realized
the wonder of its blessings

Primal Thought

There is a creative force, a
universal substance, a supreme
consciousness, an ultimate
reality ~ I call it
'the Absolute'
~ everything in this book
will stem from this truth.

Table of Contents

Within A Miraculous Realm
by
Richard J. Oddo
'A Spiritual Warrior'

First Edition ~ Feb. 1988

All essays, poems, parables and
stories are handwritten and edited
by the author

All artwork is hand drawn
by the author

Ninety five percent of all material,
printing and mailing costs have
been paid for by the author, with
the remainder coming from
loving donations

This book is Published by ~
Richard J. Oddo
Spiritual Warrior Press
P.O. Box 7012
Halcyon, Calif. 93420

ISBN: 0-945637-00-4

A Warrior's Predilection

Freedom is above and beyond the manifestation. It is its soul, yet not bound by, for it is the link between the manifest and the Absolute.

Our heart is freedom's temporary home of emanation, and physical existence is freedom's appearance; the mind is unconditioned freedom, while our thoughts are illusions of freedom — all are of one spiritual reality, and freedom is its essence.

I am a spiritual being whose only attribute is freedom. Freedom is the eternal spark of the Absolute coming into manifestation. It is my sacred trust to nurture my freedom through the experience of living, ever conscious that my freedom is my true nature and primal essence of my spirit. Ever present in this moment, my freedom will shine forth to share its vibrant gift of love; for the call will come soon, and I shall return my freedom back into the oneness . . .

Art Plate #2 ~ The warrior is joyful for no apparent reason. He is not blind to the sorrow and anguish of the world, but it has no more reality to him than a dream. The warrior makes it his conscious choice to dwell Within a Miraculous Realm...

Within a Miraculous Realm

My body is encased in a perception of mystery, and within it my spirit sojourns in freedom; for eternity has placed a precious moment before me, and it is my challenge to grasp its essence. I have humbly accepted the ways of a spiritual warrior, and live joyously within my heart — for here my spirit abides, and I need not travel upon this land any longer. My vision has taken me into a Realm of Respect, and it is a miraculous land indeed, for the wonder and mystery that enfold me can only be viewed by the soul. My essence of life is beyond this world, and within this eternal home I commune in peace, in a sublime tranquility of breathless wonder.

I feel the pulse of this universe and live in the flow of its energy, but this is only a mirror to the truth of existence which is already within me. I am here, and there is no where to go, and nothing to do, and nothing to seek — I am here in the midst of life, breathlessly watching its parade of wonder, and rejoicing as it unfolds. What mystery has been woven into us — what a miracle we all are.

We are here, and yet we are not. Our essence is pure and whole within the Absolute, and we cannot stray from our home. Life is the ultimate challenge, and it is our prayer of existence. Today I will walk thru this lush field of aspens, but the reality of my essence will forever be journeying Within a Miraculous Realm.

I have chosen this symbol to represent the higher nature within us all – it is our manifested true self as aspect of the Absolute, and is present universally and equally in all. It is our true nature that perceives this world, and is likewise present as the perception, for perceiver and perception are one, and cannot be divided. The enclosing circle represents the undifferentiated whole of the Absolute, for there is one reality, and we abide within the encompassing totality as the essence of its manifested form. We are the universal expression of one pure energy, and as such our true nature is the life and essence of the one ultimate Reality . . .

Preface to 'Wanderings of the Heart'

Scattered throughout this book are eight of my personal adventures that have etched a memory within my heart. They all carry the same title, but each is a unique experience of an unforgetable occurrence; one that not only had great beauty and challenge, but also heightened my spiritual awareness. For my hiking is very much my meditation, and each one an avenue to raise my consciousness. This is the attitude of wonder I strive to maintain, and it sets the mood for my adventures, as I sojourn within this increadible realm. And as I walk breathlessly within this mystery of perception, I have found the realization, that it is not in this world that I humbly and respectfully walk, for my spirit has taken me wandering within my heart . . .

8

Granite or Crystal

The mind may be expansive, vibrant and unlimited, but words and books are not. There are a few hundred words that express the inner feelings of the heart, and every spiritual book contains these same words, mixed together in every conceivable order. There is only one truth, and each attempt to speak it or write it, is merely the re-ordering of the same overused, limited words. The same basic truth has been repeated thousands of times, by thousands of different souls, all thru the ages. In person they were able to convey a vibrant energy of life along with the words, but in a book this vital energy is missing, and must be supplied by the reader. Thus even if a book be full of truth, few will be able to understand it in its limited, dead form. So here I present another dead piece of literature, by an untrained, simplistic author. But within these pages I present my heart, with the hope that this dead book has energy vibration — for even though a rock be dead, it can still transfer energy if its form be of crystal. So within this dead treatise I have given my love and soul energy, in hope that my sincere, dedicated life of freedom as a spiritual warrior will be conveyed. May you find within these pages the love with which they were written, and a catalyst to spark your realization of the divinity that you are. And may this book not be as a dead piece of granite to you, but have the energy and vibrancy of a clear, pure crystal ... LOVE R

Spiritual Equals

We are all spiritual beings of freedom — there are no differences of sex, color or belief when it comes to our spiritual identity. The Absolute has no aspects of conceptualization, no distinctions and no dualities. We are spiritual essence within the Absolute, and even though in physical form of sex and color, the spirit within us all is the one, undifferentiated, pure Absolute. We are one family within the fabric of manifestation, and all humans are of the same brotherhood, no matter if they be man or woman. The biological differences are for function within this magical realm, but the spirit which brings life to us all is beyond time, space, form, birth and death, and I see one and all as this divine aspect. So for convenience of writing, I will use in this book the masculine pronouns of 'he', 'his' and 'him', but in all cases it is the intent of this author that both 'he' and 'she' be indicated. Both man and woman are exactly equal spiritual beings, and this simple realization is needed if harmony of human relations is ever to happen. There is no superiority of physical form — greatness comes thru understanding and living fully in spiritual realization, and both man and woman are exactly equal in opportunity to grasp the truth and live fully in its light. Everyone of us has within them the potential to rise to the highest light. It is our determination and sincerity which creates the possibilities, and the possibilities are limitless, no matter who you are. We are all spiritual beings, and anyone can lift themself to the freedom of a spiritual warrior, and live in realization of their true spiritual nature.

A Spiritual Warrior

I call myself A Spiritual Warrior, yet I am dedicated to peace. My battle is personal, and at all times I am in a state of vigil, as I fight the delusory ignorance of my worldly nature. We all abide within the world, but a spiritual warrior recognizes a higher nature within himself, and fights to maintain this realization moment by moment. My war is peaceful, and I am in no jeopardy of defeat, for my spiritual essence is the only reality; but the battle I wage is one of remembrance, so that I will not slip into delusion. I fight my own slothful ignorance within this battleground of manifested relativity, and the weapons I use are my sincerity and respect; and I have reaped a worldly victory of joy and love, within this miraculous opportunity to experience the battle I call life, for it is the most glorious challenge our spirit can accept.

Gone are the days of weak acquiescence; an inner strength and courage is necessary to face a spiritual life. The war I wage is to realize my true self nature, and abide in the truth of its being. But, just because I call myself a spiritual warrior, it doesn't mean I honor a spiritual concept you can relate to. My vision is inward, and my revelations unto myself, for I cannot be generalized or categorized — my individual expression is unique, and my relation to the world is in sharing this uniqueness. Thru the mastery of my life, I have come to understand one fact — I am a free spiritual being within the essence of the absolute. And because I fight to maintain this realization, and live the simplicity of its truth, I humbly and respectfully call myself a Spiritual Warrior . . .

The Absolute

Throughout the ages, man's highest potential of understanding has been to develop a relationship between creation and creator. Every society has had its aspiration linked to the primal questions of origin — 'Who am I?', 'Where am I?', and 'What is God?'.

I am a spiritual warrior, and I can only supply the warrior's view as to the basic questions and doubts of life. In a book, names are necessary for relating, so I will integrate all the personal and impersonal names associated with the Divine, whether it be The Reality, Primal Energy, Tao, The Void, Creative Force, Brahman, Great Spirit or all the hundreds of other names, and use the wording 'The Absolute' to indicate the ultimate reality beyond thought, and use the word 'God' to be the personal aspect of the Divine within manifested existence. But even though I have given a name to the ultimate reality of life, I do not conceptualize a form. The warrior names for the sake of convenience, but does not identify, analyze, conceptualize or give form or attributes to the name. The Absolute 'is', and there the thought process stops. No matter what your attitude, one is faced with the fact that there is 'isness'. If you identify with a creation, or a divine energy, or a pure reality, or even a void that contains all, one has before him the primal substance of an 'isness'. Even if one says there is nothing, this initial nothing is still something of differentiation. In the dualities of something and nothing, a warrior goes beyond to a point of no concepts, and simply says 'The Absolute'.

Within thought, God is only a concept, and whether it be a personal God, or an impersonal reality, one's concept of God is still just a thought process of the mind, and the concept one identifies with, will dictate the God he will find and acknowledge. Every man and woman, no matter if primitive or sophisticated, will build a series of concepts to pin down every aspect of the creator called God. God is thus a product of their thought, and as such is but an illusion unto them.

A warrior has one profound realization and builds his world from it — The Absolute cannot be conceptualized, for it cannot be built or created by one's thoughts, nor is its existence dependent upon thought concepts. The actuality of the Absolute is the only reality, and that 'isness' will forever be fact unto itself, and no thought process can bring it into a higher light. For someone to study God, in the hope of understanding God's identity and attributes, is merely a search into their own conceptual thought. Man has built an identity with his thought, but since we are spiritual essence of the Absolute, thought cannot be our true identity, nor can thought ever be the reality of the Absolute.

In deep meditation thoughts are not present, yet one is still aware, for existence is not dependent upon thought. In a state of no thought, one abides as pure essence of the Absolute, for in its reflection we are God in manifested actuality. There is no birth or death of the spiritual essence of our being, we simply 'are', and all existence is part of that 'isness'. The questions of 'why', 'how' and 'where', in relation to this manifestation, are not part of the warrior's concern. A warrior recognizes his existence, and grasps this unique opportunity to traverse this mysterious experience called life, for each moment is the adventure of a miraculous perception. At this very moment, the analysis of the present moment is superfluous. If one tries to analyze the moment, then one will lose the precious realization of it, for the Absolute 'is', and does not reflect upon itself, but rather reflects thru itself. The Absolute does not yield to questions and answers, for it is the totality, and thus self explanatory and self evident. It is complete and whole, and in no need of discovery; thus we all abide within it, in varying degrees of consciousness, as the moment fulfills itself.

Past and future are not a reality within the Absolute, for they are thought concepts within our mind, and thus are illusory. The moment is here and the warrior lives it, not questions it — to a warrior, this very moment of existence is God. Since he knows that the moment and God are within him, he drops the concepts completely, and simply resides in the non questionable reality. Thus God is no longer an illusion to a warrior, for God is not a warrior's concept. God is not an attainment of a conceptual goal, but rather a realization of spiritual union to be lived in the present moment. If one could attain God, then one could lose God — God is not outside or inside, God is the only reality, and everyone and everything is part of this one encompassing totality.

Reality is not a thought concept to figure out, but an experience to live. With no questions, there are no problems; and since we are the spiritual essence of the Absolute, then there are no goals of discovery, or paths of attainment. And since we all must be here in this ever present moment, then none of us has any hurry to get anywhere. With no rush and no goal, one becomes desireless and unattached to the world's folly, and instead abides in a constant awareness of the spiritual reality of this present moment. The warrior views the manifested world as a mystery — not asking where, how or what it is. Whether illusion or reality makes no difference, for illusion is also part of the totality of the Absolute. The warrior is in this perception of manifestation, and whether dream or not, his actions have volition — so he dedicates to a purposeful life of understanding and challenge. This is the purity of a warrior's freedom; it is a simple life of spiritual realization, built of the manifested rocks of sincerity and respect. He knows he is spiritual essence, as actuality of the Absolute, and lives this realization; thus, with no path, goal or concepts to burden his heart, the spiritual warrior is free...

Parable - The Young Crow

Among the birds, crows are very wise. One day a baby crow was cawing with his friends, and their conversation puzzled him, so he went to the ancient crow, who just happened to be a warrior crow, and asked him, "all the other crows were talking about something called 'air'. They said we lived in it, and that without it we couldn't fly. They said we can go thru it, but that it was very strong, and could knock over this tree; and that water went right thru it, yet it can hold us up. I'm very puzzled; what is this 'air', and where exactly is it?" The ancient crow was very amused and answered, " the 'air' you are looking for is all around you, it is even within you. You cannot part yourself from it, for it is your home. It nurtures you, and gives life with each breath you take. It is always surrounding us, yet it is invisible and has no odor, sound, taste or feel, yet it supports all these perceptions by its presence. If it wasn't there, nothing else would be there either, for it holds everything in place, but has no body of its own. You can gently go with it, or it can carry you along, and its force is so powerful that it can shake the heavens. Since no one can find the 'air' by looking for it, you must simply witness its effects to be aware of its presence. And remember, all the mysteries around you, are held within the one supreme mystery called 'air'. "

Comment : The Absolute is the one reality in which are contained all mysteries. The manifest is our reality, but it is real only in relation to the true reality of the absolute. The Absolute is beyond all physical perception of sight, sound, taste, smell and touch — it is the essence of all perception, and sustains life within its fabric. It nurtures all life as its true home, and holds all existence in relationship within this realm of its mystery. If you wish to view the Absolute, then you must witness it by its effects. Your existence, and all of life around you, is the Absolute's miraculous effects...

Art Plate #3 ~ If you bring the light of spiritual wisdom to focus on any worldly form, you shall find the same equal aspect of the one reality within it. There is only the Absolute, thus all energy is of one essence, and the form is only reflective of the infinite possibilities that energy can adopt. We must view the form, but more importantly, we must remember and understand the essence that gives it life...

Sincerity

Nothing can be done till one is fully convinced they are a spiritual being. Only this conviction will bring about the determination and dedication necessary to bring one into deeper and higher realizations of life. This dedication a warrior calls sincerity.

To speak of conviction and dedication is easy, for words are easily preached, but a spiritual warrior is one who goes beyond words, to live his life as an outpouring of love, sharing and respect. A spiritual warrior is totally convinced of the one basic fact of life — that he is a spiritual being and essence of the Absolute, and life to him is the grand opportunity to unfold his spiritual wings in every situation of life; not just in a temple or church, but everywhere and at all times, for life to a warrior is a constant abiding in the truth of his divine heritage, and the joy of his ability to share his realization. His demonstration comes moment by moment, as he lives a life of steadfast determination to do his utmost to rise higher into the light within him. It is a pledge of sincerity to himself, through purity of thought and strength of action.

It appears as if a warrior was trying to earn his realization with his determined actions and sincere efforts, but a spiritual warrior knows full well that there is nothing to earn. We are the essence of the Absolute, and no greater goal can be attained, or truer path of life achieved, for our true nature is part of the totality, and in constant union as God. A warrior always does his best, but not as an attempt to earn or prove anything, for it is his sincerity of life which moves him to grasp this moment, and apply himself fully to it with love and respect. Thus the sincere actions of a warrior are his greatest joy and most cherished experiences, within a miracle he observes and unites with.

The endeavors of a warrior take on a different character than the action of others. For most persons, work is a means to some future goal, thus their heart is not into their current activity. A warrior works for no future goal, for the work itself, in this present moment, is his only goal; thus his heart is into whatever he does, for he feels blessed to be able to work at all. The action of work is just one way to experience the vast array of miracles that surround and weave thru us, for work is part of the divine experience of life, as its aspect of purpose and sharing. A warrior's sincerity builds his attitude, and work is just part of the outpouring of his respectful attitude, for his work is the outward appearance of the total dedication of mind, body, heart and soul. All his being is equally determined in his unity of purpose, to outwardly manifest the divinity within him. His spiritual work is expressed thru every action of his existence, and there is absolutely nothing else of any interest or importance besides his sincere and dedicated life to spiritual realization in this present moment. This is the spiritual warrior's only priority, as he lives the sincerity of his conviction.

Art Plate #4 ~ What difference would it make if my stomach was full, but my heart was empty — I might as well be dead. My body may starve, but as long as I am graced to roam this bountiful land of beauty and wonder, let my soul smell the flowers, and breathe in the fragrance of life's miraculous existence...

The Miracle

This marvelous, awesome, mysterious world is the grandest of all possible perceptions to behold; but if you cling to it, than you shall lose it. This miracle we call life is not understandable by intellectual thought, but it can be experienced by living in the miraculous 'now'. Life is a moment by moment happening, and any attempt to possess it or hold it, is to lose the present fleeting moment. Any attachment to the transitory, is to lose sight of the reality. As we perceive, the miracle unfolds within our heart and mind, but in our thoughts we distort the true miracle of what is happening, into what we desire. We paint the delicate present with illusion and fantasy of the past and future, thus we see no miracle, but only reflections of our thoughts and desires.

Observe this moment — look around you thru the miracle of perception, and examine this mystery that enfolds you. Can your fantasies ever build a more stupendous miracle than what is unfolding around you; and since your illusions didn't create you, then you are part of this awesome mystery. This is a marvelous, alive miracle that is within you and surrounds you. Is this not enough to awaken you to a dedicated life of grasping this wondrous moment fully. Realize the amazing fact that 'you are' — what an astounding miracle this is. A warrior is overwhelmed by this incredible realization, and dedicates each second to honoring its reality.

Every activity is a spiritual experience, for there are no common events — each occurrence of life is a miraculous explosion of wonder. We live, breathe and die by a miracle, and one phase of existence is not any more miraculous than another, for consciousness is our true nature. There is only elements of the earth contained in our body, and they all have the appearance of being dead matter when taken separately, yet we are alive. There is something within us, as a creative essence of the Absolute, and it brings life as conscious awareness into all manifest existence. This creative force is totally mysterious, and that is why we are the miracle that we are.

It is inconceivable that we actually possess unlimited perception. Everything necessary for this extravagant journey is present and within reach. To perceive this miracle is to bring the warrior into communion with life, for to touch the Earth softly and gently is the warrior's art. This beautiful earth is the provider of life, and it bestows everything necessary in abundance. To ask for more shows lack of awareness and respect for the increadible bounty already provided, and the most miraculous bounty is our unlimited freedom to experience each unfolding moment to the depth of our heart's awareness.

The depth and vastness of this vibrant, conscious miracle must humble even the greatest of minds, for we cannot even comprehend the immensity of its premise, let alone grasp its totality. Here a warrior bows his head in ultimate humility, humbled by his meagerness. His only consolation for his lack of understanding is the fact that he is part of this miracle. He is a free spiritual being, the essence of the Absolute, and a miracle unto himself. So he raises this fact over his head as a banner, and marches respectfully, sincerely and humbly into this miracle called life. The warrior rejoices with each new adventurous experience, accepting the challenge of living in the ever present moment, and dedicated to unfolding his wings of freedom into higher and deeper realizations of the miracle that he is.

Parable ~ Twin Sons

There was a man with twin sons, and on their 20th birthday he gave each a new car. Now, the two sons were of different nature. One son was after answers, he always looked to the original source in an attempt to understand. Thus with the car he saw a mystery to unravel, and set about the task of dismantling it, and trying to figure out all the intricate workings of the vehicle. Thru all his life he researched into the question of the car's performance, but at his death he was still mystified, and never once did he actually get to drive the car.

The other son gratefully and respectfully accepted the car. He also saw the car as a mystery, but his nature was to do his best to use the car as it was intended. Thus throughout his life he used the car well — for education, work and raising a family. At his death, the car was also a mystery, but it had provided a means to commune closer with life's reality.

Comment : Life is a mystery. This miracle is put before us in relative existence. The sincere, conscientious man has two choices. He can try to solve and understand the mystery — but in so doing he will misname it, never figure it out, and lose the opportunity to ever experience the wondrous perception unfolding before him. He may have found communion with his source, but it will always be a searching, desirous and attaining form of communion, where separateness is formed as a selfhood seeking an intellectual bond within a higher reality.

The other choice is to acknowledge the miracle before us, and see that we are part of the mystery also — and as such, realize that we need not figure out or seek answers to life, but abide in our true nature with respect, sincerity and dedication. We can use this grand perception unfolding before us, and gain a great communion and realization in so doing. But no matter which course one may take, the mystery of life and God will forever remain a mystery.

Parable ~ The Mystery

There once was a planet where all the people became obsessed with solving the spiritual mystery of life. Work was stopping, and the civilized society was disintegrating. The people beseeched God so vehemently, that finally God appeared to the world and answered all the questions of life's mystery. Within a few weeks thousands began to die, for now they had no incentive, and life appeared meaningless — the mystery was gone, and with it went all the challenge of discovery.

Comment: The greatest of all miracles is mystery. This miraculous mystery is the spark that ignites our eternal and internal fire. We bemoan this path of finding our true nature, for this challenge of life presents many difficulties in understanding the meaning of life. But why create and cling to a problem. It is far more rewarding spiritually to look to this grand miracle of mystery, and abide in the challenge of discovery. Life is before us, what a grand adventure we have been graced to evolve within. Let us wander in mystery, and be ever respectful of this incredible opportunity to abide in the beauty of our miraculous existence.

Art Plate #5 ~ Life is the challenge of our
spirit — there is no need to make it stagnant
and dry, when it can be full of vibrancy and
wonder. There is no race to finish life's
miracle, for we are here to dance to the
song of our heart. Why speak your life as
a dry dialog, when you can sing it as the
poetry of your soul. In purity and
simplicity we can all share in the chorus
of life's miraculous song, and let us all
sing it joyously with an open heart ...

Joy

Joy is a warrior's supreme accomplishment, but the word joy has a unique meaning to a warrior. In the world, joy is associated with pleasure under favorable conditions, something good or satisfying to bring pleasure of thought or body. But to a warrior, this worldly joy is just part of the dualistic experience of life — his joy is beyond dualism, and intrinsic in itself.

To a warrior, joy is a state of being, regardless of the circumstances and conditions present. His enjoyment comes from living fully in the present, and seeing the challenge and adventure of this vibrant, miraculous, unfolding moment. His joy is present in whatever experience he is graced to witness, for each has the potential to bring knowledge, understanding and realization with it. Whether the experience be pleasurable, or the conditions favorable is not the factor that determines his joy. The warrior simply enjoys the experience of life, and extends it to all physical and mental activities. If a situation presents itself, the warrior is in the midst of it, enjoying the play and learning through it.

Warriors love to laugh, but their laughter isn't necessarily produced from the joy they experience. Their laughter is generated by the paradox evident in this world. Their laughter may arise for no outward appearance — the humor is within them, for they are witness to the irony of the ultimate paradox. All thru the ages, man has freely exchanged his precious time in the present moment, for illusion and fantasy thoughts of past and future. With his own thoughts he has forged a chain of concepts, desires and attachments. Man is free in the ever present 'here and now', and chooses of his own free will to be a slave to his concepts and thoughts. The warrior sees the irony, and has great compassion for the folly of the world's endeavors. He laughs as he dances thru this play, for he cannot take this transitory world seriously. The experiences of life come and go, and the warrior enjoys each one as the challenge of a grand adventure. And as perception appears and disappears before the windows of his heart, he laughs and rejoices at this incredible opportunity to be alive within a realm of dream and wonder.

Parable ~ The Song of Life

Two men were walking in the park. The sun was radiant, and the song of birds filled the air. One man joyously pronounced, "ah, how the beauty of their song fills my heart and feeds my soul." The other man replied, "that's a beautiful verse, but what exactly do you get from their singing?" The first man honestly answered, "well to tell you the truth, I really don't know."

Comment: We don't have to understand the song of life to appreciate the opportunity to hear it. All phenomena is a mystery—some will provide communion, and thus your spirit will soar joyously in freedom—other experiences will have no song for your ears. Don't try to figure out life, it is a marvelous mystery. Just listen for those miraculous moments when life is singing its joyous song of love, and walk serenely within its wondrous opportunity.

Respect

Thru all the years of my spiritual growth, I have tried to live within my heart. All my experiences were seen thru the insight of love, for I truly felt this to be the highest aspect of union with our source. Even though I still feel that love is the most primal virtue of my spiritual nature, I have slowly evolved my passive, unconditional love into a deep, heart-felt and ever active respect. It is a growing experience of union, thru an active awareness of my spiritual actuality as essence of the Absolute— beyond the wishful attitude of love, and into a devoted prayer that is my life.

Love is often blind and spontaneous, and it can also end. Respect goes very deep, for it grows slowly and is nurtured by the experiences of life, and as it grows it is strengthened by the awesomeness of this mystery, and the sheer marvel of our existence. Love is my staff as I wander, but it is within my respect that I sojourn. This manifestation is perfection itself, as the inconceivable stroke of the ultimate reality. I can only do my part humbly and wander it breathlessly, ever alert and aware within this wondrous being of existence we call the universe, for it is alive to its last atom, and each second breathing forth in creative genius. How can I not feel awed by the miracle of this stupendous masterpiece; how can I not feel from the depths of my soul a love beyond love, so deep that I can only allude to its grandeur, so deep that no words can ever describe the warrior's joy of living. But in this glorious moment, a warrior recognizes the ultimate love, and humbly calls it respect.

Wanderings of The Heart

Arches National Park ~ September 1982~

We live in a realm of miracle. In southeast Utah one can easily breathe the power and magic in the air in the autumn months.

The day was crisp, bright and sunny as I traveled thru Arches National Park to a less visited area called Klondike bluffs. There I explored its fantastic array of sandstone formations, which holds arches, pillars and windows within its secret fold of massive stone ridges. Finally as the sun beckoned to the horizon, I viewed a column of stone rising out of the top of a craggy rock ridge. The west side of the ridge had a sheer 200 foot drop, so I approached from the east side which afforded some easier climbing. Once on top of the ridge, I very carefully climbed up the 75 foot, crumbly stone pillar til I reached the peak, which fortunately was flat and about three feet in circumference. Since the view was outstanding, I decided to sit and meditate, and watch the sun set over the 12,000 foot peaks of the La Sal mountains. I very carefully removed my clothes, being ever so cautious to maintain my balance while removing my pants, and then I made a nice cushion from them. It was warm and still sunny, but big, white, fluffy clouds were approaching extremely rapidly from the north-east and backing themselves up against the La Sal range. My view was outstanding of the Colorado river drainage, and all the fantastic canyons it has created. My view stretched unimpeded in all directions, and I could see a surrounding ring of mountains, including the Roan and Book cliffs, the Henry's and the Abajo's, which had been sliced thru by canyonlands. I was being gently caressed by a soft breeze, but the white puffy clouds were racing above my head and pressing harder and more compactly against the La Sal peaks, and were quickly turning themselves into a thick, dark gray menacing mass. The clouds were in a thin layer, so I still was enjoying my bath of sunlight. All of a sudden a peal of thunder cracked forth, which was rapidly followed by one bolt of lightening after another. It was as if an incredible grand show was being heralded to start for my exclusive viewing. Even though there were clouds in front of me by only a few miles, I continued to remain in the sunshine, with no strong wind or rain ever reaching me. The rain began to dump down in torrents on the desert floor below me, as it quickly turned into a flash flood careening down Salt Wash. The lightening was flashing in quick succession from the black canopy of clouds, yet the top of the clouds were still white and fluffy. Within 30 minutes the clouds expended themselves, and all the rain and lightening ceased, as the clouds broke into billowy clusters that allowed the sun to shine its filtered rays thru the patches of clouds, giving the entire panorama the most celestial feeling one could imagine. But the show was not over by a long way, for all of a sudden the sun and clouds joined at just the right angle, and there exploded before me five giant rainbows that stretched a 1000 feet each, from the desert floor up to the scattered cloud canopy above, with the magnificent La Sal peaks silhouetted behind the glorious array of colors. I was beside myself in joyous ecstasy of wonder, for the miracle before me was beyond description, and unfathomable even when viewed in person. The glorious vision lasted for 20 minutes, til the sun slowly descended behind the La Sal mountains, and then a new array of colors lit up the sky in magnificent splendor. The brightly colored rocks of Utah were matched in color, as the sky and clouds lit up in florescent hues of red, orange and gold from the sun's dying rays, and ever so slowly darkened themselves into magentas and purples. I was lost in a realm of wonder, but realities head suddenly arose, and I realized that my lofty perch was a dangerous one at best, let alone attempting a descent in the dark. So I carefully stood and stretched out my arms to say my loving fairwell to this miraculous desert, that had given me such an awesome display of its power, and to offer my sincere respect for this unique opportunity to perceive and experience, which is the greatest treasure that life can bestow.

My legs were a bit numb, and getting my clothes on was no easy trick, and even harder was descending the pinnacle with no light, but my joy was so overwhelming that I felt I could fly even if I did fall. The euphoria of the experience was so superb, and I had communed so completely with this wondrous realm, that at that moment I felt would surely be a great time to die. And as I sat in reverie that night, I realized that it was also an excellent time to live.

Art Plate #6 ~ What difference does it make if one is balanced upon the smallest pinnacle, if he has the ability to fly. This pinnacle of relativity cannot bind our spirit, for the place in time and space that we are balanced upon, is still the firm foundation of the Absolute; and why should we fear, for if we drop to the abyss below, we only return home within the totality of our essence. Hug the pinnacle, or soar in freedom, either way you remain within the totality...

Art Plate #7 ~ Freedom has no bounds—
it grasps this experience of life, but does
not cling to it. This precious gift of freedom
is our true spiritual essence, and on its
wings we can soar magnificently within
this realm of wonder...

34

Freedom

We are all free souls of the spirit, unique signatures of God. A warrior lives this freedom — right here, right now, in every activity of his life. By the exercise of his free will, he becomes master of his life — he is no one else's master, or does he bow his head to anyone. A warrior's actions are his own, his freedom is his responsibility. He endeavors to erase all conceptions, prejudice, fantasy and comparison — they are barriers to realization. The warrior strives to arrive at a state of living where he is free in the moment, with no thoughts, pure in action, and with love as his guide. Without a life devoted to love and sharing, his path would be dry and purposeless. He gives of the freedom of his heart, for he has everything necessary for this extravagant journey called life. He recognizes this miraculous opportunity to share of his love and express his freedom.

Freedom is our true nature, it is the pure inherent spark of our spirit's essence. With each desire and attachment, we forge a chain to anchor us to the world of form, thought and concept. To break this chain, and live free in our original pure nature is the essence of all spiritual life. No one can give you a map of 'do's and dont's', or 'rights and wrongs', this is acquired thru the maturing of one's consciousness. It is the nurturing and growth experiences of life that provide the necessary perspectives. Thus a warrior welcomes all situations to bring the possibilities of growth and insight, and he accepts validation only unto himself.

A warrior is willing to change and adapt his life as often as the circumstances of the moment dictate. He does not seek stability, for this will eventually cause complacency, and a subtle rigidity into accepting the stationary positions concepts — thus his freedom slowly wanes and his purpose dissipates. A warrior is perpetually pushing himself, and providing the circumstances of change and constant growth. In this way he remains flexible and always aware of his priority in life, and alert to the opportunities presented before him.

This is a solitary journey to awakening — others may be present, but the path is of inward realization. If there is no one present of equal dedication to share of your joy, then one must sojourn alone. If others be present, then let there be a glorious chorus to joyously sing of the spirit — but if no one be there, then accept this moment and sing alone. A warrior does not seek the company of those who do not live true to themselves, and are not dedicated to living a life of ever deepening realization. One must have no fear to interact and relate to the world, but your precious freedom and time should be shared with those who are likewise dedicated to freedom. Love and share with all who come into your life, but only seek out those who are true to the freedom of their soul.

Each individual has different ways, but that is no barrier for two spiritual souls to commune in the adventure of life. Nation, religion or philosophy is no hinderance to the free, dedicated souls of this world joining in the mutual celebration of life's bountiful challenge. We are all brothers and sisters of one spiritual nature, expressing ourself thru this manifested miracle — let us all join, and share the love of our heart and the freedom of our soul. But even if you find others, or if the whole world joins in, this is still an inward journey of revelation — and no one can guide your heart and mind, as you traverse this solitary road back home. Your realization is your responsibility, and in acceptance of this challenge you gain purpose and freedom.

A warrior's life is one of complete freedom. No outside influence, like money, job, prestige or family can alter his life of spiritual living. His dedication and sincerity is a pledge to himself, and he asks no one of the course his heart must steer. He is a spiritual being of the Absolute, and need call no one master—his channel is direct to God.

The illusion of the world is a powerful influence to keep one chained in slavery. But the desires and attachment to the duality of the world is only the first chain to break, and it is made easier when one has experienced the incredible bliss, thru love of a master or saviour. This love thru surrender is the most difficult chain to break, for it is at this time that the devotee has the most joyous time of his life. But freedom means no attachments—one can realize the Absolute only if unattached and desireless, and the attachment of a devotee for a saviour or master can be formidable. So eventually, if one is to become a warrior, his religious concepts will drop him. Otherwise he will always be a devoted religious follower, and a warrior follows no one — neither a person or a concept. A warrior loses his superficial contact with God, and develops a direct knowing, based in realization of his true nature as the spiritual essence of God. A religious concept can be a joyous concept, but it is a limited concept, and not complete freedom — God is not a limited concept, and the Absolute is complete freedom.

Not many are of the mood and realization to pass thru the bliss of worship and ritual, to come into a direct understanding of the Absolute. As long as there is a master, saviour, religious object or holy place between you as a spiritual being and God, then you'll never taste complete freedom. There is only God, and you are part of that totality — no arbitrator or mediator is needed for your holy contact. You have a direct link to your source, and need look no further than your true nature, which is the essence of God. God is, therefore you are. No amount of reasoning or conceptualizing will ever figure out the simplicity of it all. You are that which 'is' — a warrior abides within this absolute freedom, and will attach to nothing, and desire nothing — he is the Absolute, and is already one with everything.

Even though a warrior is free, he still has the same basic needs as anyone. He acquires what his simple needs require, no more or no less — but he does not expect these needs to be fulfilled. They are a gift of perception, and treated with respect and reverance, but with no attachment or expectation. If one, or all of them is removed, he will not complain or be bitter, or have regrets. He can die thru the lack of needs, but he won't feel cheated in life, for he formed no attachment to his needs, or to his life. He lives joyously while the opportunity exists, and when the process of bodily death arrives, he experiences it as one more mysterious adventure. While roaming this wondrous realm, he uses and rejoices — but when it is time to leave, he says his loving farewell and focuses on the new perception of awareness. He has no time for regrets, only time for realization.

Every act of recognition and identification of an 'I' or 'selfhood' in time and space extracts a piece of freedom. With name, job, property, watch, home, bills and other social dependence goes a loss of simplicity, and a tightening of the free expression of life. The true cost of any activity, object or thought, is measured in the loss of freedom it extracts — count your costs in freedom lost. Unless one be desireless and unattached, then each activity, object and thought will bind one in illusion, and extract freedom. Just let life smoothly and harmoniously interact around you, watching this joyous show, and not trying to possess it or control it. This is the art of the warrior — to live fully, but not cling to it.

A warrior has nothing to defend. His life and possessions are simple, and his way is clear. He does not try to possess, control or cling to objects, or his thoughts — he has nothing but his freedom, thus he has nothing to defend. All paths or ways are built in the thought, they are illusion of concept. A warrior stays free of his thoughts, and is guided by his inmost spirit. His true nature of spiritual being is ever free and unattached, thus not in need of seeking or discovery — it is free and clear of thought, and the warrior abides in that freedom. If no path need be taken, and no goal is to be reached, then the warrior need not defend his ways — his every endeavor is the dedication and sincerity of his spiritual freedom. Desireless, unattached, free of thought and concept, he is as a 'no one', yet he's alive and vibrant, but still he is no one. The warrior is in the moment, here and now, totally free and with nothing to defend.

There is a very subtle balance in a warrior's attitude. He can perform the same activities as someone else, but there is no hurry in his actions, no rush to be on to the next situation — he has nothing pending. Because of this nothing pending attitude, he can perform each activity to its optimum — whether he be making dinner or walking in the woods, each action is given his full attention. No situation or activity is any less important than another — all are equal in his eyes, so there is no rush to finish one activity to get to another. His purpose and challenge of existence unfolds in the moment, in each and every action he embraces. In this very moment, right here and now, no matter what he is doing, it is the most important activity of his life. The warrior has only this moment, and to live this moment fully, in the awareness that it is his life's experience in miraculous unfoldment, brings him freedom and realization. With nothing pending, he must do his best now — with nothing pending he can live in this moment, unattached and desireless, and without thought, concept or clinging — with nothing pending the warrior dances in this miraculous moment to the beat of his heart, and is free...

Art Plate #8 ~ From within us the light of realization shines forth to illume our perceivable world. Each one of us has the radiance of the sun, for we are all the same pure essence of the Absolute, and with this energy we light our world of consciousness...

41

Parable ~ Leap To Freedom

There were three antelopes in a city zoo, two had been born there, and one had recently arrived from the wilds of Africa. All day long the new antelope would lament over his lost freedom, and how beautiful it was outside of their compound. One antelope was of the mind that they had everything necessary where they were — food, shelter and safety. He complained of the confining space, and how much greener the grass was outside, but he had no wish to risk losing what he already had. The other zoo born antelope had the spirit of freedom within him, and attentively listened to the descriptions of the fields of plenty that the wild antelope spoke of. So after a few days he announced to the others, " the wild one has seen a far better life, I am now convinced and will take action tonight — join me in escaping, for I must now find my freedom." Late that night, the brave antelope took a mighty leap and jumped the fence, but the other two were afraid to go. So on went the brave antelope, sneaking thru the city park and down alley ways, heading instinctively for the mountains. It took all night and the next day of secretive travel, but sure enough, he did reach the mountains, and found luscious fields of tall grass with deer there to browse with. His joy was uncontainable; he had no idea the earth held such incredible bounty. Back at the zoo, the other zoo born antelope preached the danger of the attempt, and was sure the brave antelope was dead. The wild antelope was very sad, for his heart longed for freedom, and yet he had no

42

courage to strive for it. Everyday he stared at the fence and wished he could round up his courage, and leap to freedom.

Comment : We are all within the cage of the world, and locked within the compound of our concepts. Most will vigorously complain of the constriction of life within society, but nevertheless, they will still accept their position of dependence — for security of life is their main objective. They will never seek a freedom beyond their tight restrictions, for they know of no greater freedom, and refuse to believe that one exists. Some do have a great longing, and have tasted a freedom beyond the rigid structure of the world, but lack the courage necessary to begin the definitive journey. This is a solitary journey, with no guarantees or prescribed course — so they will stay locked into a cage of concepts and lament. Their heart will sicken, for they know there is a better way, and they will seek the company of other lamentors. There is a rare few, who once hearing of the possibility of freedom, are stirred from their slumber and take action — not calculating the costs or dangers. Once convinced, their warrior spirit must take purposeful action or they would die of sorrow. With dedication they strike forward, not knowing where to go or what to do, and yet their courage and purpose will safeguard them thru the alley ways of lessons and experiences — till they reach the green grasses of freedom. There they will find other free souls to commune with, and share the bounty of this world, and the love in their heart. Grasp your freedom, and know that you are not alone in your quest...

Responsibility

Your life, well being and spiritual realization are your responsibility, and no one else's. We are all spiritual beings, equal in the primal essence of the Absolute. We are all totally capable of mastering our life, and ruling our destiny. With relinquishment of our right of responsibility comes loss of freedom, and the loss of opportunity to live our true spiritual nature 'here and now'.

Now is the chance for you to awaken; thus it is your personal challenge to provide yourself with every circumstance necessary to realize your true self and live within its light. This miracle called life is no silly joke, your spiritual realization is at stake — it is your responsibility to live to the highest capability of your consciousness, for you are the divine essence of the Absolute, and each of your acts and thoughts has significance. Let your endeavors flow with purpose, for each act is the demonstration of your spiritual wisdom.

A spiritual warrior depends on no one, for at all times he is master of his life. No peer pressure or external force can make him do anything in detriment to his best spiritual judgement. He is master of his decisions and makes them carefully, based on spiritual intuition. He doesn't give the responsibility of his decisions to another, for they are his avenue of freedom and solely his determination. Once his decision is made, he frees himself of it and awaits the next experience of life — thus in letting his thoughts go, it allows his spirit to flow.

The warrior recognizes that other persons and books can provide a route of questioning, but the answers he finds only in himself, for he doesn't expect something exterior to give him what can only be found within. We are always surrounded by avenues that can spark insight, but no person, place or object can bring enlightenment to another. Awakening is brought about by a receptive attitude; it is a keen awareness which allows our consciousness to acknowledge the wisdom already present within us. We must be perpetually alert to grasp the catalytic circumstance which provides for our unfoldment into higher consciousness.

Within us is the provision for all our spiritual needs, and any looking to external sources will only bring disappointment, for thru dependence we relinquish our freedom. Never expect or desire others to do something you are capable of doing yourself; or to deliver God, joy, truth and happiness, or to provide something missing in your life — no external source can provide your needs, for within you is everything necessary, and any outward search will always go unrewarded. Your inner spiritual nature is awaiting recognition, thus it must be our priority to take every opportunity possible to demonstrate the abilities inborn within us, and abide in the confidence of our spiritual inherent capabilities.

A warrior does his best at all times, for there is no one to rely on for spiritual awareness and understanding. Realization cannot be bought or given away, so it is each individual's responsibility to do their utmost to live fully in the light of their pure spiritual nature. Grasp this rare opportunity to discover, for it is life's purpose to gain as high a realization as attainable. The only priority of life is to live as a spiritual being, in the light of our spiritual reality. Feel the freedom that has always been within you, and let it unfold into ever higher radiance.

45

The Peace Maker

A warrior's life is his prayer. He lives every moment as a dedication to the highest spiritual principles of love and sharing, fostering the deepest respect for what he is — a spiritual being of freedom. This is every warrior's way of purposeful action, but each warrior will have a different way of demonstration. Sharing is the spiritual warrior's purpose — without sharing, his heart and mind have no direction, and his freedom would go unfulfilled. A purposeful task is not only of necessity, purpose is the very life of our spiritual being — to find a meaningful task to enable its outpouring of love, is the only endeavor worthwhile in a spiritual life.

Once a warrior has realized his spiritual freedom, he must be perpetually alert to be able to be of service. Love and sharing are as possessions to a warrior, and he must give of them freely at all times and in all situations. The warrior does not set himself up as a judge to decide who to bestow his service to, he shares with all for the pure sake of brotherly love. He loves all unconditionally, no criteria must be met first — he loves, shares and gives of himself to everyone. He is master of himself, and judges no one else. We are all equal spiritual beings within the Absolute — God is the whole, and we are equal aspects of that totality. The warrior realizes this and humbly wishes to share, for in this oneness all activities are aspects of sharing (either negative or positive sharing), so the warrior makes his sharing one of love, joy and peace. He is blessed to be able to share, for thru his sharing he realizes his unity with the whole. The warrior loses his sense of self importance, and understands that he is not a separate reality unto himself giving out blessings, but that he is part of the whole, communing within himself as brother and sister. All his acts are in light of this universal brotherhood, of which we are all equal heirs within the totality which is God. Thru his sharing, he abides in the consciousness of deep communion with his source, and establishes his unity in the whole. Without love and sharing, a warrior's life would be like the bursting of an empty heart - like a shallow, stagnant pond, instead of a deep crystal lake, teeming with life, and overflowing to serve.

A warrior sees the trap of finding fault with the world, or his brothers. Life is here and we are part of it — there are no excuses, questions or answers, it is self explanatory and complete unto itself. The warrior harmonizes with life, and avoids the trap of comparison. Within comparison all negative emotions have their root. Comparison builds a vicious cycle — first one compares the given situation, object or thought; then immediately judges the compared relation in accordance to their concepts and established view; then in consequence one criticizes the supposed lesser or faulty of the two, and finally in time will come condemnation. The original comparison is a thought catalyst which invariably entails the other thoughts to follow — nearly all negative thought follows this pattern. All comparison and generalization is wasted thought and effort, for each item, place, person and thought within this perceivable manifestation is unique unto itself. Where all standards differ, how can comparison have validity. Look to the uniqueness of its wonder and mystery, not to the stagnant comparison of your conceptions. All thoughts of comparison

47

are futile, and in the element of time prove stagnating to the thinker. Thus a warrior avoids comparing, and always tries to see the individual quality and beauty of all separate aspects of life. Every person, circumstance and activity is a miracle of itself, and only in viewing its unique expression does one find realization in the harmony of this unfolding mystery of life.

The warrior is determined and dedicated in his ways of life, but he does not attempt to push his views unto others. Many warriors prefer not to speak their personal views, for how can a personal view be debated — so most remain master of themself, and their view their private kingdom. The warrior lets others live the course their heart dictates, and encourages them to seek more light and truth in whatever path they follow. Unless one comes to a warrior, and asks him to share of his wisdom, he has enough understanding and love not to interfere. If a situation presents itself before him, he will be ready to share — but he does not go around searching for situations to meddle in. He respects and loves others enough to let them handle their own affairs, but if he is needed, then his heart is ever ready to share in communion with his brothers. It is very difficult to leave other people and situations alone when one possesses the knowledge to correct them, but it is usually ego centered thought, or selfish desire, which makes one feel they should interfere. We cannot actually help others, we can only love, share, encourage and set an example by which others can learn to help themselves. It can harm others or a situation, to apply one's personal concepts of 'right and wrong' to circumstances external to them. Other persons or situations may be in the stage where they need to be, and if one hasn't been asked to help, then what he might feel to be helpful, can actually be a hinderance. If asked to help, the warrior lovingly applies his wisdom and energy, his offer of service is always foremost — but if his help is not needed, then he withdraws into personal communion of his soul. The world is not in need of saving, it is perfect in itself — it is not a mess to be fixed up. It is harmonious and whole, and it is our responsibility to harmonize with it, not try to change it. Live true to yourself, and keep seeking ever brighter light, and thus do the one truly beneficial deed you can do for humanity and yourself. In this way you can be an example of dedication and sincerity, and thus the 'whole' will rise correspondingly.

Within our circle of relations, it is common practice to hold others back with our thoughts. This is not a conscious effort, but one of being familiar with others, and wanting to keep everything in life stable — a fear of the inevitability of change. Everyone wishes to control the circumstances surrounding their life, and thus they extend it to holding everyone around them into a fixed conception, forming their attitude and consciousness. But nothing is fixed, and there can be no control. In their thoughts, they try to hold everyone to an assumed position, and refuse to acknowledge growth and change — thus they hinder other's opportunities of growth and learning, and dull their experiences of adventure. They lock others into a concept, and refuse to let them out, and this causes many problems in relating. Religious and spiritual persons make the same error, by not allowing

49

their brothers to advance and grow spiritually. They form concepts and expectations of the same muddled up person to be present year after year. Whatever realization and wisdom that has been gained by their brother, will be seen in the light of past years and compared to past ignorance, thus the wisdom expressed in the present moment will be missed. The interaction between the brothers, becomes the frustration of one brother trying to relate his new growth and insight, to another who is more inclined to hear of the old problems and failures. Thus their communication becomes stagnant, and the breakdown of friendships and relationships results. We are all in the process of growth, a continual evolution of changing, growing and evolving— some very quickly and pronounced, and others more slow and steady. A true sign of love and respect is to be aware that everyone around you is growing, and to share and encourage in their unfolding evolution. Love means to spur them on to higher light, not to hold them back with your concepts in your delusions of darkness. Life is a nurturing process, and we are all capable of being of tremendous inspiration, help and encouragement to each other. See your brothers as they are in the present moment, and provide the chance for them to rise higher than they were the day before. Don't hold anyone back by thought or deed, instead help inspire them to move forward into deeper realization. This is not a race or competition, we are here to share in the blossoming of consciousness. Those who gain realization of spiritual identity must share and inspire their brothers to reach to their highest potential. The dream of this warrior, is that the youth will use the greatest masters as stepping stones to ultimate realization, and in universal brotherhood find their freedom.

The warrior is not narrow or dogmatic, he is open to all ways of spiritual growth. He acquaints himself with religions and spiritual processes of growth, so as to be harmonious with his brothers, and understanding of their ways. All teachings, religions, philosophies and spiritual practices are part of the whole of which the warrior is part of, and because he understands them all, he understands himself. He has read the words of other religions and masters, but he speaks only the dictates of his own heart — never the thoughts and concepts of others. The mastery of thought is the warrior's greatest challenge. He is not trying to please the crowd, but to share communion of his heart and the depth of his spirit. His purpose is to maintain his words, thoughts and actions on a higher level than the divisions of religion and spiritual dogma. He is always trying to remain in the consciousness of the Absolute, and to raise others to this higher light where there are no divisions, but only love and sharing. There is enough division in the world. A spiritual warrior is one who bridges the differences, to share of the spiritual reality that we all can be one with. He knows that all of us are part of this unity called God, and that we are all one family, all brothers and sisters. We are all spiritual beings of this unique, miraculous manifestation, and we are all here to share the love of our heart and the wisdom of our being. He knows that we shall all unite in love one day, for the spiritual warrior is the Peace maker.

Art Plate #9 ~ Our love is so delicate. We are as any plant, and need an ample supply of the waters of compassion and tenderness. These are the vital nutrients that build our spiritual maturity. To starve one of love is to produce a barren wasteland fit only for the weeds of human brutality. Any fool can trample this childs spirit, and injure his pure heart of love. We are the guardians of his love, and it is our responsibility to provide a fertile ground for him to blossom. Nurture this child with the light of your soul, and in wisdom allow him to be pure. He will thus build no walls, and we shall all share abundantly of the fruit of his love . . .

Parable ~ The Beloved Hermit

There once was a very old hermit, a warrior of the heart. He lived outside a small village in a little hut, with few possessions and little money. His life was very simple; he had a nice garden and all the animals loved him — his life was full, and his spirit happy. Each day he would walk to the village, and if he heard someone speak that they were in need, the hermit would immediately say "I'll try to help" — even before they could say what kind of help they needed. He wasn't interested in the nature of their need, his interest was in sharing and helping in any need of his brothers. But since he was old, he couldn't work hard (though he would try), and he had little money or possessions to give (but he willingly offered them). The villagers would watch that no one took advantage of him, and made sure he didn't give away everything he had, or work himself to death. The village joke was — if you thought you were in need, then you should go to the hermit and find out how well off you really are. Even though they kidded the hermit, everyone loved him for his sincerity and willingness to share. One beautiful day the hermit passed away, and the news went thru the village. A collection was taken up, and everyone gathered to pay their last respects at his funeral. Everyone there had been helped in some way by the old hermit, and the tears were flowing at his passing. Everyone was so sad that their beloved hermit would no longer be there to share his love. The priest said he was honored to be able to speak the last words for such a fine man, and said the following, "If anyone be in need, the hermit was there to share. He had no money, possessions or strength left to give, instead he gave abundantly of his genuine love and great compassion. Never asking what was needed, he always shared and gave what he could. He could usually help the actual need of the person very little, but the peace and love he brought contributed greatly to the brotherhood of man. Once, the parrish had need of money, and the hermit reached in his pocket and gave everything he had. The amount he gave was not important — the significance lay in his depth of love, and the bond he created between brothers. His goal was sharing — not how much money he could give, but how much love. He freely gave what he could from the blessings he had, and generously passed them on to others. Whatever your need, the beloved old hermit was there to share."

A week later in the same village, a very rich man died. He had lots of money and possessions, and no jokes were ever made about him. He had dedicated his life to acquiring as much for himself as possible, and had no time for anyone or anything else. The priest read the normal passage from the bible without much enthusiasm, because no one attended the funeral.

Comment: Measure your life by the sharing of love, and the communion you bring to our brotherhood — not by the attainment of wealth or possessions. Be ready to share at all times, it does not matter what the need is. Your gift of love and your willingness to share is the greatest help and comfort to someone in need. Have no attachment to what you have, you are only sharing what has been given to you — your spirit takes nothing with it when it releases the body. Have no desire to acquire more wealth, with the thought that you can thus have more to give, what you have is sufficient. The amount of money given is of little importance, the amount of love given is. In giving, the purpose is not to fulfill another person's expected desires, but to share what is in our capacity, and to give it with love and joy. The one who shares will never be lacking, for their storehouse will always be full of love, and will receive abundant love to perpetually replenish it. Our ultimate reward is peace, and communion of our soul with all souls, in a common brotherhood of love and sharing.

Parable - Trap of Comparison

There were three friends who had visited each other often for many years. They had very different life styles, and each loved to talk about current events in science. One lived in the city, another out in the country, and the last lived in a motor home and traveled about. Their conversations were always about the marvels in the world of science, but one day they made the error of comparing their personal lifestyles. The city man said, "I'm quite concerned about you two. In the city I have all the conveniences available, and if there is trouble I can call someone to solve it, and work is always available. But neither of you have these advantages, and I'm always concerned about your well being." The country man was bewildered and responded, "I think your quite mistaken, what you call conveniences are traps of your freedom. I take care of myself, and if I need help there are friendly country people to lend a hand. I despise the city, with its phony people, trash and violence, and wouldn't live there for anything. I worry about your safety, and about our traveling friend who has no one to rely upon." The traveling man was amazed and replied, "I think you both are blind. You tie yourselves up in your little cubby holes and peek at the world occasionally, worrying about everything and always fearful of disaster. You're tied to your home, land and job, and have to answer to a long list of friends as to every little thing you do. Neither of you know the freedom of doing what you want, when you want, and going where you please, with no attachment or concern. I am free, and wouldn't live in the city or country. It is the two of you I worry about, that you'll never open your eyes to freedom." The city and country man both started to explain at once, that the traveling man was wrong, and that they were happy and free. Suddenly they all stopped talking, for they realized there was nothing they could say. They all said their goodbyes and departed, and that was the last time they had a visit together.

Comment : Everyone sees the world thru the perspective of their reality, and this is based upon their individual concepts. Everyone feels they can start their perspective from their personal position, for we each feel our concept to be the correct or superior one, and others to have missed the way. Thus everyone falls into the trap of comparison. We compare our concepts and delusions with all those around us, and since each one is different and has a unique perspective, the concepts will always conflict — and thus starts the unfortunate circle of not relating with our fellow brother. Once comparison is brought between two brothers, then each must defend their concept, and thus rises the serpent's head of judgement—for in the judgement of others we lose our integrity. Once integrity is lost, then argumentation will develop between the brothers thru the next serpent's head of criticism. In criticism we lose respect for our brother and disclaim his concepts completely, and irrationally heap faults upon him. After argumentation comes the dissolving of brotherhood, and the last serpent's head of condemnation. No relating further is possible, and our eyes are closed to the original communion. Every negative act of the past is remembered, and all the positive acts of your brother are forgotten. Bigotry and hatred develop, and lines of war are drawn. This unfortunate pattern is followed both in individual and national relations.

Each person knows that everyone is different in their ways and attitudes, and yet they still compare their unique way with others — as if their way is the correct way. Their concepts are the initial cause, and comparison is the avenue it follows to form separation and conflict between brothers on this planet. Concepts build a fool, and comparison is the game a fool plays. Let us begin to see with the eye of wisdom, that each of us is unique, and respectfully treat ourselves as such — peace will come only then.

The Mood of a Warrior

Relax into this moment and maintain a constant, sustained effort. Even though this statement appears contradictory, it is not. This moment is all we have, it is our kingdom and our refuge. We have no greater goal than to harmonize with it, and blend effortlessly into this gracious opportunity of experience — to relax into this moment of our great fortune. But a warrior is a person with fire in his heart, and energy bursting in his soul. His task is to be ever alert to live and grasp each opportunity, and experience this adventure to its optimum. He is fighting the internal sloth, and ever raising his head upward into higher and brighter light. His effort is a constant vigil, sustained by his dedication, and ever freshened by his humble respect. His purpose is alive; his nature is relaxed. The warrior could wish for no more than to be fully alive this very moment.

The outer discipline and activity are only a small part of his total effort — this part is relaxed and joyful. The real sustained effort is all internally felt. To subdue the mind into serene reflection, and stop its illusory thoughts, is the magnificient undertaking of the warrior. The illusion is real unto itself, so to control one's thoughts is like a partial death — and at the same time it is a rebirth into the spiritual body of consciousness. This effort is done as each moment unfolds, and it must be a relaxed, sustained effort — a constant vigil of awareness.

Relaxed in his effort, and sustained in his dedication, he can now seek the perfection of the warrior's mood, for it is a state of supreme awareness. There is no generality that fits a warrior, he is one unto himself, and his only common trait to other warriors is his dedication to freedom. Whatever his outward behavior may be, he is not attached to it. He laughs at his own behavior, as he laughs at everything else — all the world is folly, and he is part of it. The warrior's advantage is that he understands the folly of action and thought, and even though he is part of this world of folly, he views it from the perspective of spiritual experience, and laughs at the seriousness of this world drama. He is within this world, but the world is not within him. He doesn't hide or shy away from life. He has many periods of solitude to keep his perspective and deepen his insight, but when time comes to enter the marketplace, he does so with gusto. His energy and spirit are tested by his drive to experience all of life — his continual evolution in the moment. A warrior will quickly learn and master any activity of the marketplace, for he puts his full attention into whatever task is at hand. Clear of mind and free of any preconceptions, he joyously undertakes work as part of the experience of life, in this miracle of unfolding perception.

A warrior is convinced of his spiritual nature, so nothing can distract him from his ultimate purpose of experience. He knows he can depend upon no one, so he perpetually does his best. In every activity he maintains his warrior's mood, not in just a selected few. At all times he is aware, and thus he is not surprised by unforeseen events, for he is always expectant of the unexpected.

The warrior profoundly uses his senses, and has tuned them to perform superbly. He doesn't just glance at the world, but

views its intricacy intently — he smells the
message of the moment, he hears the song of
harmony, he tastes the richness of energy, he
feels the pulse of the vibrant earth — for the
earth is a being he loves to the depths of its
recesses, for it nurtures him and provides the
opportunity to experience life and gain his
realization. As the warrior uses his outer
perceptive fields more intently, he also uses
his inner conscious energy more profoundly.
He keeps his heart pure so he can send forth
love in his abundance of sharing, and keeps
his mind clear to express forth the wisdom
of his oneness in relation to the whole. He
harmoniously abides in this ever present
moment, and fearlessly observes the unknown.
    The warrior's mood is one of wonder, for
the miracle enfolding us is beyond words or
thought. The warrior doesn't necessarily go
around speaking spiritual truths, some speak
little or not at all, for he has realized the
uselessness of speech. In speech we can only
speak fragments of the truth, thus all
speech misses the point. At best it is a
partial expression of inner feeling, but it
can never grasp the totality of our heart — thus
speech mostly divides, and only rarely
unites. The absolute is beyond words and
thought — so the warrior abides in serene
reflection and unites with his true nature,
and lets words and thought go. His life is
a moving experience, not just a sitting
contemplation — he learns and shares by
action and intuition, not by talking and
dreaming. At this very moment, there is
nothing to stop the warrior from living the
dictates of his heart. Whatever is necessary,
the warrior does — if work, study or earning
be necessary, then he gets busy undertaking
it joyously, for this is his life unfolding
right now, and his task of realization is at

hand this moment. A warrior doesn't sit around waiting for circumstances to be just right; by the dynamic action of his unbending intent he actually produces the circumstances most favorable to his spiritual growth. He is master of himself, and thus affects the conditions and persons around him. All his life is centered around living in the present moment and grasing it fully, with no thought to past or future. The warrior is here, right now, and all his realization and power stem from abiding in the consciousness of being ever present in this miraculous moment. All the world is his wonderland, and his life is the dream of his making — and if the warrior be in a dream, he will be master of it, and it will be glorious.

Parable-Life is a Strawberry

A warrior was traversing the wilderness, when suddenly a mountain lion appeared from the trees and started to run towards him. The warrior ran, but within a short distance he came to a high cliff. There he noticed a rope attached to a rock going down the cliff, so without hesitation he climbed down the rope. But upon looking downward, he was surprised to find another mountain lion at the bottom of the cliff, waiting hungrily for him to descend. The lion above was reaching down for him, so he had no alternative then to hook his leg around the rope and stay put. All of a sudden, a chipmunk came running over to the rope above his head, and tasting the salt on the rope, began to chew at it, causing the rope to slowly break. Within a minute the

rope would be eaten thru, and he would fall
to his death and be devoured. As the warrior
gazed in front of him, he saw a pretty, little
strawberry plant with one big, luscious
strawberry hanging from it. Without any
hesitation he reached his free hand up and
plucked it. He then brought it to his mouth
and kissed it, and ate it — saying to himself,
"how sweet this strawberry is."

Comment: This parable depicts the epitome
of the warrior's mood. The warrior is always
in the present, living the experience of the
moment. He carefully and quickly assesses
the present situation, making the best
decision possible in the circumstances that
present themselves. He immediately forgets
his past decisions, and gives no concern to
future fears, so that he can live this moment
to its fullest. The lions represent our past
decisions, one's of possible regret for most
people. The chipmunk is our future fears,
expectation of the unknown for most. The
strawberry is the present moment of life —
only a warrior can so completely abandon
himself, and pluck the moment to savor
its sweetness, and forget the past and
future. The warrior's reward is the joy of
the present, with the opportunity to
experience a life fully lived, in freedom
from the illusion of thought. His death will
arrive at its appointed time, so he
abandons future fears and past regrets,
and dies as a warrior — serene, clear and
ready to savour the experience of death.
    Perhaps this seems too lofty of an ideal to
be real, but the mood of a warrior is indeed
real. Perhaps an incident that occured to
this warrior will bring the parable down
to earth. As I was hiking in Canyonlands,
I decided to traverse a cliff area out to a

spot of magnificent views. I had hiked and climbed for three miles till I came to a portion of the cliffs where the wall became sheer. I was in the center portion of a 1000' sheer wall, and could neither climb upward or down. But, in front of me there was a narrow ledge undercut into the rock wall that was about 12" wide and 18" high. If I wanted to proceed to the area of the view, I would have to crawl across the ledge with a 500' sheer drop below me. I assessed my abilities and proceeded. I pushed my pack in front of me, and crawled on my belly with one leg dangling over the 500' sheer precipice. I had to crawl about 12' before the ledge widened, but half way along the ledge I came to a pretty, little stone arch hidden inside the ledge's recesses. I stopped and gazed at its symmetry and beauty for several minutes, forgetting completely where I was and my situation. Finally, looking away from the arch, I had to laugh at the dangerous situation presented before me. a moment earlier while I viewed the arch I was on a journey thru a tunnel of beauty, and now in the present moment, time placed me on a dangerous cliff to oblivion. I became joyous in the realization that my true nature cannot die, and without fear or concern I slid the rest of the way across the ledge. My respect for this wondrous miracle sang forth as the moment brought realization of this mystery called life. The realization of my spiritual essence had dispelled any fear, and I was vibrantly alive and in love with this miraculous moment. The view turned out to be grand, and I exuberantly laughed and sang at the glorious opportunity to experience the challenge of life.

Wanderings of The Heart

Lizard Head Wilderness ~ August 1986 ~

New Mexico now lay behind me, where I had just finished climbing five peaks over 12,500 feet in the last eight days, and now I headed for Colorado. My intention was to attack the big peaks of the grand Rockies, but the weather held me to be satisfied with more 12,000 foot peaks. After several weeks of inclement weather, I decided to head for sunny Utah, but on the way I stopped at the Wilson Mountain range, which holds the Lizard Head Wilderness. This proved to be a blessed stay, and for three weeks I hiked its terrain in beautiful, sunny weather.

During this stay my climb of Delores Peak was my highest and afforded the finest view, and my traverse of the Lizard Head was the most dangerous and toughest hike, but the day that really stands out as unique was my climb of Sheep Mountain. At 13,183 feet, Sheep Mtn. is no rolling hill, but the climb was of no real danger, just very tedious. Beauty surrounds this cone shaped mammoth, and as I hiked thru the woods to its base, I saw deer and elk, and a great abundance of wildflowers and birds. The climb itself was very steep, and I had to use my hands for several thousand feet to help my ascent up its rocky flank. As I reached about mid way, massive thunderheads began to accumulate over the Wilson Range — this is a common occurance each afternoon in Colorado's high mountains, and means the liklihood of rain and lightening in isolated patches. One mountain may get soaked and the next peak can remain dry, so as I watched the clouds turn increasingly black, I increased my speed of ascent to hopefully arrive at the summit before the rain.

I was sweating and panting furiously, as I climbed as fast as I could up the talus slope, and as I finally viewed the top just in front of me, I made my final effort to sprint to the summit. The peak comes to a round point, and as I stepped on the crest, and was finally able to lift my head from the constant attention downward to watch my footing; and as I finally, after hours of strenuous climbing, was able to capture my reward and absorb the panorama view I longed to see, just as I lifted my head for my very first look—Ca-rack—a bolt of lightening struck the peak. I jumped straight up, turned in mid air, and made an even quicker descent down the side I had climbed. But after descending 50 feet I stopped and said to myself, "I didn't climb all the way up here to turn around and run down the peak without seeing the view." By now rain was falling, and lightening was cracking all around me and down the adjoining ridge. So I very quickly grabbed a bunch of talus and built a round rock wall, just big enough to sit under and draped my poncho over it, making a nice, little rock house, and there I sat cozy and dry, and had my lunch without a care in the world. The flashes of lightening were blinding, and the bolts struck the peak repeatedly, and the thunder deafened me, but my lunch was good and I was dry, and I was enjoying the spectacle as long as my body was alive to perceive it.

The odds may have been against me, but I am a warrior, not an odds maker, so I let my spirit sing free, and enjoyed the show. In the time I took to evaluate the situation, I had my doubt and concern, but once my decision was made to stay, I took the steps I felt to be necessary, and then freed myself of concern or speculation. At this time a warrior must trust in himself and the spirit within him, for his spirit is eternal, and thus whatever the outcome of any situation, is an avenue of experience, adventure and challenge — this is the warrior's purpose, and it is the mood and attitude he must maintain.

So as I ate, I listened and watched, and the show around me amazed my senses and delighted my spirit. After the grandest twenty minute light show imaginable, the rain slowly subsided and the lightening moved to the next mountain, and I was able to crawl out of my little rock house, and climb back to the top once again. The sun was now sending beams of celestial light thru the broken cloud mass, and I found myself spinning around slowly, taking in the spectacular view that stretched at least 75 miles in every direction. What a grand view of the massive peaks of the Rockies, with so many crystal lakes and lush valleys between them — the view was breath taking and well worth the effort and danger to behold it. The air was crisply alive, and as the sun shone its radiant light upon me, I felt full of life and vibrant — I could say I felt electric.

I remained on the peak for an hour, soaking in the beauty and grandeur of nature's finest effort. Reluctantly I said my loving fairwell and began my descent, which proved to be a bit dangerous because of the rain. There were now little waterfalls trickling down the slopes, and elk were browsing at the base of the peak. Five more miles of dense forest, lush meadows, babbling creeks, songbirds and flowers lay on my course as I slowly wandered my way back home. How grand it was to feel the earth, on that glorious day that lasted a thousand years.

~ The next time you watch a lightening storm, remember, I may be watching also, from the top of the highest peak ~

66

A Good Day To Die

There is no yesterday and no tomorrow, there is only today. Everyday you arise is today, and as such is the last day of your life, thus we are all going to see our death arrive on today. No one has ever died yesterday, or will anyone ever die on tomorrow — the day of death that everyone must inevitably face is none other then today. Because of this monumental fact, every day must be recognized as an excellent opportunity to live, for only thru the temperance of death does life explode into wondrous existence; and if understood as the miracle it is, both life and death will be seen as one aspect of the same mystery which brings existence into manifest form.

Each day the warrior sincerely and respectfully faces life and joyously proclaims that 'today is a good day to die'. Since his spirit is unborn and undying, he is humbly paying respect to the miracle of manifest existence, and pronounces these words without any fear, and in view of the miracle he is. The warrior does not fear bodily death, and is ready to accept its mystery whenever it unfolds. He does not look for death or encourage its embrace, but neither does he hide or run from its face. He knows death is an inevitable part of this manifestation, and lives his life to the brim while the blessed opportunity exists, so that his death will be the final crescendo to a magnificently orchestrated life.

This miraculous 'now' is the only moment we have, and to live in this perpetual moment makes each day a blessed event in which to grasp the challenge of life. The only aspect that brings the miracle of life into a relative perspective is the transitory aspect of death within it. Only death can provide the impetus

To rise above the slothful attitude of treating this miraculous adventure of life as a commonplace occurrence. How can we take life for granted and be bored with its wonder, when death will be facing us today and sweep away all who surround us — there are no survivors in this world, and our body shall also return to dust. Only the temperance of death can provide the soberness to respectfully grasp this miracle of life, while death so graciously watches on.

Death of body is not a concern to a warrior, and when he boldly faces life and proclaims that 'today is a good day to die', he has only partial inference to a bodily death. A warrior's main reference is to the spiritual task he has embraced, for each day is the challenge and opportunity to die to the selfhood he has created. He must boldly die day by day to any concept of an individual self, and live within the spiritual reality of his true essence. Only thru death of physical dependence, limitations, concepts, desire and attachment, that form a selfhood of separateness, will he be able to abide in his true nature, beyond the illusion life has painted for him with its relative manifestation. Today is the most precious time your spirit will ever possess, and only when your spirit is allowed to grasp this life in freedom, and adventurously challenge its existence, will it know the purpose and essence of life — and only then can you say with understanding, that 'Today is a good day to die'.

The Final Blessing

We shall all be blessed by death.
For every seafarer
    finally wearies of his voyage,
    and strains his eyes
    for a port.
And all travelers
    tire of the road,
    and long to reach home
    eventually.
Without death,
    life would stretch
    into monotony.
For only death
    can give perspective
    to the reality of life.
Death tempers our spirit,
    and adds challenge
    thru its touch of finality.
We have only one true friend,
    for who else but death
    can bring us back home,
    from a dream of useless wandering.
Ah yes,
    what a blessing
        death shall be.

Art Plate #10 ~ There is no death, but only the reordering of life while our true nature observes the experience in wonder. Form is in constant evolution, and will change continuously thru out all eternity, but our spiritual essence is beyond change, for it is the primal substance of the Absolute, and thus it has never been born and cannot die. So our spirit will continue to float within this realm of experience, and whichever perception is next, is of no great concern...

It doesn't matter
when I'm dead and gone,
for I was never here
to start with...

Adventure of Experience

Time is within relativity - it is the measurer of the events of our life, and as we perceive the moment, we can mold it to fit our consciousness. A warrior living in the moment, seeing life as an unfolding adventure of experience, and awestruck by the mystery and wonder, will find that each day appears to last like a year. Each year to a warrior is a lifetime of change and growth, as he observes and participates in the blossoming of life. What joy and peace there is in grasping this present moment of miraculous unfoldment. People of the world seek to lengthen their lives, instead of concentrating their experience into the given time each of us will be graced to live. Here is the secret of eternity - it is not in living a boring, fruitless life extending forever and longing for death, but in taking whatever precious moments that have been given, and living them with gusto. It is to live life fully in the present, with no expectations of more life or other worlds, and with no fantasies of this life or attachment to it — just to live desireless in each unfolding moment, as the celebration of the blessed chance of experience, for this miracle before us is the grandest adventure of your most profoundest dreams.

The worldly man whose mind is fixed in past and future is always at odds with life, hoping thru past regrets to get something better in the future. His life seems short because his view is short, a warrior's life seems forever because his view is grandiore. Time is relative - it is based on attitude and perspective in the unfolding moment. Live full in the warrior's realization and you'll be surrounded by the consciousness of eternity.

Life is a challenge, and challenges are not good or bad, but simply a grand chance to experience purpose and adventure. There are no problems or dilemmas, there is only life to experience, and each experience is a new opportunity into learning and growing. The task of a warrior is the continuous assimulation of the experience unfolding before him. This is his grand chance at life, and he doesn't intend to waste it by living within his illusory thoughts, imprisoned within concepts of past and future, and attached and desirous of stability. The warrior is a being at war - the battlefield is his heart, and weapons are his mind; he uses his freedom to attack this perception before him and reap a victory of joy, love and peace. He is responsible for the outcome of his battle, so he sincerely dedicates, with humility and respect, to a challenge of adventure. With no past fears or future expectations to disarm him, he makes his stand right here and now, and fights for the life of his spiritual realization. The warrior humbly recognizes what he is, not as grounds for regret, but as a living challenge to inspire him to go beyond the limitations which surround him. He is not looking for an easy victory, but after the total realization of his spiritual being. His aspiration is alive as each action bears witness to his sincerity and dedication of purpose. Moment by moment the warrior lives his experience of adventure, joyous in the opportunity to perceive this miracle and see the wonder of its mystery, as he sojourns within it in freedom.

Art Plate #11~ There are no bounds to encase your true nature, so don't place limitations upon yourself. Live within the freedom of the expansiveness of your heart, and let your spiritual vision extend forever...

The Ultimate Challenge

A warrior lives life as the ultimate challenge. For most people, there is a search or path to a futuristic goal, but goals are attainments, and thus one can fail in reaching their desire. Life within reality is beyond attainment, thus it has no goals - only within thought are there illusory goals. Even though goals are illusory, there is purpose within life, and the purposeful living of it.

Most seekers are so busy looking for the elusive goal, that they lose this moment's joy, and skip right by the purpose of the search. The goal of any path is secondary, it arises from within our thoughts, but the purpose of the search comes directly from our spiritual being. The heart finds love and joy in the search, while the mind finds awareness and relation within the search. Thoughts can provide fantasy goals and limitations to the search, but the ultimate impetus and motivation comes from our free spiritual nature. Our true nature recognizes no goal, but it does see the ultimate purpose in life, and that is challenge. The purposeful living of life is the warrior's ultimate challenge. The purpose within existence is a motivating, energizing union within experience. It is our spirit in free flowing spontaneous exuberance in the midst of challenge, and in communion with our source. Our true spiritual essence is freedom, and it abides in the midst of challenge.

If one sets up fantasy goals, then it only follows that they will experience fantasy victories and fantasy defeats - the inevitable pendulum swing within the world of desire. But if experience within this moment be your purpose, then challenge is available at all

74

Times. No object, person or concept can be the real purpose, for they would represent an attainment, and purpose in life is beyond the relative desire, and is in the realm of spiritual experience. Challenge is the ultimate purpose — it is beyond seeking attainment, and is an aspect within the realization of our true self. This is why a warrior lives an active, strong, purposeful life — it brings him into harmony with his true nature, and thru challenge he finds oneness in it. The man who first went to the north pole did so with purposeful action, his goal was to be first at the pole. But that was only a secondary goal produced by his thoughts, the real purpose and goal was challenge. He could have gone to the south pole, or climbed Mt. Everest, or walked on the moon, it wouldn't have mattered. What his spirit sought was challenge, and thus his ultimate purpose was union within his true nature. His spirit needed to grasp the experience of life and live it to the maximum, by the challenge of his heart's dictate.

Life itself is the ultimate challenge, and whatever experience your heart provides is your avenue of personal challenge, and your purpose of living. Whether it be art, science, research, exploration or whatever, it is your challenge of the spirit, and the flow of your nature. If your heart and mind be recognizing the challenge, then purposeful living will follow, and joy will fill your experiences of life. Purposeful living will of itself find a challenge, and thus will develop purpose. Only then can the spirit exude forth its inherent energy— with challenge the spirit vibrates forth great energy, but without challenge the glow of the spirit is dull and listless.

Personal motivation is necessary for realization, and challenge is its vehicle of discovery.

Realization of one's true nature is a dead realization, if no expression of life goes with it. The one who sits in a cave all his life and does nothing, can find realization of his true nature, but without relating within this perceived manifestation, his realization is dead. It has no life or vibrancy — he has accepted no challenge of life, and thus he found no purpose within life. It is a travesty to waste this precious opportunity to experience the adventure and challenge of life. A warrior will travel alone to places of great solitude and beauty, there to find communion and realization of his true nature. He will find inner realization within his solitude, but it will be lifeless. So the warrior comes back into relation with the world, in the manner his heart will dictate. There he will experience challenge and accept a purposeful life, and establish a live, vibrant realization. He relates to all aspects of life, whether in the marketplace or in solitude — his challenge is life itself. His true nature can then shine forth its love and wisdom as he accepts the challenge of the moment, and lives it as the ultimate purpose of life.

A warrior makes the best use of the possibilities presented. He doesn't go around trying to rearrange situations to fit his personal preference, his challenge is to experience life the way it is, and be joyful for the opportunity. Challenge does not have to be a heroic endeavor, all situations of life present possible challenges of mastery and awareness. Look to the adventure of the circumstance and find its challenge, anything can do if your heart and full attention be into the situation. Every activity is the flowing of life force, and it is the attitude of the individual which allows communion of their inner nature and increased conscious awareness. But in the heart and mind of a warrior, challenge is sought in a dynamic range of possibilities. A challenge involving action and mind allow the attention and awareness to be brought into finer focus, and greater energy released. Our spirit is part of the ever flowing pattern of energy that the manifestation is made of — with purposeful challenge we find the exuberance of life energy within a dynamic personality, but if challenge is lacking then enthusiasm for life is low. The spirit requires the flowing of energy, and this is provided by challenge. It is our priority of life, and our purpose of living, to find that challenge and become in tune with our true nature. This allows the warrior to remain in contact with the fleeting moment, and provides his avenue of realization. Thru his purposeful living he finds insight into his true essence beyond the relative. His purpose and challenge become united, and pave his way for communion within himself.

Parable ~ Purpose is Challenge

There was a warrior renowned for his great hiking ability. One day he told a few young hiking companions that he was going to Alaska, and intended to walk across it. The feat seemed impossible, but the youths had great confidence in the warrior, and asked to join in his adventure. The warrior agreed — the necessary supplies were bought— and off they flew to Alaska. An airplane

was arranged to meet them every two weeks
to bring supplies, and for emergencies. The
route picked seemed impossible to accomplish
in the short time the season allowed,
nontheless off they started on their trek. It
was hard going, and the weather always a
concern, but the scenery was breathtaking
and the spirits of the group always joyful.
Great spectacles of nature abounded, and the
wildlife was extraordinary — they all felt
deep love for the beauty and majestic serenity
experienced along the way. But the days were
getting shorter, and it appeared more and
more impossible to traverse the rugged land
to their destination. After several months of
wonderful companionship and deep insights
into life, the warrior gathered the group
together and said, " the winter storms are
approaching, and the days are too short
now to possibly make our destination. Since
the plane arrives today, I think we should
say our farewell to this magnificient land,
and depart." For the first time during the
entire trip the youths were disheartened, and
one ventured to say, " well, I guess we failed."
"Failed at what?" asked the warrior. The
youth replied, "we failed to walk across the
wilderness — wasn't that our goal?" The
warrior laughed and explained, " if that was
your goal, then I'm afraid you are defeated,
and sadly you've been defeated by an illusory
goal within your thoughts. A warrior has
no goals, no illusions, and no concepts of
attainment, thus he is never defeated — he
recognizes no goals, only challenges. Our
purpose in walking the wilderness was
for challenge and communion of our true
nature. While here, experiencing the challenge
of life, our spirit soared free in this
marvelous realm of mystery. We lived the
moment purposefully, ever joyful at the

opportunity to experience the adventure of life. The spirit lives by challenge, and though there was no goal to attain, we did have the purpose of giving our spirit a great challenge—to unfold its wings of freedom, and soar to the heavens. You speak of defeat, but the entire trip you were joyous and never complained. You saw great beauty, and communed with wildlife, your fellow comrades, and deep into your own nature. This is not defeat, this is a great victory of purposeful living and providing challenge to your spirit, and accepting the purpose of life. We are here exploring the wilderness within ourselves, and our purpose is to realize our true nature — and the challenge is to maintain our awareness of this realization as we experience the adventure of life. Victory is ours for living life as the ultimate challenge; defeat is for those who find no challenge in life, and thus see no purpose. Our purpose was our challenge, and the challenge was to experience this majestic beauty, be joyful in our communion, find love within the mystery, understand ourself within the relative, and be aware of our true nature — the challenge was to realize ourself, and thus it was our purpose also. We didn't even have to leave our homes, and could have been just as victorious there; but our spirit loves challenge, and thus we are dancing to the love of our spirit." And with that, the warrior and all the youths sang and danced, and celebrated their great victory of purpose and challenge.

Wanderings of The Heart

Escalante Primitive Area ~ October 1986 ~

This earth has hidden lands of awesome character. One such spot is Escalante primitive area in Utah, and it was my great fortune to have an incredible experience within its magnificent realm.

I drove my home down the hole-in-the-rock road, over a rocky dirt road for forty miles, til I reached where willow creek starts its descent to meet with the Escalante River. It proved to be no difficulty to drop down a side canyon into Willow Creek, and begin my episode of adventure within its ever restricting fold. Willow Creek began wide with bearly an inch of water trickling down the canyon, and along its course were majestic willows, lush bushes and ferns scattered throughout. After several miles of leisurely walking, I came into the domain of Broken Bow Arch — it is truly spectacular. The arch stands near a 100 tall, and is beautifully shaped as a creased half circle set inside the towering walls of the canyon, with giant overhanging escarpments that have long trailing ferns within its shaded recesses. The scene was one I couldn't refuse to linger at, so I found a spot of perfect viewing and had my lunch, and a long communion with the awesome character of this wondrous spot — and this long delay almost proved to be my undoing.

Eventually I forced myself to leave and continued my exploration down the creek. My plan was to walk down to the Escalante River, and then to backtrack several miles to where Forty Mile Creek intersected with Willow Creek, and follow it back up to the mesa, and then find somewhere to climb the cliff to the plateau and cut across it back to my home — about an

eighteen mile triangular course, which looked
nice and simple on my map.

So down Willow Creek I joyously walked, when
all of a sudden the wide canyon walls abruptly
narrowed to six feet wide, and the walls rose
straight above for 500 feet. The trees and bushes
ended, and the water funneled into this tight
crack canyon. Even though the water was only
6-12 inches deep, I still had to remove my
shoes if I wished to continue, so off with the
boots and down the tight chute canyon I went.

After a few hundred yards I came to the
junction of Forty Mile Creek and Willow Creek—
they were like two enormous, narrow doors
rising straight out of view, and gave me an
ominous feeling. The water now doubled in
volume, as I continued down the awesome, twisting
canyon toward the Escalante. For two miles I
continued barefoot in the cold water, twisting
ever onward til reaching my goal, and then I
reversed my course and returned to Forty mile
Creek. By now it was starting to get late, and
my feet were like ice, but I assumed that Forty
Mile canyon would be similar to Willow Creek,
and that after I walked a few hundred yards
it would widen its walls and I could put my
shoes on once again, and have a nice, leisurely
walk up a tree ladened creek.

The Escalante area is both unpredictable
and dangerous, and as I started up Forty
Mile Creek, I had my first omen of misfortune
by stepping into quicksand, and this omen
was to be repeated every hundred feet for the
next four miles. The canyon did not open up
as Willow Creek had been, but stayed very
tight walled, and I had to walk barefoot for
the next four miles in 12 inches of cold water
with no possible way to escape. On 4 occasions
I heard the sound of tumbling water as I twisted
thru the incredible winding maze of rock. I
could never see further than 25 feet in front of

me because of the winding action of the walls, and when I would hear the sound of water it always meant a waterfall. Sure enough, I would round a corner and there before me would be a large, deep pool with a waterfall behind it. With daylight getting short and too much distance behind me to backtrack, and with the belief that at any moment the canyon would widen, I reluctantly crossed one pool and waterfall after another. The canyon walls were rarely wider than six feet, so my method to cross the pools was to stem the walls by placing a hand and foot on one wall, and my other hand and foot on the other wall and slowly inch my way up the canyon walls, and then go horizontally til I crossed the pool and waterfall. It was either this method or swim, and I was already cold. The walls were wet and slippery, with moss and ferns growing on them, and my numb, bare feet made the traverse even more difficult. All went fairly well, that is if you could call falling thigh deep in quicksand dozens of times well, until I came upon a very large pool and waterfall. At this point the canyon walls widened to seven feet, and this forced me to try a very dangerous manuver — I placed both feet on one wall and both hands on the other wall, and delicately inched my way up the wall and over the pool. I had slung my shoes over my shoulder, and as I tried to descend to the top of the waterfall, my shoes and long hair fell into my face, covering my eyes. I reached one leg down from the slippery, moss covered wall and desperately tried to find something to place it on, but my other foot slipped and I fell down the waterfall into the pool, bruising myself as I landed on a submerged rock. But getting wet or bruised didn't matter now, for what really counted was the fact that I was running out of daylight, and I couldn't possibly reverse the last four miles thru the water and quicksand in time to reach Willow Creek before it got dark. Now if I was to run into a really large waterfall I would be trapped, and have to spend the night in this cold canyon standing in 12 inches of ice water — the possibility looked very grim. My great hope now wasn't of returning home, but merely to find a dry piece of earth to sleep on. But I am a warrior, and my spirit lives by challenge, so even with the cold water, quicksand and claustrophobic walls, I was deep into the adventure of this rare, incredible experience.

All at once I heard the worst possible sound imaginable — it was the dreaded sound of a very large waterfall. And sure enough, as I rounded the next corner, there in front of me was a 25 foot waterfall and the canyon walls were too wide to stem across — I was trapped! But upon closer examination, I discovered a way up the side of the waterfall, and quickly scrambled to the top. The waterfall marked an abrupt change in the canyon, for now the walls spread, and there was a dry sandy bottom dotted with low bushes. How joyous I was to be past that maze of twisting, wet rock, and on dry earth once again. But very little light remained and the canyon walls still rose 400 feet above my head, and I hadn't the faintest idea how to get out of the canyon and up unto the mesa above, where I needed to cross the plateau to reach my home — once again I was trapped.

Quickly I put my boots on my poor, frozen feet, and started heading up the canyon. After I had barely covered a hundred yards, I was blessed to see a coyote in the canyon bottom about a hundred feet in front of me. I dearly love coyotes, and would have liked to sit quietly and observe him, but I had no time to lose. So I watched for a brief minute, then reluctantly moved toward him, figuring this would scare him away. To my surprise he did not run, but loped up the canyon a short distance and then waited. He repeated this action twice, each time I would catch up to him. Finally he approached the canyon wall to the south, which was the side I needed to climb; he then proceeded to head diagonally up the canyon wall, using a very narrow, almost imperceptible path, and continued to wait every once in awhile, so that I could keep him in view and follow his movement. I was very leary to follow him up the 400 foot vertical wall, but without thought I knew this is what I had to do, so up I went. Without encountering any real difficult spots, the coyote lead me up the narrow path to the top of the canyon, and when I arrived at the crest I expected my coyote friend to be there waiting, but as hard as I surveyed the mesa, I could not locate him. I ever so respectfully thanked my brother coyote for his gracious help, and also offered my sincere gratitude to the power and spirit which guides us both. Quickly I climbed the closest hill, and to my amazement I spotted my van about three miles away. Even though darkness quickly arrived, I had set my course and followed it true, til I joyously reach home once again. My triangular loop was completed, and my body was bruised and bloody, but my spirit was so exuberant that I shouted for joy and sang in praise of this glorious opportunity to experience the grand challenge of life. My purpose to experience this wondrous realm was so close to my heart, that my communion with life could not have been closer, and in this union came the realization,'that today was a good day to die', and thus I lived to the highest light of the warrior's dream.

Seeking The Way

What is the purpose and goal of life? Do you seriously believe a book or person can tell you the essence and mystery of life — that is a personal realization. It is each individual's responsibility to come to an understanding of life thru insight, experience and dedication — this is the number one priority of living. But perhaps you feel it would be nice, if someone or a book would just tell you the purpose and goal. This is precisely the problem now, everyone wants to tell you their limited, relative opinions. Not only do we have thousands of books and proclaimed enlightened souls expounding their personal views, but there are even more souls from the past, whose conceptual opinions are still honored.

So who are you? Do you have no soul and spirit in which to discern your self nature of God. Can you not look deep into your heart and hear the vibrations which have echoed thru all of eternity, giving rise to the presence of our original source. You are the emanation of the Absolute, God in manifestation. Why should God, manifested as you, need a middle man to proclaim his being — God blasts his trumpet of existence loudly thru every act and thought of your life. You need not listen for a faint whisper, or a still small voice; God is yelling his presence, and demonstrating his reality throughout this universe at every second. What goal or purpose do you look for? — just realize your spiritual unity in God, and shout the call of spiritual freedom as the essence of God. There is only the Absolute, you cannot lose it or find it, but simply be at peace within it. Find peace and purpose in knowing that you are the divine essence of the ultimate reality.

Each warrior is a free individual, he is master of his life and follows no one else. His heart is his only guide — it is his path and his goal. He will adopt a unique life suited to him alone. It is of no avail to try to follow another person's ways, you are not someone else, or in different circumstances. You are here, right now as you, and it is your responsibility to find the way most suitable to you. Redirect and refine your ways of life as often as the circumstances around you dictate. Use as your guide the criteria of 'how close are my life's experiences bringing me to a deeper realization of my true nature'. The only way to measure the experiences of a person's life is by the depth of realization they bring. Seek according to your capacities, do not compare yourself to others around you. You cannot see their heart's realization, the best you can do is to feel your own heart's longing and follow its direction. If you are true to yourself and follow your heart, you will always find joy and purpose. The decision who will dedicate to a life of realization can only be made in the heart. In a pure, joyful heart, all efforts will bring deeper awareness and a more expansive consciousness, thus the way is open to realization.

Seek realization in your daily world, it can be found no where else. Whether your daily world be the marketplace or in a monastery, your insight into awakening will be available in the situation you are presently in. This is because enlightenment is already within you awaiting your recognition, and the outward circumstances can at best be a catalyst to inspire a concentrated effort of understanding. The situation around you is not the factor that sparks revelation, it comes from within you, no matter where or how you may be experiencing this perception. One may be in an externally unpleasant situation, but if their attention and receptivity be focused, then great insight may develop. Another may surround himself with the glories of nature, on a beautiful day and serenity of mood, and yet if his awareness be unfocused, no insight will come. When the eyes are closed in meditation, the depth of union with one's true nature is not dependent whether he be in a jail cell, or out in the wilderness. All realization is inwardly sparked, and the best that outside influences can do, is to inspire one to focus their attention and awareness to allow the insight to surface. Holy persons and places can only inspire one, they can never actually elevate one's consciousness permanently. At this moment, you may feel that you are in unfavorable circumstances to be able to make contact and abide in your inner nature. This is the foolishness of thought trying to complicate the simplicity of life. All times and places allow equal opportunity to realize your true nature. Every situation is external to the real task of moving inward into union of our true self, and abiding there in love and wisdom. No matter where you are, or what you are doing, you can withdraw your attention outwardly and turn it inward in meditation. All situations are there to gain knowledge and insight, not for fighting them and painting fantasies in your mind of ideal circumstances that will hand you the sacred realization. All situations have both favorable and unfavorable aspects available. It is our task to view them as they truly are, and thru the experience we can learn, harmonize and grow – not fight and complain. The warrior is always in the awareness to learn the lesson that each particular situation has to teach, thus he is attentive and alert in the present moment. He is always surrounded by the perfect circumstances to spark insight, thus at every moment he is ready and aware to receive the realization that he has dedicated his life to. At any moment or any place it can happen, outside influences do not matter — it can happen this moment, so the warrior is joyous and alert in the patience of his heart.

It is not necessary to leave the world, but one must elevate their consciousness and attitude, for we all tend to seek stability, and thus stagnate our freedom. A warrior recognizes this attitude of clinging to security, and thus purposefully effects changes in his life, by simplifying and reordering his habits. When one is in the midst of change, one is usually fully awake and aware, and trying their best. Thus a warrior seeks continual change intentionally, it keeps him at his best. Calm and purposefully he goes into solitude, or into the marketplace, and puts himself in a state of challenge. It is a direct attack on man's timid nature, so that his freedom can be exercised and strengthened by a sincere, determined effort to reach his optimum of realization. A warrior strives for balance to always be at his best— in solitude he gains insight, in activity he gains perspective, both are needed to embrace the full realization of his true nature.

Embarking on the ways of a warrior is not a decision of the mind. To some, freedom is so paramount that everything else has value only in its light — thus a warrior is born, not made. There are different types of warriors, with their common link being a dedication to the challenge of life before them, but only thru fortuitous circumstances will one be able to dedicate to the freedom of a spiritual warrior. The process which builds a warrior begins in the same way for everyone — one will be dedicated to a particular dogma or concept, it can be religious, spiritual, philosophical or even worldly. He will follow its premise till he reaches the highest point of its limited, conceptual thought, and there he will find himself alone and still unfulfilled — his thoughts are not his own, and his heart longs for some undefined communion. The victory of his past endeavors seem as defeats, for he has lost his irreplaceable time as the magic of the moment slipped by. He is now at the crossroads — he can become closed or embittered by his attempts, and remain superficially satisfied in his shallow worldly victories; or he can open his eyes to the futility of attainment and begin listening to his heart, and thus embark on the ultimate journey of freedom toward the sincerity, dedication and realization of a spiritual warrior.

A warrior has his ways of life, but he has no path of life as defined by a goal. If one identifies with a path, then one feels there is something to do — he then becomes trapped within the conflict of a 'doer' to perform the actions. Where there is a 'doer', there is the dualities of right and wrong, plus questions to ask and problems to solve, thus the moment is lost in a quagmire of conflicting thoughts, and freedom is gone. Path and goal are concepts of illusory thought born within ourself to inflict purpose into our life. We need no illusion of purpose, we already have a true nature of freedom, which is abounding in purposeful effort to experience this unfolding mystery of perception. Why lament for need of a goal,

we are already complete and whole within our
pure heart and unconditioned mind — our true
nature need not be looked for or sought after,
but just realized. We are the spiritual
manifestation of the absolute; it is the reality
of our being, and we need do nothing but
abide within its freedom.

So the path falls away, and the
realization arrives that there is no pressure
to achieve — there is nothing pending.
Activity will still go on, but the actions
become desireless. They are actionless actions,
for no one is there performing them. One
is in the moment, and illusory thought is
not of the moment — when thought is gone,
so is the person. One is now free to
spontaneously interact in the circumstances
that unfold, making life an experience of
unfolding adventures, and joy is the natural
outcome of such a life. All tasks become equal
in essence, and one realizes that it is not what
we do that has importance, but rather how well
we do it. The subtle paradox is then seen, that
it is not wasted time to spend our lives in
peaceful contemplation — there is permanence
in serene reflection, for reality has no needs.

So the warrior's life is really an
attitude of awareness, he has his ways and
lives them sincerely and truthfully. He
follows no person or concept, and is master
of his life alone. He is not attached to his
activities, or desires anything more than the
simplicity of being aware in this miraculous
moment. His heart is at peace, and his
mind tranquil. He wanders a solitary
journey to nowhere, and is overjoyed at the
realization, that after all his endeavor and
struggle, the path and the goal turned out
to be none other than himself.

Art Plate # 12 ~ We seek after a goal
outside, yet it is our own true self we are
seeking after. When we stop this lonely search,
we shall realize that our true nature is
already present within us ...

91

The Pathless Path

Throughout the history of man's search for realization, there have been basically two paths used by all seekers — the path of the heart, and the path of the mind. The path of the heart is the positive approach to finding God, it is the way of the ascetic. Methods and practices are essential, and time is needed for their perfection. Much spiritual work must be performed and devoted to. One is looking for God, and communing with God thru prayer — an emotional union thru the heart. The path of the mind is the negative approach to finding God, it is the way of the mystic. No methods or practises are necessary, time is of no importance, and no spiritual work need be performed. One is waiting for God, and makes himself available thru deep meditation — a non emotional union beyond the mind.

This is basically the two paths that all aspirants choose. Thru both paths profound changes in attitude, and some realization is possible. But both represent paths to future goals, and thus the ego is ever present spinning its illusive web and fantasies of prospective attainments. Either path will take one to a magnificent plateau, depending upon one's dedication, but there is always something missing. Deep insight is lacking on the path of the heart, and the path of the mind is dry. There must be harmony between the two aspects of our nature ; heart and mind must unite if ultimate freedom is to be realized. Every great master has had both love and wisdom, both compassion and insight. Their true nature was in harmony, thus the ultimate realization of themself was their path.

Thus by example of the masters there is another way — it is the warrior's way of spiritual freedom. It is not a method or path, and no goal of realization is sought after. This is the pathless path. One lives a purposeful, dedicated life, and as a result, one realizes their true nature. It is a union of heart and mind into the harmony of the moment. There is great love, joy and respect present, but it is not focused by illusory concepts to some projected goal. The heart's love is vibrant, and within it the challenge of the moment is accepted and realized. In the mind there is insight into reality, and awareness of the ultimate purpose. The mind is alert to the ever present moment, and projects no expected goal, or a realm beyond it. Calm and clear, the mind finds purpose in perceiving the unfolding mystery around it. Thoughts, concepts and fantasies do not rule a warrior's heart or mind. Harmony of heart and mind bring a natural realization of one's true self, as the warrior perpetually lives the experience of the unfolding moment — whatever the experience may be, he is aware, attentive and alive within it. His awareness is always focused on the overall view of life, where all aspects of perception are equal, thus he gives his full attention to every activity. Whether active or meditative, he is present in the moment, seeing the mystery of its challenge. Though active, he is not doing anything special, for there is no attempt at attainment, or to achieve a goal.

Time is the warrior's friend — dedicated and active within it, he seeks nothing from it. He lives purposefully, and his ways bring joy into the moment, but he has no attachment to them. He is clear in heart

and mind, thus there is no clinging within
the emotion of a heart concept, or within the
dryness of a mind concept — he is not
trapped in the desire of a concept of a defined
goal, or any path leading to it. His heart
and mind are free, thus the realization of
his true nature is the acknowledgement
of himself. Even though the realization of his
true self, and freedom of his spiritual being
are his only priority and consideration, he
doesn't have a path or method to achieve
them. They are not goals attained thru a
path, they are realizations arrived at thru
his purposeful living. With joy in his
heart and freedom in his mind, he finds
union with all of life. As love and wisdom
guide his way, he merrily sings and
dances down the road to nowhere.

Art Plate # 13~ The road to nowhere is the road back to yourself. The view in the world is one of desire, attachment and concept, thus its limited perspective makes the spiritual path seem obstructed and difficult to follow, when in reality the way is wide and clear, and leads straight to our heart.

God Praying Within

Within this book I have used the words 'God' and 'the Absolute' almost interchangeably, but in my intent there is a difference. The difference is one of concept, for both 'God' and 'the Absolute' are representative of the totality and ultimate reality. The Absolute is beyond thought and concept; nothing is part of it, for it is the whole and not dividable— thus the warrior identifies his ultimate source as essence of the Absolute. God is also the Absolute, but personalized within our conceptual thought. This manifestation is within God, and God is within all, making God a personal relationship within the conceptual mind. When thoughts are present, one knows of his unity in God; when one is serenely quiet within, he intuitively feels the oneness of the Absolute. Even though thoughts and concepts are illusion, the warrior uses the name God in full knowledge of its ultimate meaning behind the relative. Thus he can sing with God, and as God, as his joy overflows in spiritual communion in perceiving this wondrous manifestation; or he can drop his concepts, and silently unite his true nature into the essence of his original source. This allows the warrior to abide within the paradox of God's power and love being easily felt and recognized throughout this manifestation, and yet the Absolute is unreachable, unthinkable and untouchable. The warrior's art is harmony, he recognizes the illusion, but realizes its relative realness. So he finds joy in relating to a personal God, and he finds freedom in realizing the ultimate reality — it is the harmony of heart and mind. He knows he is a spiritual being, and this relative world is part of his spiritual experience — he is part of the relative and also beyond it. He can open his eyes and commune as God in the relative, or close his eyes and dissolve into the absolute — his consciousness determines his awareness.

There is nothing one can say, think or write about the absolute, it is the essence of our spiritual being, and each must realize it thru intuition and revelation. The Absolute simply 'is', and thru realization of our true nature, we can abide within the unity of which we are all one.

About God, we can enjoy ourself and speak to our heart's content. At all times the shrine of God is in your heart, no external edifice is necessary, for at all times your love, sharing and respect are devotional prayers to God within you. No seeking is necessary, just live true to yourself and recognize the blessings that this miraculous moment bestows continuously. No pilgrimage or holy spot has ever brought one closer to God — God dwells within us all equally, and is present in all manifestation as the totality of it. We need nothing external to feel God's presence; God is internal, and the light is perpetually present as your very life. We are part of the miracle which is God, and no looking is necessary, for we are the primordial substance — with this awareness, one is always in the presence of God.

There is no outside force or external God to pray to. Prayer is the recognition of your true nature as an integral part of God, and knowing that you are a spiritual being here for the experience of all perception unfolding before you. Prayer is a perpetual stillness of the heart, a surrendering to yourself as an aspect of God. Prayer is not beseeching an entity outside of us for favors, but

97

acknowledging and abiding in the presence of God within us. We need not speak outward to God, but listen inward for insight thru intuition, which is the voice of God within us. In silent meditative prayer one can feel God's essence as one's true self, but if one is chanting and beseeching, their communion is only within their concepts. God is our true nature, and we need only realize this unity to be in perpetual prayer — a prayer which is our life, as the spiritual beings of the one reality, which is God.

The warrior's personal communion in God is strictly personal. He needs no person, place or object to be an intermediary between him and God. God is within him, as him. How can a church, religion, dogma or ritual bring God closer to him, God is him, for he is a spiritual being in God. Religions are not our spiritual source, our source is within us. Religions are part of the world, they are intellectual and social forms of conceptualization. The sincere and dedicated individuals within the religions are spiritual souls of purpose, attempting to make deeper contact with their source. But the church itself is a convention of the world, and has lost touch with their original revelator, replacing the initial insights with ritual, dogma and formality. Thru simplicity and purity one abides in God, in complexity one searches for God. All spiritual souls need to unite in a common bond of brotherhood, for we are all the same essence radiating from the one God. Prejudice of spiritual expression within the family of God has never made sense. Every revelator has emphatically stated that God is within us; how is it then that all the religions fight for dominance to an external God. The religious world fights over details of

God's form and attributes, and all these conceptions are just illusions of thought. Every human attribute has been piled upon some external God to worship, defend and fight over. We need join together and realize our unity of essence, and stop conceptualizing our differences. God is the reality, and we are spiritual beings, free and equal of this one ultimate reality — God is not a concept, God is the only truth. The world will find harmony when each one of us becomes the master of our personal relationship within God. We are all equal, unique signatures of God, and each of us can commune directly with the essence of God within them. Each individual can be as a religion unto himself, and his path as God will be the prayer of his life.

It is the romantic notion that all religions, doctrines and philosophies will bring one to God. God is not external to us, God is within us — no looking or searching is necessary. One need only abide within the consciousness of their realization of God's presence. Religions and dogmas keep one looking for God; one is kept so involved with the social aspects, rituals, concepts and philosophical fantasy, that the sincere devotee can find little time or courage to abide within the light of realization. All doctrines must be released to allow the sincere, dedicated devotee to move inward, and recognize himself as the essence of God made manifest. There is enough religious division, each individual must turn within and follow his highest light, leading to the ultimate freedom within their true nature. Let no one tell you their biased opinions of right and wrong, or their conceptions of good and bad, you are the spiritual soul of God, and have a direct source to all love and wisdom. Within you is the guidance of the eternal, you need but still your thoughts and listen with your heart. Let the personal experiences of your heart dictate your way — listen for that intuitive voice within you. You are the essence of God, and your intuition is your personal guidance as God — be true to it, and joy and understanding will always be leading the way. In the world, harmonize your heart and mind to live joyously within this unfolding experience of life; but when turning within to God, let your heart be your guide and your soul your altar, and silently listen in communion of God praying within you.

Art Plate #14~ Within you is the miracle of life, and with its blossoming comes the opportunity to pass on the real treasures of this world – love, sincerity, respect and humility. The materialistic concepts of the world are a poor inheritance, for they burden the soul and delude our spiritual vision. If you accept the responsibility to bring forth life, then first find an understanding of your true self, and thus you will raise your child in spiritual wisdom, for wisdom is the greatest inheritance you can ever bestow ...

Life is a Prayer

As realization blossoms, one begins to intellectually understand that their religious life is a quagmire of conflicting concepts. They now realize that God is their very essence, but still they desire to have some form of communication with a personal aspect of God— so within this conflict they face the question, 'How do I pray?'

God is not external to us, God is our very life, thus the warrior realizes that it serves no purpose to pray to a concept of an external God; for we are God within manifestation, so we need not pray unto ourself. So how does a warrior pray or offer devotion then? As with everything in a warrior's life, prayer is simplicity itself. The warrior recognizes that praying outward in thought only re-enforces an inner development of concepts. So the warrior drops verbal prayer, and instead lets each action of his life speak his prayer for him. His loving attitude in daily expression, and his sharing with all his brothers, and his devoted life of sincerity and respect to the true spiritual nature within him, are his moment by moment prayer of unceasing devotion.

In every activity and situation, the warrior does his best as the prayer of his life. His truth in living is his prayer, and since he is true to himself, his prayer is true to his source. He has true respect for this blessed opportunity to experience this miracle of life, and thus his humility and respect build an attitude in which every moment is his chance to prayerfully live his actions as a devotion to his true nature of God. Thus it can be said that a warrior's sincere and respectful attitude is his true prayer in life.

But if one still feels that verbal prayer

is necessary at this time to bring them deeper into the moment, and provide a closer communion with life's miracle, and a deeper respect for this blessed opportunity to live, then of course they should still pray. But remember that your prayer is not directed outward, but rather it is the acknowledgment of the divinity within. It does no good to pray outward for guidance, and not recognize the divine light already within you. Pray within to the miracle of your existence, and pray to your true nature of God and all of life, as the manifestation of God's reality. In silent communion let your love be your prayer, for prayer is not for asking or questioning, prayer is your communion of the divinity that you are. But always remember this— what good is prayer if your life does not reflect it; thus prayer is not a separate activity a warrior does, prayer is a warrior's life, and every act reflects it. This moment is the most precious moment of existence, so the warrior abides within it respectfully, humbly, alert and conscious, and with this attitude every circumstance and act he performs is done as the prayer of his life. The warrior abides in wonder within this miracle, as the prayer of his most cherished dream, for he is God in reality, and with this realization he sincerely makes his life the prayer of God.

Art Plate # 15~ Our heart is the center of our being, and lights our world of spiritual vision. As our love pours out, we bath the world with our compassion, for without the sharing of love, this world can contain no joy ; thus our spiritual experience within this miraculous realm will go unfulfilled, and true understanding will always be lacking. Let your heart guide your way, and know that you'll never be lost...

Heart and Mind

Our true self as a spiritual being has the dual nature of heart and mind, and if awareness of our spiritual nature is to arise, then there must be harmony and balance between them. If the heart is allowed to rule completely over the mind, as many devotees of God attempt, then one loses the opportunity to relate within this relative world. We are here to perceive, not hide in the fantasy of the heart, and divorce ourself from our world of daily experience. The vast majority leans the opposite way, by allowing their mind to rule their heart. They identify with their thoughts, and see the world as their true home, and their body and mind as their true self. Spiritual realization can arise only when one harmonizes his dual nature of heart and mind, and lives spontaneously in the moment.

The warrior abides in peace — his heart loves all unconditionally, because he sees everyone as part of the totality of God; and his mind provides relation and interprets the experience of the present moment. The warrior doesn't try to subdue his heart or his mind, but realizes his spirit cannot function without either. Our spirit's vehicle of experience and expression is our heart and mind — in harmony they relate as compassion and wisdom, but if out of balance, one reflects within oneself an illusion of separate existence, and loses relation of the true nature of their essence.

The warrior's life is the art of harmony. He does not seek the extinction of the rational process of thought, only the cessation of fantasy, illusion and conceptual thought, and the desires and attachments that arise from them, and also the past rememberances and the future expectations that cause the delusion of thought

To eclipse the present moment. This is the framework the ego resides within, and it keeps us from living the moment fully; it deludes us into thinking instead of living, while the precious, irretrievable moment slips on by, and we are left with only memories of fantasies. This moment is as precious as your life, for that is exactly what it is. To stop rampant thought does not hamper living; rational thought is still there as problems arise, or in relating to the world, but the useless perpetual inner dialogue is curtailed. This incessant thought is the hardest, yet simplest task to accomplish. It is the true spiritual work of the warrior, for nothing can be realized till the mind rests in the true abode of the spirit. The warrior is free when his mind has stopped its clinging to fantasy and illusion. His heart will now have a partner free of delusion and abiding in wisdom, and living attentive in the moment to answer the heart's need of direction for the expression of its love and joy.

All dualities stem from heart and mind. Good, bad, true and false are not dualities, they are products of thought, and of conceptual relativity. Thoughts of themselves are not bad, they are unconditioned. The harm done thru conceptual thought is that it holds one in delusion, and thus the mind can provide no direction to balance the heart, thereby losing contact with the fleeting moment. The duality of heart and mind is not like good and bad, but as an aspect of the manifestation of inter balancing cycles. This polarity is within all of us, and any interference, such as illusory thought, puts one out of harmony with their true nature — the precious moment of experience is lost, and the spiritual eyes are blinded.

Without illusory thought, one still possesses the positive emotions, but the negative emotions will have no place to abide within you. Love, joy and compassion have a natural home in your heart and are expressed as part of its nature. But negative emotions are generated of thought and have no home, for they are illusion created by desire and attachment. Stop illusional thought, and the illusion of negative emotions will stop also.

We are all in ignorance, but the purer our heart and the clearer our mind, the more intuitively we can feel our true home of pure consciousness — it is the spiritual essence which is our inner light. The ego that tries to look deeper with a process of thought, will find nothing but its own illusory dreams. Still the voice within, and you will find a place to abide in a tranquil sea of serene insight — it will be there and no amount of reasoning can explain why this is so. Just shut off your thoughts by an intent of your heart, no force will do, and you'll find both a tranquil peace and a deeper understanding. Eventually no intent will be needed, and your mind will seek its pure state of no thought of its own accord. Love and wisdom can then radiate as your heart and mind join as one, and within this joyous moment you will find your unity.

Thought produced fantasy vanishes when the mind is focused in the present — it is the death of your illusion, but since it is not real, there is nothing to die but a dream of its own making. Your being is the spectrum of reality, and you need add nothing to realize your true nature, especially not thoughts of illusion and fantasy. You can intuitively feel your spiritual identity without the need to mentally confirm yourself to you. All thought brings the mind into disturbance, and while it is reflecting, it loses the moment and the opportunity to experience this magical realm of perception.

Relax into this moment, there is nothing

To be done, nothing is pending — your heart and mind have the opportunity to grasp the freedom of this unique experience, because this moment cannot be chained. Your own thoughts build the heavy chains you bind your spirit with. Your attitude is reflective of your conscious choice, for this manifestation is the avenue for a joyous leap of the spirit into a realm of wondrous experience. We have blossomed into being, both free and vibrant, to perceive this adventure in an unbridled spiritual attitude, and only in a childlike innocence will we find spiritual purity.

In this very moment, with our heart pure and mind still, we can reach into our source. The Absolute is the only reality, and all we need do, is to abide in our true essence. There is nowhere to go, and no place to come from— we are here at this present moment, and the truth of realization is acknowledging this fact. We are a spiritual being within the totality of the Absolute, and no amount of thought, study, discipline or ritual will ever bring this illusive enlightenment. This knowledge is nowhere to be found, but within your true nature of being, and you need seek or do nothing — you need only to realize the divine presence within you, and live in this knowledge. You need not go anywhere, your true self is contained in the present moment, wherever eternity has placed you. We are all capable of this definitive journey of simple self discovery — to complicate this realization with techniques and rituals is to lose the subtleness of its presence. It is like running around madly with our eyes closed, looking for a puff of smoke — we need to open our eyes to detect its subtle presence. The process of meditation, prayer and spiritual gatherings are for opening the eyes, and to give perspective of direction — then the techniques and methods can be used to keep one dedicated while approaching the presence of the smoke — once there and convinced of its reality, the methods can be dropped, for they are no longer of use. The smoke realized, one can stand silent within it, just to find the realization that we also are smoke, and part of its engulfing presence. We drifted out of the smoke and will return back into it. The subtleness of its presence permeates everywhere, for everything is made of its essence — thus we were never separated from the reality of the smoke's totality. Our eyes were opened to see and realize our true source, and once opened, no search was found to be necessary — our look outward became a realization inward.

The opening of one's spiritual eyes is measured in the element of time. It can be a sudden illumination, or as with most seekers, it can require a considerable amount of time — it requires time and sincerity for techniques and disciplines to unweave the complicated tapestry of their illusory thoughts and living attitudes. We can abide in our spiritual nature this moment, but most aspirants need years of simplifying and purifying their life and thoughts, till they can joyously abide in a pure, loving heart and a serene, peaceful mind. How much time it takes is relative to how quickly one can be completely convinced they are a spiritual being.

Time is of no importance, once dedicated and sincere, realization will come of itself when conditions are conducive. It usually depends on how much thought is present, for concepts and fantasy are hinderances to realizing one's true nature — they bring knowledge, not understanding. The initial questioning into one's self and attitudes will be started by some form of catalyst; and while experiencing life, many catalysts will be encountered to keep one motivated and evolving. Any catalyst will do, for they are all part of your attitude at its present moment — we all form catalysts for each other to provide the opportunity to realize ourself. Gurus and masters thru out the ages have dedicated their lives to be catalysts, and provide a spark of inspiration to help others to delve deeper into their true self. Unfortunately, most people maintain their attitude, and thus build concepts about the master around his unique quality, and start worshipping, clinging and desiring — thus they miss the chance of catalytic self enquiry. They see the master as a path and goal, instead of seeing themselves as complete and spiritually whole. A master is not necessary to acheive realization, he is just one of many possible avenues to spark a dedicated inner search of truth. A master can possibly bring profound understanding, but he can also be the source of possible stagnation. Any activity, situation or person can work as a catalyst — the glories of nature, meditation, physical endeavors, sharing, yoga, prayer, etc. are all possible avenues of stilling one's thoughts and receiving a catalytic spark to bring communion into one's source. Be aware at each moment for the opportunity to grasp the mystery of our being, it is the adventure of life knocking. It is your invitation to drop your illusory thoughts and sojourn this wondrous land with a joyous, unfettered heart and mind. At each moment, you are in the presence of your spiritual reality, free to capture the unfolding experience of life. At this very moment you can cease being a man or woman, and start being God. It is time to unite your heart and mind, and allow your spirit to roam this miraculous realm in freedom.

Parable ~ Heart Leads The Way

At a spiritual gathering, a bhakti (a devotee of God) and a jnani (a follower of the discriminating mind) got into a conversation. The jnani had brought great distress to the bhakti by telling him that his path would not lead him to realization. The bhakti wept, "I don't know what to do, I don't want to lose God." "Well", the jnani replied, "if you don't believe what I say, then let us journey to an old master of great wisdom. I've never met him, but my teacher told me to visit him if ever I lose my way and can proceed no further. I think that's where your at, so let's go see him." The two journeyed to a little cabin nestled in the trees, and knocked on the door. Soon, an old man appeared - he was the master of many teachers, and a great warrior. "Welcome, my friends", he said, "only ones seeking the ultimate truth come here. Come in and we shall talk, but first say hello to my pet lamb; the poor little creature got attacked by a wolf, and had its legs bitten off." The two disciples looked down, and there in a small bed lay a little lamb that appeared to have no legs. The bhakti burst into tears and knelt down to caress it compassionately. The warrior turned to the jnani and asked, "well what do you think of this lamb?" The jnani dryly replied "it is of no ultimate consequence within this illusory world if it has legs or not." The warrior laughed and said, "your answer is true, but it comes only from your mind, you might as well leave for you can find no realization of the truth here." The bhakti was still crying over the lamb, so the warrior lifted the lamb and undid a rope that had tied its legs under it, to give it the appearance of having no legs. He then invited the bhakti into his home, saying that the time has come for him to approach the gate of realization, and enter into full awareness of the truth. The jnani was utterly confused and pleaded, "please wait, I don't understand, he has no conception of the reality, and I have thought this matter over thoroughly, how is it that he is ready and I am not." Compassionately the warrior replied, "for the very reason you just spoke — he has no conception of illusory thought, but only purity of heart motivating his spontaneous actions. Whereas you have only thoughts of attainment — your concepts fill your being with delusion, not light. You know the truths only by word and thought. Your realizations aren't of your true nature, but only of your intellectual illusions; you have concepts of your true self, but no actual realization. There are two natures within us — the heart and the mind, and all dualities of life arise from them. Without the heart there is no love, joy, beauty or sharing; and without the mind there is no understanding or relating this world into relativity. The heart gives purpose, and the mind guides this purpose. Now here is the paradox — the heart serves, and without the mind to guide it in this relative manifestation, our physical being could not function. But when one seeks the reality beyond this transitory world, and wishes to rise into higher light and abide in the reality of their true nature, then it is the heart that must lead the way. Once the disciple is pure of heart, unattached to thought, desireless of motive, spontaneous in his action, sharing of his love and joyous within the moment, then the mind can unite with the heart and bring its attention and awareness, so that complete understanding will be realized. For once the union of heart and mind be completed, then one's true nature is grasped. Our true nature is always there, but to live in constant awareness of it, your pure heart must first lead the way – then your consciousness may abide within it, unhindered by attachment, desires or thoughts." The jnani pleaded, "but what am I to do?" The warrior answered, "the way is the same for all – our nature as absolute is always present, we need only realize it. For the bhakti, he is ready to forsake the concepts of attachment of a love outside himself, and use the guidance of his mind to understand the reality within himself, and abide in that awareness – his heart is pure, now he is in need of mind's consciousness to commune with. For yourself the way is harder. You have built a formidable barrier with your intellectual thought. Your concepts allow no room for heart, therefore you miss the joy, beauty and love of existence within this miraculous realm of perception. You're too busy conceptualizing about the reality, to actually live in the moment where reality exists. Your thoughts of your true nature are illusion, they are not the reality; your real nature is much more than your mere thoughts and concepts – there's more to you than you can ever imagine. To find your avenue into the mystery of being, you'll have to ask your heart for guidance. You have only dry knowledge and dead thoughts, what you need now is live intuition and joyful adventure. It's time for you to stop reading a book about realization, and start living the poetry of life. This is a dance here, one needs energy and exuberance for life, a zest to experience this wondrous, unique miracle – this brings the heart to life with joy, love and beauty, and as it soars, your awareness will ride along with it into the unfolding moment. Only in uniting your heart and mind will understanding bring realization of your true nature. Then you can joyously abide in your wisdom, and your spiritual essence will at last be free, and the absolute ever present in your consciousness."

Parable - Realize or Die

An old man heard that a warrior was in the vicinity and went to see him. He explained that he had been searching for truth all his life and still had found nothing. He had tried many religious paths, only to become disillusioned — and now with old age, only bitterness of life's failure remained. He pleaded for help, "what can I do, I'll do anything to gain enlightenment." The warrior seriously replied, "you've surely tried everything, there is now nothing left for you to do but kill yourself." With those words he placed a knife before the old man. The old man was frozen in fear, no thoughts in his mind, just a sense of entrapment. Suddenly the old man shouted, "that's it, I've seen my true nature, my life is precious to me, I want to live and experience. In this moment of fear I saw I was trapped by my own thoughts, desires and concepts; when my thoughts left me so did my problems, I need search no more, I am the goal I sought. I'm free at last." The warrior confirmed, "yes, everything you've said is true, you were holding yourself back with your thoughts, and needed a catalyst to recognize it, for you a very strong catalyst of realize or die. But this insight you've just had is an emotional outburst of sudden light, like all experiences, it will go into your memory and be slowly forgotten. You've attained a glimpse of your true nature, but don't think this is a complete depth of realization. You must maintain this insight by a constant vigil of awareness, as you live in the ever unfolding moment. In this way deeper understanding will develop, and your consciousness will abide as your true self, ever joyous in this miraculous moment unfolding before you."

114

Parable - Choice of Two Trees

Within a farmer's orchard there were two delicious apple trees. One day the news spread that a plague of locusts was coming. The two trees were very worried, and one tree said, "I have a plan; I will turn all my leaves and fruit very sour, and that will save me from the locusts." The other tree replied, "that does sound like a good plan, but I could not bear to sour all my beautiful fruit – I will just have to rely on providence." The locusts arrived and ate all the fruit in the orchard, except for the sour fruit on the one tree. The sour tree was very pleased, and told the moaning sweet tree that he should have listened to him. The next day the farmer surveyed the damage, and was amazed that there was fruit left on one tree. He tasted the fruit and said, "no wonder the locusts didn't eat this horrible fruit"; and with that he took an axe and chopped down the sour tree. And with the coming of a new season the sweet tree blossomed anew, and produced an abundant crop of beautiful, delicious apples.

Comment: The reward for uncalculated love often goes unseen. Our true nature is one of love and sharing, and if this is altered to reap benefits for ourself, there may be short-term, superficial, worldly rewards; but in this compromise, freedom and love are buried under worldly desire, and this selfishness sours our heart, and brings upon the death of our spirit. Love is its own reward, for we are a spiritual being; and for one who is true to themself, the fruit of this relative existence may be sparse at times, but at least it is always sweet.

Art Plate # 16~ Each of us has grown within a forest of concepts, and its canopy is thick and dense around us. We are all equal in that our roots are nurtured from the same physical source, yet we each have the freedom to grow away from the ignorance of our prejudice and preconceived concepts, and into the light of spiritual understanding. Always seek for greater light, and though you appear to be illumed from above, the wisdom of our true nature actually radiates our world from within...

Communion Beyond Concept

If you feel that God is outside of you, and that there is an identity as yourself as creation apart from a creator or God filled reality, then your conviction will force you into the position of adopting a path to a futuristic goal of a hopeful union with God. This is almost the universal pattern of all religious seekers — they have an outside goal to reach, thus seek a path to attain it. It is all very logical, for the whole process of seeking begins and is perpetuated in one's thoughts. It is all illusion of conceptual thought, for if your thoughts are stopped then the path collapses, and the goal is found to be none other than yourself. God is your true nature, for you are the spiritual essence of the Absolute, and all existence is part of its totality.

If within your delusory thought you begin seeking a concept of God, then any path you choose has the terrible possibility, and almost sure inevitability, that because of an untrue act you commit, your thought concepts will determine you have slipped from your chosen path, and have now fallen away from your goal of reaching God. If one adopts a path, then one can slip from the path; if one sets up a goal, then one can fail in their attainment of it. Thus one will fall into the greatest misery imaginable — they have lost one illusion by the adoption of another illusion. If one tries and fails in the marketplace there is only regret, but if one adopts a path to God and fails, then the suffering is the most real agony imaginable. The suffering is only illusion, but since it is accepted as part of the total concept, then its relative realness makes the sorrow as a reality. When a devotee of God feels they have fallen from union with God, they have now placed themselves into a conceptual hell. They set up an illusion of an outside union of creator and creation, an expected joy beyond this world; but as the illusion set up demands of an unattainable goal, then came the pendulum swing, and they found the counterpart of an unexpected sorrow within this world. The path of the devotee is a continual process of elated highs and depressive lows; it is the hope of attainment of a futuristic goal, mixed with the reality of failure of their present illusion.

Paths are illusion of concept, and attaining the illusory goal is not possible, thus sorrow is the inevitable companion of the seeker. The rigid concepts keep the path narrow, so it is easy to fall from its demands — there is much sorrow in falling. The goal is ever in the future, and since it is an illusory concept of attainment, one is always failing to reach the elusive goal — there is much sorrow in failure. If a path is accepted, then the sorrow it produces is real unto itself, for within the concept all aspects have relative realness. If you believe you are your thoughts, then the illusion of sorrow is its own reality.

All this suffering can be avoided by realizing that God is the only reality. You are a spiritual being emanating from the one and only source. Your spirit is eternal — you live, breathe and have your being as God. You cannot be separated from God, for God is the totality and the only reality — God 'is', nothing else 'is'. Thus there is no seeking necessary, and no suffering from falling from the path or failure to attain the goal. The goal of God is the reality of yourself — you are within God, and God is within you. In this realization of your true nature, you can find your communion within God.

The warrior is not a seeker, thus he does not ride the pendulum course of joy and sorrow. The mark of a warrior is his constancy; he lives in realization, not in the emotions generated by illusory concepts. To understand that your thoughts and concepts are illusion is to find realization of your spiritual essence. Freedom is not a goal, it is the supreme awareness of who you are.

The paths of my past have been many, for my dedication is sincere. As I sojourned this land alone, I was guided to the ways of a warrior. Unfortunately, I quickly fell into the illusory thought of conceptualizing a warrior's path. There is a great difference between living the ways of a warrior, and following the warrior's path. The warrior's path is just as much an illusion of the mind as any other path, and contains all the pitfalls of sorrow if failing to attain the goal, or not being true to the concept. The 'ways of a warrior' is quite different though — it is the simple living in the present, and experiencing this wondrous miracle to the fullest. It is a realization, not an attainment. A warrior merely has his own simple, unique, truthful ways, and is sincere, respectful and joyous in his opportunity to experience life as it unfolds. He is not seeking, or desires any goal — his realization has brought him into an understanding that he is the goal, for he is the spiritual emanation of God, and in continual communion with the source of his being. There is one totality, one reality, one truth, and he is the essence of it.

The difference between the ways of a warrior and a warrior's path can be shown by an example. If one makes his dinner and is fully attentive to the preparation, as if it were the only activity of importance; and then eats fully aware of his meal and savors the experience, then this person is alive in the present and living the ways of a warrior. But, if one makes dinner with no attention to his actions, and eats unconsciously with his mind ever active in thought, and hurries to finish so he can get to the tasks of a warrior's life, then he is not in the joy of the moment, and is trying to live a warrior's path. He will miss the essence of life, for his goal is illusory and of the future, thus it is a non-realizable attainment. The difference between the two lives is not as subtle as it sounds. If your thoughts are active, and your activities rushed, then you cannot be fully alive and conscious in the moment. Only if your thoughts are quiet and your heart at peace can you be fully attentive and aware of this unfolding moment. This is the essence of realizing your spiritual identity — this ever present moment frees us from concepts and paths, so that we can abide in the reality of our true nature — it is a goal that is our 'self'. Relax into this moment and live true to yourself — here you will find the freedom of realization; it is a communion with your source, a communion beyond seeking, a communion beyond concept.

Parable ~ The Precious Ring

There once was a man who owned a ring, and loved it so much that he thought it more important than anything else. He was constantly worried of losing it, so he kept it in a pouch in his pocket with his hand firmly grasping it. When he would meet a friend, he would take out the ring and place it on the third finger of his right hand and show it off. One day while walking he bumped into a friend, so he very quickly pulled out the ring and put it on his third finger. The conversation was very engrossing, and when they parted he was deep in thought. Suddenly he remembered the ring. He looked on his right hand

and the ring was gone; he opened the pouch and the ring was not there either; he looked thru all his clothing and found nothing. Repeatedly he searched the pouch and his right hand, and then began looking on the ground and retracing his steps — crawling on his hands and knees. He found nothing and started asking everyone he saw if they had seen his ring. He was frantic with grief and crying so hard that he had to wipe the tears from his eyes, and that's when he discovered his precious ring on the third finger of his left hand.

Comment: The religious concept of God is as a precious object to most. They set up ways to protect and ensure their conceptual union by rituals, dogma and paths. But the danger of losing their desired attainment is always present. When thru weakness or forgetfulness they slip from their desired union within their concept of God, then great sorrow will occur. They will seek and look everywhere outside of them for that which is ever present within them, and ask advice of others to help find the goal which was never apart from them. The search is in the wrong place; the seeker looks for an attainment of a concept of God, instead of communion within the very truth of his existence. He is anxious to show off a prize of illusory attainment to everyone, a God as his precious object of conception. But reality will fill this delusory path with sorrow and loss, til his tears force a deeper look within the purity of his heart. There in his heart he will find freedom from his concepts of desire and attainment, and come into communion with the source of his very being — at long last he will find the reality of God, abiding as his true nature.

Art Plate # 17~ I traveled the world over in
search of God, till I was utterly exhausted. In
despair I sunk my face into my hands, but as
I lifted my face away, I stared at my hands
and was amazed by the miracle they were—
my hands were a masterpiece of creation. I
suddenly realized my hands were not separate
from God, but an aspect of the divine, and so was
I and all of life, for how could anything exist
apart from God. I didn't have to look for God, for
I was in fact God in manifest form. My long
search for God was at last fulfilled, by the
presence of God in the palms of my hands . . .

122

Parable ~ Seeking a Doctor

A doctor was hiking in the hills, and while climbing over some rocks he took a fall. He struck his head and cut himself, and when he regained consciousness, he couldn't remember who he was. Upon seeing the blood on his head, he grew concerned and set out to find a doctor. He went to the closest small town and began to look for a doctor — he asked everyone he met where he could find one. The looking brought only disappointment, and he soon became discouraged. Deciding to eat before continuing his search, he looked in his wallet for some money, and found his business card with his name and profession listed. He at once remembered who he was and laughed heartily at the idiocy of seeking a doctor when he in fact was a doctor, and then proceeded to cure himself.

Comment: The seeker has amnesia — he has forgotten who he is, and of his union in God. He looks everywhere to fulfill his desire of finding a God that is present only in his concepts. He will travel on pilgrimage, and seek advice from others to try to stay on his path to the hopeful goal. But upon looking into his heart he discovers that he is already in union with God, and had never been apart from his source. He remembers his true identity as the spiritual essence of God, and realizes the obvious — that no search is necessary to find himself. What joy and laughter the realization of one's true nature brings. Thus we are all capable of curing ourselves with the simple recognition of our divinity, and abiding in this knowledge moment by moment — for here and now is the blessed opportunity of experiencing life as our perpetual prayer.

Parable - Face To Face

A man went to a warrior and asked the question which had always brought him into religious doubt - "Where is God?" The warrior replied, "God is everywhere to be perceived if you have eyes of spiritual discernment." The man responded, "please, that means nothing to me, could you actually show me God. I wish to see God face to face." "alright," the warrior answered, "I'll bring you face to face with God, but it will be up to you to see God." The warrior took the man down a hallway and came to a shut door, and said, " God is in this sacred room. It is dark in there, so be not afraid - just take three steps into the room and look in front of you till you can see God - be patient, for God is most definitely there." With that the warrior opened the door and pushed the man inside and shut the door quickly, before the man could see into the room. It was very dark inside and the man could see nothing at all, so with hands outstretched, he gingerly took three steps forward and halted, and there peered into the darkness. Slowly his eyes became adjusted to the dark, and he was able to make out a figure before him. He became excited to think he may actually be in the presence of God, and peered intently till he could clearly distinguish that there was definitely a figure standing a few feet in front of him. He concentrated and strained his eyes for more light, wanting desperately to see this spiritual vision. He felt euphoric and filled with spiritual strength at the thought that he was finally in the presence of God.

Suddenly the door opened, and the room was flooded with light. The man turned around and saw the warrior approaching him, and then he looked in front of him and saw himself in a full length mirror. The warrior could see that the man was obviously disappointed and chagrined, so the warrior said, "you stood in the presence of God and used your spiritual sight, but now you are disappointed because God is not in your worldly sight. You wanted to be face to face with God and that's what you were, for you are God in reality. But God is not some entity outside of yourself to search for and beseech, or to stand in front of. With spiritual sight of discernment you can see and experience God as the reality of all life around you; and most importantly, you can realize God as your own true self of existence. Just close your eyes and you'll once again be within this dark room, and there you can use your spiritual sight to be face to face with the essence of your being, and that essence is God."

Wanderings of The Heart

The Hoover Wilderness ~ September 1985~

The day broke sunny, as I raced the sunrise into the Hoover Wilderness of the high Sierras. The trail I followed led me up a broad, lush canyon with giant walls towering above me. After nine miles of gentle ascent, the valley floor rose abruptly into a granite cirque, with snow covered ledges and waterfalls cascading down the cliffs. The trail was now at an end, so I continued on by climbing the walls til I reached the 12,000 foot ridge above. I now traversed along its crest til I came upon a spectacular array of black twisted pillars rising out of the granite peak. The hundreds of volcanic pillars rose like statues of ebony set in a stark granite backbone. The vision they brought to my mind, was that I now was entering into a sacred temple on the moon. Ink rocks they are called, and stand as Titans upon sheer granite cliffs that drop over 3,000 feet to the cascading creek below. Upon the stark summit I rested, surrounded by magnificent peaks, massive granite domes, sheer canyon walls and cascading creeks, that enfolding me for 75 miles in every direction. Gazing upon this grandeur could only bring the wondrous feeling that I was sitting on the throne of creation. For hours I could do no more than bask in the awesome display of nature's miracle, but since this miracle is cast in the mystery of time, I recognized the necessity to attempt my descent down Ink rocks and into the paralleling canyon to the one I had ascended. The drop to the adjoining cirque proved to be difficult, and I was forced to slide from one black pillar to another — a grand opportunity to be a mountain goat til the angle lessened in severity, and I was able to follow a small cascading creek down to the lake in the granite cirque surrounding me. The 1000 foot walls now engulfed me, bringing amazement and gratitude that I was even able to descend. I charged down the valley toward home, for I had nine miles still to go, but the beauty of 500 foot waterfalls and crystal, pure lakes set in lush medows slowed my pace in reverie of appreciation. The stream became larger as hundreds of rivulets merged into its winding course. After four miles I came upon a pretty meadow lake with a beaver dam trapping its course. I was overjoyed, for my eyes have never been graced to behold the sight of a live beaver in a wilderness pond, so I waited patiently. But the light of day was weakening, and I still had five miles to go, and it was not my wish to traverse the dense forest on a moonless night. So on I went reluctanly, but soon came upon another beaver dam, so once again I waited. Twilight was approaching, so off I went with no vision of my flat tailed little brother. The next mile held one dam after another, and I waited briefly at some, but realized I must move quickly. Finally, the trail, which was strewn with trees from the beaver's handiwork, came within a few feet of a beautiful two level pond. This time I didn't look at the pond or for a beaver, instead I looked up and within and earnestly asked, "Mother, I've run out of time, I can only stay one minute, then I must leave, please let me see a beaver". I then looked down, and there in front of me, about ten feet away on the bank of the pond, was a husky, forty pound, squinty-eyed beaver just entering into the water. It swam to the center of the pond, and then climbed up and over the dam and into the lower pond, and finally disappeared into its beaver lodge. I watched flabbergasted at the event, and it took about one minute. I then, with deep respect and gratitude, said my thanks, and then double-timed it back thru the pines and giant cedars to my home parked in the woods, just as it got pitch black. The twenty miles of exploration was a physical reality, and yet my sojourn was an adventure in my heart, for the beauty was the reflection of my respect, and the beaver was the realization of my true nature. I can do no more than humbly offer my prayer, for my life is my prayer as the essence of God that I am.

The Solitary Journey

In this solitary journey to nowhere, the path and the goal are one. Consequently, there is no hurry to arrive, for we are the one we are walking towards. Tranquil and at peace we shall recognize ourself, and be content in the knowledge of our ignorance. We need only be true to ourself, to arrive where our hearts have always been...

Art Plate #18 ~ There isn't a grain of sand
or drop of water that doesn't have as its core
of being an essence of life, and just because
we can't relate to them, it doesn't cancel out
their existence. All form is vibratory expression,
and all aspects of it have the same true
nature as essence of the Absolute — there is
one reality, and all energy is an aspect of
its totality. If you can't recognize God around
you, then you won't acknowledge God within you...

Warriors Are Not Followers

If you love Christ, then your love must extend to all spiritual masters. I did not say you must follow them, I said you must love them. Not only do they live dedicated to realizing God, but the message of Christ was to love one another. So if you love Christ then you must love all your brothers, including prophets and leaders of other faiths. You must love all spiritual followers, and also those that aren't religious. But if your love for Christ is only a shallow word, then your love will be limited and conditional to only those that your intellect chooses. If you follow a master, then you must obey the precepts of the one you follow. If you honor Buddha, then you must honor all your brothers; if you worship Krishna, then you must worship all of humanity. It is a mockery to expound your love for Christ while speaking ill of your neighbor, or say you honor Buddha and slander another religion, or show worship to Krishna and fight another nation. The love and ideals of the master must be alive within you and find demonstration in each activity of your life, as the very truth of your being.

The warrior honors and respects the ideals of all persons, but he follows only the dictates of his own heart — he is a free spiritual being, and his way is his own. All masters are spiritual warriors, for they are sincere and dedicated to living their heart's dictate. They follow no one, or preach any one else's message. They are master of their life's course, and speak to everyone the message of their heart. No master ever followed another master, he is unique unto himself and has his individual ways — even great disciples had to strike a course unique to themself. Truth in living is not dependent on following another person; one does not have to know of Christ, to live Christ's message of peace — it is our inborn nature to love and share. The words of all the prophets are written in your heart, and with spiritual sight, we can read this message of our soul and be a living master of truth.

At is not possible to follow another warrior. His path is unique and his ways are personal; his words relate to himself, and their meaning grasped only within his unique life. We are all unique individuals and have personal views within the relative, thus each path is the personal expression of the individual. That is why the realization of Christ and Buddha became a religion about them. People can't understand the essence of their unique, sincere life, and instead adopt the form. The essence can never be held, it is a personal realization that each individual must acknowledge — thus the followers settle for worshipping the idolized form, and ritualize their devotion.

No one can transmit their realization while alive, so how can their message be conveyed after the master has died. Neither Christ or Buddha or anyone else has ever enlightened some one, if they could have, they would have enlightened all souls of the world. One is not enlightened by another — no external force or object is necessary to bring one into realization of their true nature as a spiritual being. The individual must recognize his own enlightenment, and abide within that wisdom — living it fully, moment by moment, as the prayer of his life. Others can inspire sincerity and dedication, and give knowledge about the totality of their being, but only if one is receptive and aware can they grasp an understanding, and realize the essence of their true nature. Revelations are personal, and so is the manner in which one will live their spiritual life. There can be sharing of our insights, but our individual relation within God is a personal communion. To be in the presence of one who lives his realization can be a great inspiration, and if the person is receptive, then the master can be a catalyst to spark an inward journey into their true nature.

In person, the vital energy of transmission from a master is a powerful catalyst, but once the master is gone, then the best one can receive is inspiration from past words, and a memory held live within us. Inspiration provides us with incentive, but realization can only come from within ourself, when our conscious awareness abides within our true nature. It is a solitary journey, for there is room only for yourself when traveling that path within — you may share abundantly of the love that will flow from your heart, but in enlightenment one stands alone. As you follow anyone else's way, you'll only be deluding yourself with concepts of their superior nature and your inadequacy. Each one of us is equally capable of listening to our heart, and allowing it to steer a course true to our unique life. To find this mastery of being, and realize one's unity of individual consciousness with the supreme reality of the Absolute, is the only priority of life.

This writing is nothing new, throughout the ages there have been numerous warriors proclaiming the same inspiring words of freedom. We are surrounded by wisdom and love, and the realization of yourself is no further away then a bird singing, or a glorious sunset or the smile on your neighbor's face. All have something to share, all are a vital piece of this mysterious experience of life. Our learning and growing is one of attitude, our realization is easily grasped; open your eyes and blame no one for your blindness. We are a spiritual being, but our illusory thoughts and concepts blind us — in communion of our true essence we understand this, and thus our spiritual reality is made visible before us. A spiritual warrior is one who has found his vision; he is one with all souls — he doesn't compare or judge, and he doesn't follow any person or doctrine. He is free of concepts and thouroughly enjoying his soul's experience; he is master of his life and solely responsible for the growth of his consciousness. The warrior's only priority is to grasp this moment, and abide within it as the essence of freedom.

Parable ~ The King's Sons

There once was a king so powerful that he ruled all the earth — his strength was not in armies, but in wisdom. The earth was divided into sections, and each section had its own ruler. Each ruler was a son of the king, and was sincerely devoted to their father — both loving him, and respecting his authority. In one of the sections there lived a hard working farmer who was honored one day. An invitation arrived at his house by messenger of a ruler of a different section, inviting him to travel to the other ruler's land and be his honored guest. The farmer was a simple man; he knew of his ruler and respected him, and it was thru his ruler that he learned of the king. So he honored his ruler above all, and did not want to show disloyalty to him by visiting a ruler that he knew nothing of. The farmer was puzzled, and asked the messenger what he ought to do. "Have no concern", replied the messenger, "all the rulers are sons of the king and love him equally, so to see any of the sons is to honor the father. You need not love your ruler any less, but in respecting the other sons, you show respect to the king. Respect for all the sons brings this world into unity under the one and only king."

Comment: Within this manifestation, there is only God. Amoung us there are ones of sincere devotion, that have a dedicated, deep love in their personal relationship of God, and thus have become conscious sons of God. These masters love God equally, even though their individual expression of love and respect for God differs. Words, form and name will not be the same for each master, but the one same God is in the heart of all the masters. To honor and respect all the masters is to offer that love to God. Those within a religion feel it is disloyal to pay respect to masters of other religions, but one doesn't have to change faith or belief to have honor for another master who is likewise devoted to God. In finding this love, respect and understanding for all the sons of God, we will find peace in our brotherhood within this totality of God.

Parable - The Bigot

There once was a man who was extremely bigoted, and very outspoken. He was convinced that there was no God or true spiritual saints, and that religion had no honor; and he would continuously tell everyone his prejudiced viewpoint with much yelling and profanity. Within the realm of spirit, the devoted sons of God gathered to discuss this boisterous, deluded man. They decided to take action and sent down to earth the most noble of the group. Buddha approached the man, and with great compassion began to elucidate the noble truths, but the man began yelling profanities about beggars and shiftless vagrants, so Buddha knew he could bring no understanding, so he left. Next, the wisest of the group came down. But before Lao Tzu could speak the subtle truth, the man started yelling about calling the police, for he saw Lao Tzu as an illegal alien — so Lao Tzu returned. Christ had been watching and figured enough was enough; he decided to go to the man with great love and peace, and reform him at once. But before Christ could say a word, the man picked up a shovel and chased Christ down the road, yelling profanities about those damn hippies.

Comment: The truth has been spoken by many realized souls — and many sincere, dedicated saints have devoted their life to serving humanity, and bringing a message of love — and there are books, scriptures, temples, churches and religions dedicated to bringing a brotherhood of man to this earth, and peace between us all; but what good can all this possibly do for a man who is deaf and blind by his own choice. If we live within concepts of illusory thoughts, then how can the reality of our spiritual nature ever enter in. If bigotry and prejudice close our mind, and fear seals our heart, then how can the truth of living, and the beauty of this world, ever be seen. Within this miraculous moment rests the wisdom that there are no conceptions to defend, there is only a continuum of growth, if one's heart and mind be open.

  If a sincere soul, dedicated to realizing truth came before you, would you recognize him? Or, would you be so prejudiced in your preconceptions, and so focused into a dead master, as not to recognize a live one before you. Words and lives of truth are present now, the past has no exclusive claim to them. More can be gained by opening your eyes, and seeing the wisdom of your brother and sharing of his live understanding, than trying to decipher dead messages of past prophets. Wisdom is found in the living present where we are, if one keeps alert to its message and free of preconceived ideas. We must all open our minds and become receptive to the truth that surrounds us, and is woven into us as our true spiritual essence. See this miracle of life and know that you are the truth of it. We are spiritual beings within the totality of God, grasp this blessed opportunity to recognize your freedom.

Parable - Don't Follow Me

A young man heard of a great warrior and went to ask if the warrior would be his master and teach him. The warrior said, "you seem sincere, but I doubt that you will do what I suggest." The youth quickly replied, " I will do anything you request - I will meditate all day, and do whatever yoga postures you prescribe, and read everything you suggest, and I'll be your faithful servant - I'll do whatever you think best for me, because I must become enlightened. Please be my master and teach me to be a great warrior like yourself." The warrior responed, " well, you do seem to be dedicated, so I will tell you what you need to do. If you wish to realize your true nature, then don't follow me. Don't call me your master, or anyone else. you must become master of your own life if you are to gain the ultimate freedom- to do this you need to follow your own heart's dictates. Be open to all experiences, and harmonize your heart and mind to be joyous in the present moment. You are the spiritual essence of the Absolute, so you need only be true to yourself, and keep your mind immersed in the Reality." The youth was a little puzzled and said, "is that all? Aren't you going to tell me what to do, and how to do it, and what to believe in, and have me serve and worship you? What kind of advice is this? Aren't you a master?" The warrior laughed and replied, "I am no one's master but my own. I told you that you wouldn't be interested in what I had to say. My advice would lead any sincere, dedicated soul to freedom and realization, but that is not what you are truly interested in at this time. Your after someone to relieve you of your responsibility. Enlightenment is a solitary journey and no one can give you their wisdom or prescribe the course your heart must follow. Your interested in becoming a blind follower, instead of being the master of your own unique life. Within you is everything necessary to realize the divinity already present within you; all seeking outward will only delay your realization. If you felt you could gain greater insight into your true self by being around me, then you should just visit me as a friend, and see if there is anything for you to learn by the example I set. You have dedication, now let your heart guide it, and you'll find an understanding of the true nature of your spiritual essence. Trust only in yourself and let no one be your master, but your own true nature of God."

No One Special

A warrior is no one special, he is master of his life and at peace with the world. Within spiritual thought, gurus and masters who preach doctrines of salvation are seen as special people. They have been elevated by their disciples to be extraordinary people—not normal, and not touchable. They are used by the disciples to answer problems and alleviate burdens; thus the master falls within the desires of the followers, and becomes a possession of their ignorance. In so doing, the master becomes the very problem he is trying to alleviate; he becomes a source of clinging and concept to the ones he has earnestly tried to absolve of this worldly attitude. In being special, both master and disciples become entangled within the world of desire and attachment.

A warrior calls no one master, or does he allow anyone to call him master—he remains free and thus keeps freedom around him. If he has anything to teach, it is the example by which he lives his life—words are secondary and purposeful action primary. He walks the same path you do, and is not trying to stand out, but his mastery of life sometimes makes his presence obvious. Finding a warrior is not easy, for he is not waving a banner proclaiming the ability to run your life. He is not trying to fix up your life or anyone else's life. He is master of his life thru much dedicated diligence, and knows that it is your responsibility to acquire mastery of your life by your own efforts and purposeful action. He will share his experience of life, but not try to run anyone else's. We each bear the responsibility to gain realization and mold our perceivable world into any experience of adventure we choose—our freedom

138

is our sole possession, and we must be master of it. Thus the warrior cannot be your master, but he can be your friend. He is no one special, he is just yourself. The warrior is the one inside of you who has been convinced that he is a free spiritual being, and lives that realization sincerely, at every moment of his life.

Parable ~ The Prideful Shepherd

There once lived in the city a magnificient German Shepherd. He had won lots of ribbons, and wherever he went he was leader of the pack. The shepherd had never been out of the city, but one day he traveled with his owner to the wilderness, where few people ever venture. Out went the shepherd exploring, and before long he came upon a wild bunch of scraggly dogs. The shepherd thought to himself, " here is a little group I can lead while up here", and with that he pranced up to the group. He expected the usual ritual battle with the leader, and to scare him down before he would be accepted as leader. He was much larger than the leader who stepped forward, but something unexpected happened. The leader came at the shepherd with every ounce of strength he possessed; his intensity was so ferocious and his agility so keen, that within a minute the shepherd was forced to retreat for his life. The pack left, and the shepherd limped back home licking his wounds. The shepherd was very disturbed by his defeat, and went to visit the old Husky, who happened to be a warrior dog. Very ashamed, he told the warrior what happened, and asked if he could explain why he was defeated so easily. The warrior answered, "you are highly respected here in the city, you're lord of the pack. But out in the wild, there is no honor or the customary ritual battles. That wild dog was fighting for real, not for just a moment's supremacy of leadership. The wild leader is always alert, his is a life and death struggle for survival. His leanness and scraggly appearance have been achieved thru tremendous hardship, for his life is dedicated to his survival. Your battles are ritual, and you have only pride for courage, whereas the wild leader's courage was the humbleness of his great ability."

Comment: In civilization there are dynamic persons who stand out as spiritual leaders and gain much praise and honor. They groom themselves to look distinguished, and thru ritual debate they rule as leader of whatever group they wish to be among. Their pride blinds them of the message they pronounce, and robs them of their sincerity. They espound realization, but pride, honor and prestige build a wall that keeps them from realizing a true understanding. But in the spiritual wilderness, there are some free individuals who are humble in their simple living, and deep in their spiritual realization. They aren't looking for praise or honor, or to be a leader. Their life isn't for show or ritual; they are sincere and dedicated, and perpetually alert to their spiritual survival. Thru great hardships of fighting their ego and illusion, they have achieved a lean, purposeful life — their ways are simple, but their understanding is great. Their ferocity of intention to live their life in the truth and dedication of their realization is something that most spiritual figureheads would be humbled to witness. Thus many leaders who meet a sincere spiritual warrior will lose their pride and start listening and living their own heart's message.

Additional Note : Here is a true story from my travels that will show the beauty that surrounds us, but in humility doesn't parade itself. After coming out of the 'Hoover Wilderness', I stopped at a gas station. Even though it was a self service station, an attendant came out and began pumping the gas. My van is unique, and he started asking questions about my life. But his words were of little importance, for upon his face was the biggest, most beautiful smile imaginable — and whether he was speaking or listening, his sincere smile filled his face. I asked him of the joy he exuded and his great smile of warmth and love. He told me that as a young man he had read, 'we should take no concern for tomorrow, for it will take care of itself'; and he further said that ever since reading these words he has lived in that vein and his life has been joyous, and that he and his family alway seem to manage just fine. This man was uneducated, and with no prideful philosophy or theology to expound. He was simple, humble and full of love, peace and respect, and very sincere in his realization of the spiritual joy of living. Any prideful master would be humbled by his mere presence. Spiritual pride is one of the most difficult barriers to cross; it keeps one attached to the world of desire, and within the illusion of an ego. Acknowledge the immensity and awesome mystery of this astounding miracle unfolding before you. In your meagerness try to behold the enormity of the Absolute, and thus find your humility in the nothingness that you are — but remember, your nothingness is the miraculous essence of God.

The Mind Killer

Fear kills the mind and poisons the heart, it is a product of thought and is woven into all our concepts. In a pure heart and still mind there is no fear, but as concepts form, fear arises with them — these fears are born out of desire, attachment and expectation. Concepts weave our relative world, and since stability of its illusion is desired, it produces worry and fear, and attaches them to any occurrence that can mean a change within its fantasy thought. But stability is not the order of the universe; the dominant force that surrounds and permeates this manifestation is a perpetual evolution thru change. So fears produced thru stagnant thought are recognizing the fact that change will occur, and probably not as it would desire it to.

The warrior recognizes this conflict of fear within immature thought and chops it away, bit by bit. He stops clinging to a concept of a stagnant world which seeks security of its thoughts, and opens his heart to a magical realm of constant renewal and ever changing vitality. The warrior observes his habits and sees the rigidity of them, and endeavors to become more fluid and free. He breaks his need for attachments, and recognizes that desire and expectation bring sorrow eventually. Above all, he fills his heart and mind with the knowledge that he is a spiritual being, unborn and undying — he is the pure essence of the absolute, and all reality is his home. With a positive understanding of his spiritual reality, he finds nothing to fear. Change and unexpected circumstances are seen with a new attitude — a spiritual attitude that we are here to experience this unfolding drama, not to control or arrange it, but to witness it and grow within its ever present moment.

Fear vanishes for one who abides in their true nature — they are within their source, and fear is not part of the spiritual essence of their being. The warrior understands that within this realm of perpetual being, fear is not a real aspect, but only the product of errant thought. Fear poisons the mind and erases the knowledge of our spiritual heritage, it shows lack of self reflection and a timid heart. Fear means that one does not see the miracle of this blessed chance to experience the challenge and adventure of life. This isn't a position where one has to rise above fear with a courageous act, this is the recognition that we are spiritual essence here to experience the unfolding mystery of perception — every circumstance presented is an opportunity for our spiritual being to behold the wonder and magic of existence. With this spiritual attitude, fear is not present in one's mind. Even if fearful possibilities exist, they are seen as just part of the total experience, and not singled out and focused upon.

Death is nothing to fear; the body will go for it is part of the manifestation, but our spirit is the undying essence of the Absolute. There is no non-existence, death is just the miraculous release of our spirit into a further journey of unfoldment — an evolution within the realm that is our home. The spirit must fearlessly accept the challenge of life; only with a spiritual understanding will our heart and mind be fit vehicles to experience this adventure purposefully and fearlessly, thus reflecting our true nature of spiritual essence. The warrior grabs this opportunity with gusto — his freedom is his only consideration, and as he sojourns within this wondrous world, he finds nothing to fear.

Art Plate # 19~ We are alone in the midst of simplicity. Our true nature is the reality, but the further we drift from its pure light, the deeper into the complexity of desire and attachments we go—it is the web of maya. In abiding in our true self we sit in the light of simplicity and purity, and in this freedom we understand ourself and the complexity surrounding us ...

Desire And Attachment

The Absolute is the only reality, and its totality has never changed. Its fabric of existence is the manifestation, where all is in constant flux — this is the impermanence of the world of relativity. Life within the manifestation is the re-ordering and evolution of energy, and all within it is transitory. Birth and death are the ceaseless flow of conscious intermingling energies; all is within the Absolute, so death as non-existence is not possible, but only a continual involvement within the one totality.

While here in this field of perception, we are bound to it and must use it, as we ourselves are being used. By gift or grace here our spirit be, and it is the opportunity to reign supreme and free within this realm of consciousness. Our deterrent to freely traversing this wonderland of mystery, is to form concepts that this transitory, visible world is the ultimate reality, and thus become attached to it, and desirous of stability within it. Clinging to this transitory world is the death of freedom within the reality of our true nature. The manifestation has reality as fabric of the Absolute, but all is relative within it and perception is transitory, thus any attachment is futile. Perception is our vehicle of experience, but all desire within this perceivable world is formed of illusory thought, thus desire has no reality and is futile. Attachment and desire are delusions within thought, based on concepts of a world of permanence. This world is an ever changing vehicle of experience in a continuous evolution, and our only permanence rests in our ultimate spiritual identity as essence of the Absolute. This manifestation is a mirror of the Absolute, and its permanence is relative to it. Our spirit is part of this totality, both as essence of the Absolute, and as its vehicle of manifested form. To be attached to the physical world, and desire permanence within it, is to accept your conceptual thought as the reality, and not realize that the only reality of your being is your true nature as the spiritual essence of the Absolute.

Thought does not bring one closer to reality, but just enforces his delusion. Any effort to use thought to go beyond its concepts, is to accept the relative duality for the reality. Concepts are traps that lead one into deeper illusion, as thought reflects ever deeper upon itself – thoughts are fantasy reflections, and its goals contain no reality. No search or goal is necessary, we are already spiritually free and united in the Absolute. The path is motivated by desire, it is the illusion of attaining a higher reality than is already present within us, it is the ego looking for itself.

Problems and frustrations within a persons life develop as a result of desire and attachment to their illusory world of concepts, this is the individual's effort to control life's situations. Control is futile; life is a happening, and one cannot control the circumstances unfolding. Our spirit cannot be free while desirous of controlling life, or if it is attached to the results of its actions. Life must flow free and spontaneous, with no desire or attachment – only in this way can one perceive the reality behind the unfolding mystery. Our spiritual being is here to experience the process of life, not to hold it stagnant, or try to control or possess it – this miracle is the realm of realization, not a dead end to desire. Our true nature is free from attachment and desire, it is a perceiver of experience; it is our thoughts which form all illusion, fantasy and concepts, of which all desire and attachment are woven within. Stop thought, and desire and attachment stop also; there is no end to desire as long as thoughts are present. And as long as thoughts continue to produce desire and attachment then no ultimate realization of your spiritual essence is possible. Realization of your true source is within you awaiting your recognition, and it is within your conscious choice to drop your desire, attachment and concepts, and abide in your spiritual identity as the living essence of the Absolute.

~ Fascination ~

I wander life in fascination, for I have solved all my problems by recognizing that none exist. Everything is fine just the way it is, and as it changes, that is fine also. I have no problems because I have nothing pending, thus I create no conflicts in my time; and as my life comes and goes, I watch in fascination. I keep totally interested in absolutely nothing, for everything is equal, and everything is perfectly the way it should be. Time is my friend, because I do not use it linearly, but rather I go diagonally in time, by recognizing that nothing is pending now or ever. And because nothing is pending, death is also my friend, for today is a good day to die, and an excellant day to live. Whichever is presented before my window, I will watch with no comparison or judgement. And as I breathlessly watch, I wander life in fascination — this beautiful, mysterious, awesome adventure of a life, I wander in joyous fascination...

Nothing To Accomplish

There is nothing in life to accomplish. Accomplishment is the foundation of the world, and its corner stones are desire and attachment. A warrior understands the futility of attainment, and thus makes no attempt to accomplish, for he accepts no goals, and thus has nothing pending. With no future desire or past attachments, he can effortlessly abide within his freedom, for our spirit is complete and whole, thus accomplishment can add nothing to it. A warrior sees accomplishment as the conscientious use of time, so in humility he may accomplish many tasks; but though he is in the act of accomplishment, he has no attachment or desire for any goal, so there is no selfhood within the action. His spirit can thus remain free while his body is in the midst of living the experience of life, for he has no time to be trying to accomplish some other task within the world of desire, besides the living of his freedom.

We live in a world of accomplishment, and the desire and attachment for its rewards extract a price in sorrow. No one forces this sorrow upon us, we accept it of our own free will, as the result of attachment to attaining a desired goal. Freedom from sorrow exists only when a person loses his interest in attaining worldly goals, and instead gains great enthusiasm for experiencing the miracle of life's perception. This is the freedom a warrior has found, and though he has accepted the challenge of accomplishment, his only true action is living his freedom.

Here and Now

A warrior doesn't have the answers, he has a distinctive way of living that brings about a realization of the active principle of life. He doesn't look for meanings of intellect, but of intuition of being — he is here and now, and lives his life accordingly. This is the warrior's challenge, and as long as he is in the present, and dedicated to his realization, then he is master of his life and free within this realm. But if a warrior loses this precious moment into forgetfulness and illusion, then he is as ignorant as anyone else. Realization is a moment by moment happening; it is a state of abiding in a serene mind, free from the illusion of thought, and pure in the awareness of the activity unfolding.

There is no coming or going, and no birth or death, there is only right here, and right now. But no one can say where 'here' is, or tell you what time is 'now'. We are within a mystery, a dream of the moment, and the epitome is to live ever present within it. Our past illusions and future fantasies are not relevant to the present moment. Each one of us has the opportunity presented daily to drop our past conceptions of who we where, and adopt a new attitude in life as to who we prefer to be right now. Our past is gone and the future is in creation now; we need no fond remembrances, for within the purity of this moment our life can flow effortlessly and harmoniously, always captured by the magic of the present experience.

The moment is here now, not to dictate what is to be done within it, but to dedicate our full energy and awareness to bringing forth our best ability in whatever circumstance of life is presented. In such a state of consciousness, our life becomes a prayer and a meditation, for both are arts of living in touch with the moment. They are the arts of simply abiding here and now, and not asking for, or desiring to receive anything. This is the acknowledgement and joy of recognizing that we are complete and whole, and have everything necessary within this miracle, for we are a miracle also.

The circumstances of our realization are always surrounding us, and it is always the correct time to grasp the catalyst of the moment, and spark a movement in consciousness. We are enveloped by our awakening, and we need not go anywhere looking for it, or seek special places or people; we need only be alert to the action of life around us, and grasp each opportunity of insight as it arises.

Our body is always of the moment, it is our thoughts that lag behind or shoot ahead, and are rarely satisfied with where we are at the present. At this moment the body is going about its functions, but its thoughts are not in harmony with the action. Tranquility of heart is the simple harmony of mind and body, and since the body is always in the present, then the only way to achieve this balance is to bring the thoughts into the attention of the moment. Basically, this is the task every spiritual aspirant must endeavor to succeed at, for only when alert and aware in this present moment will the essence of life be captured. Our inner nature of spiritual being can guide our life smoothly and more adequately than our confused intellect. We shall find tranquility when our thoughts are subdued and brought to bear witness on this precious, eternal moment.

Here and now is where all the mystery lies hidden. All techniques of meditation, yoga, prayer, worship and rituals are simple methods to stop the useless inner dialogue, and subplant it with a conscious, aware thought, or even better yet, a communion thru silence. They all have the intent to put one in touch with the moment, and achieve harmony of heart and mind, and union with one's self nature. The final stage is to reach a state of serene observation, where the body is tranquil and yet active, and the mind is peaceful and observant, yet functions sharply as the need arises. This is the actionless actor, and the doing of not doing, for when thoughts are not active then no attachment or desire arises. The mind will now be freed from its concepts of clinging and attaining, and can abide in the freedom of spontaneous expression; and the body is freed from tensions, worries and fears produced by thoughts, and flows harmoniously in a life of peaceful contemplation and active meditation, no matter what the activity engaged in.

When thoughts are dropped, it is a time for keen attention and alertness, for at this time our true nature will function within its inherent wisdom, and we can spontaneously intuit the message of our heart. There is true wisdom in all of us that has been covered over with useless knowledge and concepts, and this has built a disorganized, unharmonious thought process. The whole point of all spiritual practice is to bring one back to a state of simplicity and purity, where the true function of mind as conscious relator of our experience can find expression uncluttered by desire, attachment and illusory thoughts. Purity of mind is only present in the 'here and now', and it must be harmonious with the purposeful living of the heart. This is a divine place of wisdom where no conflicts arise within, thus no problems are within to solve.

Most everyone lives in a world of fantasy, and this forms their conscious link with their true self. Thus their link to the magical realm of reality, has been changed into a thought form of illusion. There is no need for "make believe", life is magnificent the way it is. Right here and now the miracle of life is unfolding before us. What we perceive is not an illusion, but our concepts and fantasies of it are—what we perceive is beyond our thoughts, it is a mystery. Do not lessen this grandest of all miracles by turning it into an illusion of your thought process. Here is the paradise within the moment—it is like a tranquil, crystal lake, always here and shining forth thru its depths. We must perceive and realize its simplicity, instead of using the complexity of thought to figure it out, and thus rush and clamor into the lake to be drowned within our thoughts and concepts. The ways of a warrior are much like learning to swim—it is the respectful attitude to enter slowly the purity of the holy waters, and in simplicity he finds harmony of heart and mind in the tranquil serenity of no thought. And while this opportunity unfolds, he basks within this realm of perception, and here and now he uses this miraculous moment to float within the boundless purity of the Absolute.

Parable—Gasping for Realization

A sincere, young man looked diligently, and succeeded in finding a warrior. He begged the warrior, "you have stilled your mind and found realization, please teach me how to quiet my tempestuous thoughts so I may become enlightened." The warrior replied, "my young brother, your desire to stop your thought and become realized is the very obstacle preventing you. You see, desires are illusory thought, thus your emotional wish of attainment is your illusion. You grasp at one illusion, feeling it to be superior to the past illusion you clung to, when actually they are the same. When you drop all concepts of achieving, and all paths and goals, then your illusions will leave you, and so will your thoughts." The young man said bewildered, "but what am I to do, nothing at all?" The warrior replied, "No, there is much to do, but not a lot of thought to be conceptualized. Please come with me and perhaps we shall learn together." They proceeded to a large fountain and stood before it; suddenly the warrior grabbed the young man, and threw him in the pond, and held his head under the water. The young man struggled and finally freed himself. Gasping for breath he shouted, "what are you trying to do, kill me?" The warrior laughed and explained, "well tell me now, what did you think about while under the water?" The youth replied, "I didn't think about anything, I was trying to live." "Ah, now we have something here," said the warrior, "your true nature was in the moment, experiencing life to the exclusion of all else — no desire, no attachments, no attainments, no path and no goal. It was completely free of thought and concept, with no ego pondering the problem presented, just raw, basic awareness of the present moment. You were free and alive, right here and now, and your spirit reigned supreme in your survival of life. When you can live in this aware and attentive attitude in all your daily activities, spurred on by only your purpose of freedom, without desiring to find something above or beyond you, then you'll have gained realization of your true nature and communion within the absolute."

Wanderings of The Heart

Aravaipa Wilderness ~ April 1986 ~

My hiking ability is my finest blessing, but on several occasions my endurance has been tested to the extreme. One such incidence happened within the twisted canyons of Aravaipa Wilderness.

Aravaipa is a paradise of lushness, set in the stark bleakness of the Arizona desert. It is oasis to a thriving population of birds, frogs, fish, big horn sheep and wild pigs, all set in a deep river canyon lined with ferns, willows and sycamores. On either side of this 25 mile stretch of 1000 foot deep canyon is rolling desert with little life, but within these narrow canyons where water flows, it is a wilderness paradise.

I left my home early to hike down the river into the wilderness. Since Aravaipa contains no trails, I leisurely walked down the two foot deep creek for several miles, til seeing a side canyon to my left. Its twisted, narrow gorge intrigued me, so I decided to make this days hike an exploration up its secret recesses.

What a gorgeous little canyon it proved to be, with just a trickle of water carving its way thru fluted rock, forming deep pools and waterfalls. The course meandered for miles thru tight canyon walls, and occasionally would open into hidden little valleys loaded with trees. Frogs and birds serenaded me as I slowly climbed higher and higher up into the hills, til finally the little creek became a dry bed of sand. Junipers and Pinyon pines now filled the widening canyon, and the sheer walls became twisted formations of gnarled rock with crumbling pillars of stone. I was so fascinated by the changing terrain, that I had now walked too great a distance to make it possible to reverse my course and arrive home by daylight.

I figured this possibility could happen, so before

I started up the canyon, I checked my map, which is a very poor map of this area, and saw that the canyon where I parked my van was in a parallel canyon to the one I was hiking. All I needed to do to get back home, was to climb the ridge to my left and drop down the other side into Turkey Creek canyon, where I was parked ½ mile from Aravaipa creek. Sounded real easy, and looked simple on my lousy map, so I figured the 2 hours of daylight was well sufficient for the shortcut.

The best layed plans of mice and warriors will often go astray. The climb to the top of the ridge proved to be very strenuous, and the ridge itself was much higher than I expected, but I finally arrived, and figured all I need do was to pick an arroyo to walk down, to reach Turkey Creek below. But what lay before me was a total surprise, if not a sheer shock. I was at least 1000 feet above Turkey Creek, and 2 miles away from it, but worst of all there were dozens of deep canyons that stretched before me, that descended to the high cliffs of Turkey Creek. Since the cliffs held the canyon from my right, I had no way to know the direction of my van.

In this situation one analyzes everything carefully, and then guesses. So down the arroyo before me I went for several miles of tough going – the rocks were loose, and the bushes fought with me, and many steep drop offs lay before me, but I finally reached Turkey Creek and was amazed to see how accurately I had predicted the location of my van. My home was only 300 feet away, but unfortunately the 300 feet was straight down a sheer vertical cliff, and I had no possible way to descend. There was no way to traverse along the cliff, for the arroyos that descended from the ridge to Turkey Creek were deep and sheer walled, with straight drop offs into the main canyon. So my only option was to walk back up the same canyon I had descended, and try another

155

arroyo for descent to Turkey Creek.

Daylight was now getting very short, so I picked up my pace and reached the ridge in record time. I decided I would play it very safe and use my good hiking ability to my advantage, so I hiked down the main ridge 3 miles, and figured at this point any arroyo I used for my descent would surely reach the main canyon with no drop off or cliff. So down an arroyo I fought and finally reached Turkey Creek, and I was right, there were no 300 foot cliffs, only a 50 foot straight drop!

By now it was dark and I had to get my mini flashlight out of my pack, and decide my course, but I had no real choice. So up to the ridge I reluctanly walked, and down the ridge another mile, and then I once again picked an arroyo for descent, and felt it must be a good one. With no light the bushes not only fought me, but went out of their way to grab me, and the rocks conspired to trip me and break my legs — there was no shame in their valient attempt. Eventually I reached the main canyon, and to my utter amazement there was still a 30 foot sheer drop off. I was puzzled and getting tired, and a bit crazy I guess, for I seriously began an attempt to jump from the ledge into the boughs of the trees below and hope I could catch a branch. For 15 minutes I debated this plan, but finally decided to walk up to the ridge one more time.

I had walked only a short way when I saw something shining on the ground, but when I put my flashlight to it, nothing was there. As I raised my flashlight to walk, once again I saw something bright on the ground, so I turned off my light, and there below me was a florescent bug lighting up his world. I had never seen such a sight, and was astounded by the event, and stared flabbergarted at the miracle before me. The caterpillar had a

156

bright red light on his head, and lime green lights on his segmented body, and for his small size he put out quite a bright shine. As I watched, it dawned on me that I was quite simular to my florescent friend, as I crawled thru the arroyos with my flashlight, lighting up my little world, and we both were in a hurry to get nowhere. The humor of it struck me, and all seriousness of the situation I was in left me. So what if I had to walk around all night and couldn't get down; what difference did it make, none of us have any real place to go. I would get home eventually, so I should just enjoy the event for the unique situation it was. With that joyous realization, I sang to my spirit and honored my caterpillar brother, and happily resumed my stroll up the arroyo, and the bushes gently helped me along and the rocks no longer tripped me. Instead of walking to the ridge, I had an impulse to climb along the cliff of Turkey creek, and sure enough, I hadn't mauvered over 100 feet when I came to a spot I could descend. I now had a leisurely walk down Turkey creek for 4 miles to reach home, but I was no longer in a hurry, for I had nothing pending and no where special to go. Eventually I reached home and took my bath, and had a nice big salad, and the only difference was that I ate a little later than normal, and enjoyed my bath and dinner even more.

I had to smile at the strange events that were necessary for me to experience, in order to deepen my realization beyond the point of intellectual speculation, and into the realm of actual living. I knew very well the premise of a warrior's life, but this wondrous event made me live my knowledge and grasp it as a reality. Intellectual knowledge is of little use when one is put to a test, and only thru the joy of hardship does one gain realization, and have the opportunity presented to live it.

Within Relativity

The Absolute is the reality, and within its fabric of manifestation all aspects are relative. Anything ever written, spoken or thought, along with all physical appearance is all relative, and only has a value in relation to its center of perspective. There is no ultimate reality to the experiences we witness or the results of them, for our perception is relative within the limited boundaries of the manifest. Perception has a reality only as fabric of the manifest, but all conceptions resultant of the experience we perceive is illusory and relative. The Absolute is beyond all thought and action, for they are part of the manifest and can only indicate a relative perspective as definition of limitation. Consciousness within the relative can never grasp the ultimate, for a limited perspective can never fathom the totality. The Absolute is a mystery, it is not just an unknown to figure out, but a sheer mystery that has no solution or graspability within the relative — and from this ultimate mystery all wonder and life perpetuates into being.

The real essence of our being is of the Absolute, and our true nature within the fabric of the manifest is the consciousness of a spiritual being of freedom. This is our spirit, soul and true self, and is the doer of all our actions. The ultimate purpose is not of thought, but one of experience, thus the challenge is to perceive the unfoldment of the energy within manifestation surrounding us, and relate it to our spiritual essence. The Absolute is complete and whole, and our essence is complete and whole within it. We thus have no need to solve or figure out a solution to the mystery of life. The manifestation is not a problem to solve — it has no solution, because it contains no problem, and it has no answer for it contains no question. Its origin is the Absolute, and as consciousness within the manifest, we have only experience of this relative perception to witness and relate to.

We are not coming and going within the manifest, we are evolving and revolving. There is no where to go beyond this realm, for all existence is here. Would you lose this unique opportunity to abide within this mystery enfolding you, so that your fantasy thoughts and conceptions could produce an alternate place of perception? How can any thought ever compare with the stupendous glory of this manifest realm. We are here, let the wandering of your thought be stilled, and let the desire to seek and attain be emptied. We are the essence of the Absolute; we are the ultimate reality, can you conceive or desire for more. The goal of finding the Absolute is not obtainable, for you are the Absolute — you cannot find you, you can only realize your essence of true nature. All paths converge into this one aspect – to realize the essence of your true spiritual self that is ever present within your consciousness. This is a course of abiding, not attaining; if it were attainable then it would also be losable, and no one can lose their contact with the Absolute. There is only the existence of spiritual essence, it has never been born and it cannot die, and its roots stretch to the eternity of the Absolute.

There is nothing to achieve, only realization to live and abide within. All experiences have the same equal value, for the ultimate consequence of any action is none; but the value of any experience is great, for it is our purpose to experience the challenge of life. All experiences are equal, for it is not the action that holds importance, but how attuned and aware your attention is while doing it. We are the divine miracle, and there is nothing to achieve — we are here, and we are free. Within the actions of our experiences we roam the joy of our heart, and the awareness of our mind. Here we can relate the perception to its essence, for the perception and perceiver are one within the absolute. The perception is manifest, and the perceiver is spiritual essence, and both are within the mystery of the ultimate reality. Our physical form is part of the perception, and our dual nature of heart and mind is also within the manifest, but our free spiritual essence is united in the pure, unchanging Absolute. Our essence is beyond the manifest, therefore it is not subject to birth and death. It sojourns thru the relative, but its communion and home is in the undifferentiated Absolute. Though we journey within the mystery of the manifest, no one can ever be separated from the totality, for there is only the one Absolute, and we are it.

There is no doctrine to preach, thus there is no one to preach it to, or who can preach it. We are all within the totality, thus we are the doctrine, and any attempt to preach a doctrine brings separation and partial truths. There is only one truth, and you are it. You are the spiritual essence of the one reality - this is no doctrine, this is your very essence. If you preach a doctrine you slander the truth - this is the realization beyond the concepts and doctrines. This is nothing new, for within your heart and mind is the truth, and your essence abides in it always. There is nothing to master, and no esoteric doctrine to unravel, and no subtle concepts to fathom, there is only life to behold - and the platform to witness this marvel of perception, is the tranquil serenity of your free spiritual being.

The wisest man simply has nothing to say. He realizes that all thoughts, words, acts and even enlightenment are within the relative. We are as a dream within the Absolute, and though it be our essence, we are separated by the fabric of manifests relativity. Even the greatest of men is still in delusion, for there is no point of reference other than the relative. Our conception of enlightenment within the relative is still ignorance within the manifest, for illusion is the art of the manifest. We can expand our view and gain greater perspective, and thus gain realization of our true nature and ultimate spiritual essence, but we'll still be within the limitations of the relative while sojourning in the manifest. We can only discern part of the whole; we will never be able to grasp all of the reality.

A warrior's purposeful life brings him to an understanding within the relative, and humbles him within the vastness of the ultimate reality. His realization is a positive, direct experience within the manifest. Abiding in his true nature, he knows that we are all spiritual actualities of the absolute —beyond time, space, form and thought. We are free, ever fluid, all embracing— the pure essence of the ultimate, the one reality without a second. In this simple awareness of truth, a warrior laughs at all the dialogue, and joyfully carries out the garbage.

Tomorrow's Laughter

Today I laughed at the ignorance
    of my past conceptions.
Oh, how blinding is this illusion.
For today's ignorance,
    is tomorrow's laughter.

And still we continue to cling...

Parable ~ Knowledge is Relative

There was an intelligent man who had a young son. The boy was becoming interested in cars, so each day the man would tell him of the simple workings of a vehicle. The boy thought his father was the wisest one around, til one day the family car was running poorly, and they went to the neighborhood mechanic. There the mechanic dismantled the carburetor and fixed the problem, and re-installed it. The boy asked his father why he hadn't done the repair himself. The father confessed that he understood all the theories of operation, but had never worked on a vehicle, or had the confidence to start tearing one apart. The boy saw that the auto mechanic wasn't very smart, and yet he knew more than his educated father. Even though the boy was young, he realized that all knowledge is relative.

Comment: To one who knows nothing, a man who knows something is a genius. Knowledge is relative to its place of origin, and the circumstances surrounding it. The very wisest spiritual soul knows for a fact that he is ignorant and understands nothing, for his knowledge is relative unto a higher knowledge. Only the wisdom and love of our true nature has any reality, but if you think about the reality of it, then it becomes relative also. There is no rising above the relative, one can only realize their limitation within the manifest, and abide within a deeper understanding of our true nature and the miracle that is surrounding us. Only if we can free ourself of illusory thoughts and flow free in our actions, can we live unchained in this eternal moment, and realize that all this world is relative, and joyously abide in its wonder.

We Own Nothing

The world owns everything. If you try to possess or cling to the objects of the world, then the world will take them away by force. Whatever you have, the world will eventually repossess, for you can only borrow objects here in this realm. If you respectfully use what the world will freely allow you to use, and have no attachment to it while using it, then you will have a unique opportunity to roam in freedom. But try to cling to the objects of the world, and you'll have to fight your entire life, and still lose the battle, as the world breaks your body by death, and returns your elements back into its body. For always remember this one fact, your body, as well as all your objects, belong to the earth, and your spiritual essence can take none of it with it as it continues its sojourn of unfoldment. Your spirit will evolve, and it is your degree of consciousness which determines whether the world be the chains to bind your freedom, or whether it be the avenue to gain realization. Your only choice is whether you trap yourself or roam freely, but either way you choose, the world still owns your body and everything you call dear. You can never win any battles here on earth, you can only run from the understanding of how to harmonize with this manifestation. The world owns your body, and it is only by gift that you are allowed to experience its realm. This is the reason why the warrior is so respectful of this miraculous chance of perception. So he clings and attaches to nothing here, and the world gives him its blessings freely, till the day his spirit is set free of the world, to adventurously journey into the unknown.

Time is The Great Advisor

There is a constant flow within the relativity of manifestation, and it is ceaseless in its ever expansion and contraction — it is the evolving and revolving of energy. This is the reality, and we call this process life and death, but our concept of these terms is inaccurate. Nothing comes into being or finds extinction from being, for this manifestation is an ever present, never ending flow of one ultimate totality. The absolute is complete and whole, for it is one totality and its fabric is the manifest. The manifest is our reality where our spiritual essence finds form and expression as a spiritual being, but at all times our essence is within the absolute, for nothing can be divided from it. Life and death are expressions within the manifest that spiritual beings revolve within — it is the ebb and flow of energy, as consciousness experiences the communion of relating. All manifest reality is ever changing — it is a constant renewal and re-forming of ever varying patterns of energy. There is no stability, only a constant re-ordering and evolution of the present existence. Death as finality or extinction is only a concept of thought, and has no reality. Our spiritual essence will continue to flow with the whole and ever change and revolve, thus thru the death of form we evolve and find renewal.

The fabric of manifestation is woven in time, and as our spiritual essence enlivens a form, we find that time will be the guardian of our experiences. Everything we perceive finds relevance by the expression of time. Time is only in the present, for there is no realness to past or future time — they are only an illusion and fantasy of thought, for time is only 'now'. With our attention, we ride the vehicle of time — attention is necessary to be in the present moment, and that is the only moment time will allow. In the fabric of the manifest time is eternal, for it holds the relative in place, but has no part of it. Only time is eternal, for all existence within time is transitory, and in constant evolution. The reality of our spiritual essence is beyond time, for our essence is of the Absolute, where time is its illusion. The Absolute is beyond time, for it has no beginning and no ending, but its fabric of manifestation falls into the weaving of time, and all form is slave to its dictate. Time dissolves stability and brings constant evolution, as it measures the motion of manifests constant energy flow — this is the creating and dissolving into re-creation.

Time has no energy or power to accomplish, yet all manifest rests in its domain. It is powerless within the Absolute, and beyond power in the relative, we thus find our physical form ruled by time. Purpose in life is the opportunity to experience time for the spiritual process of coming into being. We have the chance to touch the essence of time in this magical, mysterious moment, and gain communion with our essence. Our opportunity is fleeting and transitory, so to waste this chance and not dwell in the ever present, continually changing moment is to lose this precious gift of life. There are no moments to waste — one must be adventurous and grasp this gift of life within time, and use it with respect, reverence and joy. There is no security in life; we are spiritual beings of evolution encased in time, and now is our chance to live life fully.

Time can be your joyous friend and show you stupendous wonders, or time can be your dreaded foe that dissolves your attachments and destroys your body. It is our attention that brings time into focus — with our attention focused in the present, we find an adventure of experience, and time becomes joyous and eternal; but with our attention focused in illusory thought of the past and future, we find stagnation in a world of pain and boredom.

Time is our greatest advisor. Time will tell you if you can waste your life in illusory and fantasy thoughts, dwelling over past regrets and future apprehensions. Just ask time, and time will point out that there are no survivors. Time will end our precious moments of opportunity so very soon, and we will lose the chance to behold and capture the marvels of this realm. Ask time for advice whenever you lose the moment and drift into your fantasy thoughts, time will tell you that you have precious little opportunity left, so you better let your actions flow free and live them fully. Your last opportunity will arrive soon enough, and time will allow no regrets or chances to retrieve the lost opportunities of your life, or to witness the glorious marvels of this wondrous realm again. Time is the great advisor — respect its authority, for it can show you stupendous wonders before it leads you away. The warrior respectfully listens to time's advice, for his heart has told him that time is irretrievable.

Journey of a Dream

Here I stand within a dream,
in this passing instant of curiousity,
where time seeks no answers.

Life has blossomed into expression,
as time flows out of expression,
both are rivers within the sea.

The ocean of relativity,
is forever embraced and held whole,
balanced in the void, nurtured by the Absolute.

The blue heron stands motionless,
as the galaxy races to nowhere,
and all fantasy is eclipsed by the miracle.

Sojourning a road to myself,
I serenely watch in wonder,
as the precious moment unfolds realization.

This opportunity is so fleeting,
for tomorrow I will journey back home,
and there really never was anything to say.

Who Are You?

Do you know who you are? Only in this present moment is the opportunity available to know who you are. You may have a fond conception as to who you were last year, or an idealistic dream as to who you wish to be in the future, but who is this 'you' at this moment?

We are all in the process of continual change, and as the world evolves, we must constantly adapt to it. As time re-orders our physical being, a re-ordering of our conceptual identity must go with it. Your greatest dream of yesterday, and fondest hope for tomorrow, are seen in today's light as unnecessary aspirations of an immature, developing mind. Our conception of who we are has no validity beyond the scope of this present moment. We all have a faint vision in our mind as to who we think we are, but the picture is always distorted by our past remembrances and futuristic ideals. It is the rare person who recognizes that urge within themselves to observe, understand and know who they truly are in this eternal moment.

At this very moment do you know who you are? and where you are?, and do you understand the significance of the question? Life is not a silly joke, it can have great value if one understands his inner nature. To find purpose in life, the process of inquiry must be seen thru the eye of wisdom. Beyond your physical nature, your conscious awareness as a spiritual being is evolving and growing. It is obvious that you are not as you were ten years ago. You are not the same person now, because your ideas and conceptions have changed, and with them your attitude and awareness — so who is this 'you' who is ever changing? If attitudes and awareness change, then these ideas and concepts which you think to be 'you', cannot be the real 'you', for you must have a core of being that is beyond change, and beyond the re-ordering of awareness and attitude. Your true nature as a spiritual being must be beyond the 'you' of your conceptions — it must be beyond all change, growth and evolving. You are physically here within the manifestation, and so is the question of who you are, but the one who asks the question has a core of reality beyond the relative. Your spiritual essence is complete and free within the source of all existence. Here within the totality of the Absolute, your true spiritual nature abides as the very essence of it. You are here, right now, and only now can you ask questions, for only in this present moment does the opportunity exist to inquire into our relative existence. Reflect within the perception of this moment, and be ever so conscious of this miraculous chance to abide within the reality of yourself. The miracle exists only in the present, and each moment is so very special.

Who are you now?
Where do you go?
Are you inside,
watching the show?

Who were you then?
Where have you been?
Always outside,
now turn within.

Parable - House of Three Men

There lived in a house three very different men. One man spent all his time on the back porch looking down the road. He worried a lot and was afraid to leave the house for fear of losing his way. He felt that life had cheated him, and though he knew of nothing to live for, he was very afraid of dying. Another man sat all day on the front porch looking up the road. At times he was very hopeful and enthusiastic, and at other times fell into deep despair. He had great hope of accomplishment, but seldom left the house for fear of failure in his fancied dreams. The last man lived in a room on top of the house. It had a glass roof so he could watch the sky and stars. He was happy and contented, and took no notice of the road. He traveled whenever and wherever he felt, and had no fear of doing tasks, or of just staying within his glass room and peacefully watching the sky in wonder. Even though all three men lived in the same house, they never met, for each lived within a separate world of his own.

Comment: The house is the consciousness of each one of us, and we all have these three men living within it. To the degree of your conscious awareness is which man you are, and the world you will perceive. The man looking down the road is your longing to recapture the past, and live within it. It is your delusory self of attachment and clinging; fearful of the world because of memories of the past, and unwilling to see the world as it is. The man looking up the road is your fantasy self of future imaginings. He is the wind of desire, perpetually blowing ahead to seek greater abundance and far better circumstances in situations that he visualizes; thus there is apprehension of the unknown, and with it comes hope, sorrow and despair. The last man is your true self, harmoniously living in the moment. The sky and stars are ever present, and his eyes are focused on them only— they represent the ultimate reality of God and the Absolute, and his only concern is in communion with its presence. He has no concern for the road of past and future, thus he travels freely and without fear, for his mind is free of thoughts. His glass roof is the purity of his true nature and clarity of his soul. To the degree we live within this last man is the true depth of our realization. The other men will always be there, but we need not abide in their fears and worries, but view their antics as part of the insight into a higher understanding of our total nature. Visit the illusion of past and future sparingly, and instead find your home in the reality of abiding in the crystal room of the present, with the eyes of your soul perpetually focused on the stars — the heavens of reality within this miraculous moment.

Spontaneity Lost

Today I walked so carefully,
every step an artistry of precision.
My balance was superb,
but my feet were not on the earth.
I lost the moment in careful planning.

Art Plate #20~ We sit in the midst of our diversely branching concepts, confident that our path is the correct way. But look deeper, and see how little you truly know – disentangle your preconceived concepts to discover your true nature, and abide in the simplicity of its being...

Clinging To a Concept

People want to cling, and what they cling to they call their religion. They cling to names and form of an external God — they cling to images of a savior or master, and memories of his life — they cling to books, relics, rituals and churches. They cling tightly to their concepts, for their religion is external to them — just an illusion of their conceptual thought. All clinging is formed by desire and attachment, and creates a bond within this transitory manifestation. Clinging to external concepts is motivated by social convention and not by deep realization, for the interest of most people lies in social interaction, where the safty of group agreement is desired. As people cling to their concepts, they also feel justified in defending their opinions, and among some religious groups their defense turns violent. The divisions that have been created by religious clinging of concepts has caused killing and hatred in the name of books, prophets, saviors, churches, religion and even God. The world will find peace when it stops seeking outward for God, and goes beyond its concepts to a place of direct communion.

The spiritual future of this evolving world does not rest in the hordes of blind followers, but in the sincere hearts of the doubters. The world has never been united into a loving brotherhood by the followers of concepts, as they grasp and cling to fantasies of heavens and hells. The future of peace rests with the ones tired of all the dogma, rituals and rules. They have shunned institutionalized religion, and turned to a personal communion within themselves. The conceptual names and forms are for the mind not yet mature, for they have no reality and are used as a substitute to direct communion. All existence is part of the same manifestation of the one ultimate reality, and to abide in the awareness of this conscious existence is the highest prayer possible. To establish earthly forms and concepts to idolize is to honor one's illusions and a social structure of convenience, and thus miss the real communion of one's soul in exuberant unfoldment, as life is experienced around it. For most people, God is only a concept external to themself, and not till this concept is dropped is the reality of themself seen as a vibrant, living essence of the Absolute. No search, beseeching or worship is needed, just a clear understanding of the reality present within us.

Past masters and books cannot provide a present realization. Our heart knows the message of every prophet, for wisdom and love is inherent within us as our true self, and needs only the opportunity to express it. It is buried under the conceptions of the past that have been handed down blindly, and defended violently, century after century. Unity and peace has never been achieved in this manner, but an ever increasing complexity of division. The peaceful, loving ones of today are the religious doubters who have dropped the concepts, and live true to their heart's dictate. They are sincere within their own realm of communion, and have no need to conceptualize the source of their union. Existence 'is', and we do not need to create fantasies to make it more real. Our concepts only delude us from experiencing life as it is, and realizing the wonder of our being. Be not dismayed as the world leaves its religions, for they are concepts within the mind, and only when we have evolved past our foundation of concepts, can the world find peace in a personal communion within the source of its being. Each of us must have a unique expression of our spiritual union, fostered from the sincerity of our heart. We are all of one brotherhood, and now is our opportunity to share our love, and abide in the prayer that is our life.

Certain dedicated warriors have seen this attitude of clinging, and have tried to keep their message and life from being turned into a concept to cling to. They kept their lives simple and unencumbered, and encouraged others to look within to find their freedom and communion, and not look to them, or cling to them. But after the warrior dies, the followers seek for concepts to cling to, and acknowledge only the external aspect of the warrior's life, and lose the essence of his purpose and dedication. All books, rituals, images and churches came after the warrior's death. It is easier to worship someone else and make it a socially bonding activity, then to stand alone and dedicate to the realization within you. It shows no honor to a master to build a statue of them and worship it, and forget the communion of the divinity present within yourself. If one adopts a savior and prays to him for salvation, then they lose a direct contact with their true nature. A master tries to save others from forgetfulness of God and their true nature, so it shows the master no honor to continue to forget God, and now worship and pray to a master. The greatest honor you can give a master is to allow his purity and sincerity to inspire you, and be likewise dedicated to your own ideals which come from your direct communion with your source. Plug into the universal source of your being, and inspire all your brothers to dwell within and realize their true essence of being.

The warrior clings to nothing, thus he has nothing to defend. His realization is inward, for it is the total expression of his life, not just a concept or an attainment to cling to. This world is relative and transitory, so he clings to no aspect of it. With no desire or attachment to the world, he has no need to join the social convention of seeking an external God and looking for the illusory goal. He stands alone in his temple of realization and in continual self communion of his true nature, and at no time does he follow or cling to books, rituals or masters.

The warrior clings to no concept of a selfhood, and is careful not to make 'no clinging' his concept to defend and cling to. It is easy to turn the humble attitude of no clinging into a worldly attitude, and build a concept around the premise of being 'no one', and thus become spiritually prideful. One can then start scorning others for their clinging, and feel superior because they don't cling — thus 'not clinging' becomes their concept to cling to. The warrior is ever alert as he watches this play unfold, for the mastery of life is a subtle art.

In the acceptance of other person's thoughts, and vocalizing other person's words as our own, we build a foundation of concepts, and cling to them as our own true self — thus forming the ultimate barrier to realization of one's true self. They may have value as a catalytic spark to awaken one to inner possibilities, but the spiritual aspirant must always remember that his ultimate realization must come from within, and not from concepts formulated by others — be true to yourself is the highest truth one can live.

To trade one's clinging of a relative religious concept, for the clinging to a concept of spiritual reality, is indeed a giant step in consciousness, but with spiritual maturity proves only to be a change of perspective — it remains as a concept of realization, and not actual knowledge of one's true self. It is as trading a concept of a flat world (our relation within the relative) for a concept of a round world (our spiritual actuality). But this conceptual search for truth is still within the mind, and thus brings no ultimate understanding of our true spiritual being. All concepts are within thought, and our true nature is beyond thought, and can only be discerned when one abides in the present and serenely reflects the wonder of existence, free from the clinging of relative concepts. After all the words, thoughts and books of concepts have been reviewed, it is necessary for the spiritual warrior to be adventurous, like Columbus, and strike out to discover the reality — to bravely seek the ultimate beyond the concepts that everyone has only alluded to. One must evolve into the truth of existence, and let their freedom carry them as their ship into a new world, and not carry the unnecessary baggage of past remembrances, fears of the attempt, fantasy concepts or other traveler's illusions. The new world is our ultimate destination — it is a solitary journey of awakening, where concepts and illusion are dropped, and one bravely observes his own reflection. As long as one continues to read, expound, cling and defend other persons conceptual views, then no indepth wisdom or union of their true self has been gained. Freedom is found once all concepts are thrown away, and one stands alone in the present moment to find the depth of meaning inherent in their spirit. Realizations are personal, and one cannot have or borrow the same realization as another person, nor can one take the same path they used to arrive at their insights. Clinging to other persons concepts of life is futile, for this is a solitary journey, and if realization is to come, it must be lived in the awareness of freedom with no preconceived concepts.

The externals one clings to are indications of one's maturity in spiritual life — the more concepts one adheres to, the more insecure of inner truth they are. Most masters had no objects or concepts to cling to, their outer life was a reflection of the inner truth of their spiritual being. They lived the realization of God, thus they needed nothing external to establish their connection in God, or thought concepts to verify it. Every master's message has been of unity — that there is only one reality, and we are all part of this totality. Peace will come when each of us goes within, and realizes that we are all equal aspects of God, then we can sit together in harmony without the necessity to compare personal views. There is only God, and we are that reality — let's leave it at that, and establish peace. Each of us can commune in private to establish the prayer that is their life. Let us unite into brotherhood, and leave all the complicated theories of chosen ones and exclusive realms to the immature seekers of the past. Realization is in simplicity — we are all spiritual essence of one ultimate God; we are all equal, and all here to learn, share and experience the challenge of life — let this blessed opportunity be one of love, peace and brotherhood. Commune within and realize God as your being, then each person will be as a unique religion unto himself. Let us congregate together and begin to civilize this world thru spiritual realization of the true essence of our being.

Parable — The Mountain Hermit

As a warrior was traversing the high Sierras, he came to a beautiful, isolated valley. It appeared no one had ever inhabited it, but upon descending, he found a little cabin and a hermit. The hermit had lived there his whole life, and had only met a few passing hikers. The warrior was invited to stay, and the hermit asked many questions of the world, for he was very naive. His amazement had no end, and when the warrior mentioned the ocean, the hermit became very curious and asked, "how big is the ocean?" The warrior responded, "it is very big." Taking the warrior to the center of the valley where there was a pretty, little lake, the hermit asked, "is the ocean bigger than my lake?" "Yes, it is much larger", the warrior responded. "Perhaps ten times larger?", asked the hermit. "Still much larger". "A hundred times larger than?" "Still even larger". "But this is absurd", cried the hermit, "how could the ocean be bigger than my whole valley. I've climbed to the top of my highest peak and I've seen the world — sure it's big, it probably has thousands of valleys, but I saw no place you could put a giant lake — are you sure about the ocean?" "My friend," the warrior responded, "I'm afraid that you didn't see the whole world from your mountain top. The world is a vast globe with millions of valleys, and an ocean tens of millions of times larger than your valley." The hermit was outraged and jumped up crying, "you must be lying — this is too absurd to believe — a round world indeed, I will listen to no more."

Comment: We are imprisoned in a cage of concepts of an illusory world. We cling to these concepts and cannot imagine or tolerate anything beyond the scope of our relative world. Our perception of reality is limited, and within its narrow bounds we build and relate to our constructed idea of the world, assuming that the knowledge we possess will cover the limits of reality. Even if we have a larger glimpse of reality, we will fit it into our prejudiced and bigoted viewpoint, and cling to our pre-conceived opinions. If some person or circumstance was to present the overwhelming vastness of reality, the hermit within us is very likely to bury himself deeper into his delusion and ignorance. For the ego is a hermit, and prefers no mind opening reality to trespass into its little valley of illusion.

Art Plate #21~ Where do you look to God?
Can the concept above be any more divine
than the earth below? You stand on holy
ground, for your true spiritual essence is the
reality, and wherever you stand is the
foundation of God. By recognizing God in
yourself, this will allow you to see God in
all of existence, for you are that which you
seek, and all of life is the breath of God.
There is only God, and you will forever
be that truth...

All Searching is Clinging

The spiritual movement is helping people to realize the lack of attainment, in seeking a God external to themselves that sits in judgement and requires praise, worship, rituals, temples and all the external sources used to beseech an untouchable God. Thus many are now re-examining the words of the masters, and have taken up a new search within themselves, looking for any sign within to be a devine signal — such as lights, visions, holy sounds, small voices or any internal perception. Seeking God thru perception is the same whether it be outward or inward, and is still clinging to the concept of a path and goal, motivated by personal desire and attachment. Perceptions of any nature are not indications of realizing your true nature. Any search for God, transforms the reality into your desire to possess an attainable object for your use. This miracle of existence is not separate from God, for God is the totality, and existence is its essence. God is not external to your being, so no search is possible, and no goal attainable. God is your essence, and to find your true nature you need to acknowledge yourself and all existence as the manifestation of God. What we perceive within us or outside us is all relative, but has an ultimate nature as part of the totality we call God. You cannot seek that which you are, you can only abide in the realization that your essence is that of God. Be free of your search, and abide in the joy and freedom of your true nature, as the essence of God that you are.

Parable - Essence of The Apple

There once was a Celestial Being who happened to come to earth. He landed in a farmer's apple orchard, and there met the farmer. After some pleasant talk of world like conditions, the farmer told the Being that the finest taste in all the world was that of a ripe, crisp apple, and gave the Being a nice apple. The Being took the apple appreciatively, and went back to his planet and announced his great fortune of having the finest tasting object of all the earth. All the Beings gathered around to receive a taste; they could smell the fragrance, but since tasting was foreign to them, they were puzzled as to how to get a taste. They asked the apple for a taste, they prayed to the apple, they lit candles and did elaborate rituals and wrote books in praise of the apple, but still no one received the mysterious taste. They had great faith in the farmer and devoted themselves patiently, but eventually the Being decided to go back to earth and speak to the farmer. When the farmer heard of their vain efforts to receive a taste, he said, " my friend, it does no good to look outside the apple for its taste, the wonderful taste is within the apple." The Being went back home and announced his new knowledge about tasting, and brought out a new apple and a knife, and sliced it in two. Where upon all the Beings began to examine the inside of the apple, expecting the glorious taste to be present. A little disappointed, the Being sliced the apple into hundreds of little pieces, and everyone scrutinized every detail of the inside of the apple, but no mysterious taste was experienced by anyone. Once again they took to worship, rituals and beseeching the apple to grace them with a taste, but all in vain. Their faith was strong, but finally the Being decided to visit the farmer again. When the farmer heard the story he howled in laughter and asked, "don't you know how to taste food?" The Being explained that on his planet sustenance was provided in the air. "Well," said the farmer, "I am sorry, but you misunderstood my meaning of the apple having the finest taste. You see, the taste is not outside the apple, or is it inside the apple, the taste is the apple itself, they cannot be separated. To taste an apple you need to eat it. The apple is the totality and the taste is its essence — the mysterious taste you have been seeking outside and inside the apple, is the very apple itself."

Comment: If one feels God to be separate from them, they will take up a search outside of themself. By faithfully following a master, they proceed with ritual, prayer, church and beseeching God to appear to them — they wish to possess the subtle taste of God. But since God is not a worldly attainment to possess and cling to, their search will go unrewarded. Many eventually tire of the search, and finding another master's words, will begin to look within to discover God. Different rituals, reading, meditation and more beseeching will once again prove fruitless in the possession of God's subtle taste. God is not a goal to be acquired thru any search, whether it be inside or outside — looking for a burning bush or hoping for visions and celestial sounds is just thoughts of desire to attain one's concept. God is your substance; no seeking is necessary and no attainment is possible, for God is the realization of your very being. God is the totality and you are the essence, and the subtle taste of God is this experience of life. Both outside and inside of yourself you can experience the fragrance of manifestation, for it is part of the totality of this perceivable experience, but it is transitory and relative. The taste or essence is one with the whole, for this is your true self as the emanation of God, and there can never be any separation.

No Mind

The thoughts within our mind are in our power to control, but few ever exercise their freedom to control them, and instead are witness to an endless parade of fantasy and illusion. This fruitless dialog gives the mind the appearance it has a personality, and we call this person our ego. The ego is an illusion of our memory, and is supported by our thoughts. Mistakenly, the ego is identified as the mind, but when thoughts are stopped the mind still relates within its relative world, yet there is no mind as ego. 'No mind' does not mean that your mind as dual aspect within your true nature is gone, it refers to the absence of thought developing in the mind. The mind will still be there for understanding, awareness and relating within our relative world, but illusory thought as the creator of desire and attachment will be gone. This is the state of the non dwelling mind — its wisdom and reflection is clear, for it has no thoughts or concepts to grasp, and nowhere to dwell, because it has nothing to cling to. The dialog within has stopped, and the mind is calm in serene reflection — it is a clear awareness in the tranquility of no thought. The mind still perceives, yet it is not doing anything — it is attentive within the experience surrounding it, and since its inherent wisdom is complete of itself, there is nothing to learn and nothing to do, because the mind is in need of no attainment. The 'no mind' abides within the non action of experiencing, and is not subject to gaining or losing. If there was arising and extinction, then whatever gained could also be lost. The mind is pure and unconditioned — it is the mirror of thought that give it color, shape and form. We dwell within our concepts, and accept them as the attributes of the mind, and the relationship this builds with the world forms an ego of desire and attachment, and thus we build a home of concepts to surround us.

The function of our mind is as a perceiver, but our thoughts find their origin in the memory of the mind's perception – the thoughts then reflect upon themselves and form the illusory dimension of ego. The mind is unconditioned and abides within its spiritual true nature, but our thoughts are busy seeking for our true nature in its dwelling place of past memories, and in its future fantasies, for they are also built upon past remembrances. But our spiritual nature is not in our memory, it is the actuality of our being. So the search is endless and the problem unsolvable, and thought marches on, continually looking in its place of origin, the memory. But quiet your thoughts and your true nature is self evident and realizable – the mind is already abiding within it, so no search is needed and no problem is there to solve. If you seek for it you will not find it, for it is you, and you cannot look for yourself. There is a place beyond the thoughts, it is a place of no answers, for there are no questions to ask. Our mind is an aspect of spiritual conscious energy, and thought can never fathom this mystery, so the necessity of thought proves to be valid only within its illusory selfhood. We come into being pure and innocent, and here we can perceive in the serenity of no thought, and have no concepts to dwell within – this is our original nature, it is the state of 'no mind'. Serenely reflecting within our non dwelling mind, we can abide in realization and be the mirror of our essence.

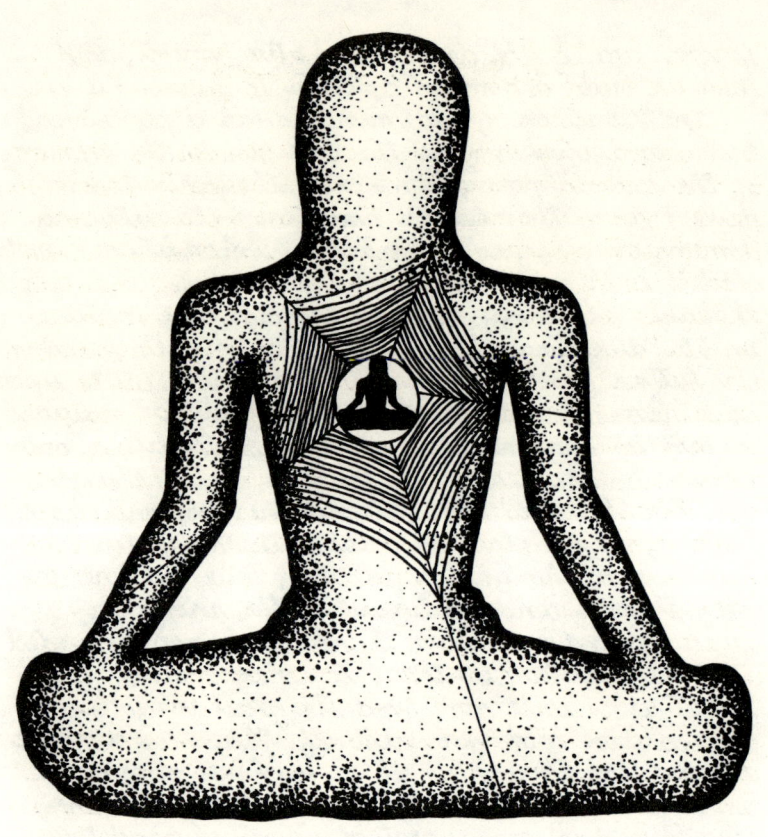

Art Plate #22~ The web of maya is not external to us - it is not the physical world, for a relative freedom exists within this manifest world. Maya is the web of concepts we build our mental world with; it is an attitude we hold internally, and there within our thoughts we imprison ourself. The selfhood we build in our web is illusion of conceptual relativity, and only in tearing apart this web of delusion do we realize that our true nature encompasses the selfhood of our illusory world . . .

Thought Energy

I have stated repeatedly that thought is illusion, but even though thought is only a reflection, there is power associated with it. The true nature of our mind is to perceive in receptive awareness, but our thought, as the continuous dialog of memory reflection, is but an illusion. Thoughts are a product of energy reflecting within the memory of our mind; the flow of energy has a relative reality, but the content of the energy as thought is only a mirror to the relative, and is thus only illusion. We are the flow of energy, and thought must flow with it, but it has no ultimate reality.

It takes energy to think, even though thought has no energy of its own. Thought is just one of the many places our energy is directed, thus it is in the position of using and directing our inherent source of power. Our energy is derived from the primal energy of the absolute — this energy is our divine spark of life and constitutes our true nature within this manifest universe. Our spiritual essence uses this energy to form our dual nature of heart and mind, and to adopt a physical form to perceive this manifest realm. The heart is an unconditioned center for the experience and expression of life, and thru it we find purpose in living. The mind is the unconditioned center which enables us to function, relate and understand, and with it we direct the heart's purpose of experience. The energy within us is channeled thru our heart and mind, and the interacting of energy, between our sences and the encompassing energy field, relates our individual perception. Accumulated perceptions build a memory, and this memory has access to our energy source, for memory is vital to every function of our existence. A unique avenue of expression of our memory is called thought, and depending upon the individuals ability to concentrate, is the amount of power that the person will be able to channel thru their thoughts. The mind requires no thought, for it has the full energy of our true self to perform all functions needed for our existence. As our mind relates understanding of its perception, the energy needed creates the enigma of thought and allows it to witness the perception unfolding, and this clouds the harmonious function of the unconditioned mind. Thought reflects within the mind, and gives rise to the concept of an illusory identity to relate its perception to, then stores these concepts in our memory, and slowly builds this unique individual we call ourself. Most people relate to this self created ego as their true self, and allow their conceptual thought to direct their energy, and thus their true nature is eclipsed. Once thought has accepted the premise of relaying its experiences to a personality, then all thought will ensue as the indispensable flow of an illusory creation. The 'I' it creates is then in command of an inexhaustible source of illusion, fantasy and concepts, and has the power of the mind to back it up, if it can focus this energy thru concentration and direct it. With concepts of intensity and determination, there is a vast amount of energy that can be focused, but with timid illusions and fantasies there is little power available. Our attention will determine the amount of energy we can channel, for we are an inexhaustible energy source looking for ways to express ourself.

The process of thought, and the concepts derived from them, only have reality to the extent of the energy channeled to direct them. The energy available to heart and mind is tremendous, and if a created selfhood rules the mind with illusory thought, then it gets access to the inherent power, and can build or destroy their physical body, and alter all the surrounding energy fields with that power. The unconditioned mind has a core of wisdom, but the ego does not; its realm is illusion, and it can re-order its fantasy world in any fashion it desires, and does so continuously. The ego cannot be blamed for its ignorance of reality, for it is an illusion which specializes in fantasy. Thus any attempt for this created ego to comprehend reality, and relate to the true nature of our essence and its own origin, is purely folly, and only results in the ego building biased concepts to hide within.

Wisdom is inherent in our true self, but knowledge has its roots in concepts of illusion, thus one can abide in the reality, but cannot know of it or understand it. Your heart and mind are linked to the perpetual source, but ego continually seeks for fantasy sources. The ego cannot gain maturity thru fantasy, and this is the reason behind all conflicts of relating between persons. Each person is a specialist in fantasizing their own illusory world, while being surrounded by an engulfing illusion that it has no control over, but always tries to control. No one can control life or another person's illusions, but everyone tries to, and this pressure removes one from the reality of life and breaks many relationships. We unify our relative world thru our concepts, but since each person is doing the same, and since no two illusions match, we shall continue to find relating difficult, unless we dissolve our concepts and meet in harmony in a spiritual brotherhood of communion beyond thought and illusion.

What makes this all so important, is that the illusion of thought, and the emotions that result from them, have access to the mind's inherent power. All emotions created thru thought are illusion, but if the ego adopts a thought, then the force of energy within the mind will be channeled thru the emotion created, and will affect all energy fields it is focused towards, including its own. We are a

being of energy, and even though thought is
illusory, we freely give it access to our power,
and thus we give thought as much of a
reality as the rest of this relative world.

All emotions are illusory thought, but the love
within our heart as aspect of our true nature,
is not the same as the emotion of love in
one's thoughts. The inherent love a mother has in
her heart for her child, is not the same as an
emotional love one has for a pleasing situation.
Without thought the heart will still be loving,
for thought does not enhance the joy and beauty
of life, but only removes one from the direct
experience of it. Thought acts as a mirror, so
it can never equal the first hand experience
of direct living. Even though the world is
perceived directly thru the heart and mind,
most everyone allows emotional thought to
interpret the world as they conceive it to be.
They relate to the world thru their emotions,
and this creates the world of duality, which
means they know only the unreality of illusion.

All emotions are relative to themselves, and
last only as long as the supporting thought is
maintained. When a child is angered, he hates
instantly, and in a few moments forgets his
concept of hate. He builds an illusion, and it
falls apart as soon as his concentration of
supporting thought wanes. Adults have greater
concentration, and consequently more power is
channeled – thus they can hold the illusory
thought of anger, grief or revenge longer, and
use the energy associated with it to affect
themselves and others. Their emotions build a
conceptual realm, and their ego dwells within it.
Spiritual persons do the converse, they build
illusory thoughts of love, and with the power
inherent in the mind, they direct this purposeful
thought and radiate beneficial energy to themself
and everyone around them. All emotional energy
is a temporary burst that lasts as long as the

190

illusory thought is held, and the power will wane as the thought wanes — thus concentration is the mark of a spiritual master. But all thought energy is directed by illusion, so it is not the avenue of a warrior abiding in his true nature.

The power of illusory thought is the essence of faith healing, for real power is behind the illusory thought, and when focused, it can exact real results. We are the energy of the Absolute within manifestation, and any focusing of this energy will have the result of manipulating the energy forms around us, or wherever it is directed. All energy is in constant activity, and any burst of energy is felt by everyone receptive to the directed vibration, and it will alter their energy to the extent of the power manifested. We are an energy field, and life is the relation of our individual capacity to channel energy within the vast, encompassing energy field surrounding us, which provides our opportunity and limitations.

The world of thought is the world of illusion, and only when thoughts stop will the world stop with it. An thought one can never accept the reality of their true nature and realize the essence of their spiritual being. Within thought there is the division of ego, thus the totality of the Absolute won't be understood. The warrior examines this situation of an illusory ego maintained by the concepts of thought, and dedicates his life to serenely living in the moment thru active meditation. Once free from the concepts of an illusory selfhood, he realizes his true nature as a free spiritual being; and as his thoughts wane, his emotions, desires and attachments dissolve, for they were maintained thru fantasy and illusion. Without thought, the warrior finds nothing to seek outside of himself, for he is the path and the goal, and this realization of his true nature has allowed him to accept his freedom.

Memory has an Ego

To understand the illusion of thought, and the ego created by it, it is necessary to examine the mind's memory. The Absolute is the only reality, and one aspect of this reality is the manifest in which spiritual beings are woven into a fabric of perceptable energy. Spiritual beings have as their vehicle of perception the dual nature of heart and mind — both are unconditioned and possess separate capabilities. The heart is our center of purpose, and the mind our center of understanding — heart gives purpose and joy to our understanding, and mind gives wisdom to our purpose. Both have the inherent energy of the Absolute to enable their functioning — the heart as giver, and the mind as taker.

For the mind to relate and understand its perception of the manifestation which enfolds it, it is necessary for the mind to store these perceptions of experience within itself in the form of a memory. Without a memory, no relating or functioning is possible within this relative world, and for this reason memory has access to mind's tremendous power. Every act requires instantaneous remembrance of its procedure, so we are in constant recall of all the necessary information to function in a relationship to the relative world. Since memory must arise before thought can take form, memory becomes the forerunner of the illusion of thought. Memory stores all experiences, and must reflect within itself to find its information, for it is recalling the past to mirror possible action in the present. All present actions are derived from past memories, and even future desires are based on expectations derived from memories of past experiences. Because of this mirroring effect, the phenomenon of an ego or selfhood arises. We cannot function without a memory, for it is everything available to the mind as recoverable perception, thus our memory views this present moment in terms of a past perceiver. This perceiver is not the mind itself, for it can neither make decisions or solve problems, but has been born of the reflection of memory in the mirroring of its own functioning. The energy of memory is the vehicle of thought. Thoughts only capacity is to watch and comment on memory, and thru this mirroring effect it gives the illusion of being the memory itself. The non-functional thought organizes itself into a selfhood we call the ego— it is the memory witnessing itself as a mirror of illusion. Ego does not have a memory, but rather the memory has an ego— it is the illusion of thought backed by the power available to memory, and arising from its energy. If there is no energy within the mind, then there can be no memory; if there is no memory, then there is no thought; and if there is no thought, then there is no illusion of ego. The ego is like a dream; even though it be illusion, it has reality within itself, and bears witness to all our acts. It rationalizes that mind is our reality, and that memory is our relation to the world, and that ego is memory's link to the present— thus the ego sees itself as the reality of us. Ego uses the memory to reflect the premise of a selfhood, and then expands this premise into the constant thinking and fantasizing that most everyone experiences. This process starts in everyone when they are a very young child. A baby has no memory, thus it has no thoughts and no ego. As memory develops, fantasy and illusion of thought are born to stabilize and bring a perspective into this relative world, and thus the ego is created as a witness to the perceptions being recalled by memory. The perception of the learned relative world is related to the child's developing ego by the surrounding adults. The relative perception is then given substance by agreement, and the illusion of thought, with ego as its relator, is the glue which binds this struggling society into relationship. This process is automatically repeated by each generation, and has an error built into its initial premise, for thought is not needed as our link to the present moment, and merely removes us from the direct experience of life. Thus we are immersed into an illusory reflection of life within the conceptual mirror of ego, and this is established as the norm, and causes the ignorance and folly of excepting this relative world, in place of the reality of our true nature.

We have created an ego to witness our memory, as it organizes our past recollections to foster action in the present situations. But how can past experiences reflecting within themselves as thought, ever put one in the present moment. This is the reason why the continuous dialog of thought is illusion, for it removes one from the present moment and builds a world of conceptual fantasy. Memory does not need a witness to its functions, for our true nature can function thru the mind with no necessity of thought, or the illusory selfhood of an ego. Memory works automatically as each moment of perception unfolds, and if thought is absent, then our capacity to function is not impaired, but actually improved, for our true self can then perform any activity in its inherent wisdom, unhindered by distracting thought. All superior acts are done when thoughts have stopped, and this is known as the moment of truth in any athletic sport or intense activity, and as the moment of awakening in the practise of spiritual discipline. It is indeed unfortunate that we allow our thoughts to take all the alive, present moments of life, and paint them over with a dead fantasy.

If one is to realize their true nature as a spiritual being, then thought must be under control of the heart, or stopped by the mind. The nature of the individual will determine which is best for him. To control illusory thought is actually a simple process, but it requires a sincerity of purpose. Thoughts take shape from past experience, and organize themselves into an illusory concept called an ego. If at this present moment you curtail all thoughts of illusion and fantasy concepts, then this present experience of sincere conviction turns this moment of no thought into a stored memory. The more your thought is purposefully stopped and your true nature experienced, the more sincere your attitude becomes, and the more memories of the present, alive moment of no thought are stored. In time, the ego begins to organize its fantasy concepts around a dedication to higher consciousness. Thus the ego adopts a path to the goal of realization, which is the process of undoing itself. Our illusory thought is very fascinated by an illusory path to a conceptual goal, but only thru this process will the proper situation allow the correct catalyst to present itself, so that the person will see thru the illusion and drop all the concepts, and abide within their true nature in the purity of no thought. Our true nature need not be found, for it is present at all times, and we need only abide in its unconditioned awareness. The great task of consciousness is to abide in the present, for in this instant all realization is possible. Illusory thought will relinquish its concepts when it realizes that it is not the true self. With thought absent, the mind can use its memory unclouded by illusion and fantasy. The mind can then supply its pure inherent wisdom, guided by the experience held within the memory, to the purpose dictated by the heart. Thus harmony can be restored into balance, and this allows our spiritual being to be realized, and free once again in its pure inherent nature.

Art Plate #23~ Within the manifestation we
see the many branching forms of relative
existence, much as one massive peak sending
forth many cascading streams of life — and
within this flow we try to grasp the pattern of
concepts that build our individual life. But this
manifestation is only a reflection and has no
creative power, for it is a relative form, and
gets its ability to issue forth the living river
of life from the ocean of reality, which though
surrounds this manifestation, remains unseen.
The Absolute provides the source of existence as
its very essence, and to this source we shall
all return within the flowing stream of
individual consciousness, there to rise again
into this journey of remembrance, that we
call life . . .

The Illusion

Life is not illusion, but it is not real either. Manifestation is an aspect of the Absolute, and there is perception within the reality of it. But what we perceive is not the reality of its true nature. All within manifestation has reality in relation to the Absolute, but our perception gives rise to concepts of its reality, and there the illusion starts. There is perception, and the perception has reality as energy of the manifest, but the thoughts of the perceiver have no reality. It is the subjective agreement formed between individuals, and collectively within society, that transforms this mystery of existence into a conceptual realm of illusion. All energy fields relate one onto another, forming the fabric of manifestation, and any thought process within it brings division as name, form and identity, and this limiting conceptualization builds our reality. But this conceptual reality is the relative world of duality, and just an illusory reflection of thought upon the fabric of reality. With the cessation of thought, the deluding character of ego, concept and fantasy cannot be focussed upon, and the surrounding experience of perception can be grasped in a more understanding light. The deluding character of this subjective perception will always be present, but the added illusion of conceptualizing this perception thru thought is in our power to control. The fabric of the manifest remains as a reality of energy, but our interpretations of our experience within it builds a dualistic, relative world of illusion, which separates us from the reality of its true nature, and allows us to see only the reflection of it within our delusory mirror of concept. The Absolute is the totality and it needs no thought or reflection, for our existence is the light of its reality.

Art Plate #24 ~ We are surrounded by the ignorance of our preconceived ideas, but at all times our true nature is within the light of understanding. We need but abide in the silent wisdom of our true self to go beyond the concepts, and see the miracle that enfolds us...

Thought is Illusory Creation

The world of thought is the realm of illusion, and it is ironic that the greatest thinkers are the ones who perpetuate this grand illusion. Statements to enforce the validity of thought have been repeated for so long that their factuality has gone unquestioned. Such statements as, "we are what we think", "you create the world with your thoughts" and "I think, therefore I am" are only confirmations of thought acknowledging itself. Statements about thought, which have been initiated by thought, cannot be the sole support for the ultimate reality of thought. Thought is created illusion of the mind in the same way that dreams are illusion of the mind. Any sincere person can go deep into a state of thoughtless meditation, and even though his mind is quiet, he will still know of his relationship within this world of relativity, and will feel his reality as a spiritual being. His thoughts are not necessary to know of his existence, or are they his true self, they are only an illusion separating him from realization.

We and the manifestation are equal in nature, and our thoughts act only to separate and divide us from awareness of our union. Our identity is not of our thoughts, for it is beyond concept and beyond the physical — our true identity is our spiritual essence within the Absolute. All concepts that our thoughts are creators or the real us, is merely thought reflecting upon itself within its realm of illusion. The purity of this moment can only be viewed in a mind free from the disturbance of thought and concept. The penultimate moment in any activity is in the depth of the cessation of thought. The deeper the silence, and the longer it lasts, is the measurer of the ultimate experience, and indicates the depth of communion within ourself. Any action or non action which leads to inner silence is meditation, and can elevate one to the highest aspect of communion within our source of being.

The world unknowingly tries to lose its thoughts thru external activities, yet desperately clings to their concepts to create a manageable world, and to alleviate their boredom; but ironically, the boredom it runs from is the monotony of its own thoughts. It is thought that removes one from living the moment, for in this alive, present moment there is no boredom. Boredom can exist in a state of thoughtless observation only if one is not attentive, for it is absolutely necessary that an alert attitude of awareness be present to give meaning to the moments when inner silence reigns. We are in a delusive circle of our own creation, for by accepting fantasy, illusion and concept as the reality, we hold ourself back from the very place we crave to be. It is the place of communion with life — where we are free within the moment, fluid in our actions, deliberate in our attempts, intuitive of decision, aware of our true nature, and abiding in realization of the reality. And this unique state of being arises only in a serene mind, when all the thoughts have stopped.

Meditate on this :
    Truth within thought,
    is still just illusion . . .

Art Plate #25~ We fall into manifestation as an individual drop of consciousness — our true nature is pure, and as yet untarnished by the world of relative concepts. As we cascade down the high, pure reaches of simplicity, we mingle with other consciousnesses and begin the process of relationships, which forces the adoption of subjective views. As each new rivulet of other individual attitudes mingle with our own, we formulate ever differentiating concepts of a selfhood. As the river of life is approached, our cascade is slowed by deeping concepts of the relative world. Eventually the river grows slow and tired, as we become rigid and stagnant in our views, and try to build a stationary world around them, and thus our bubbling innocence is lost. Finally our form drops away, as the river of life flows into the sea, and our spirit is released back into the reality of our pure essence. We shall rise again and repeat this laborious process over and over, until we can see beyond the limitations of our stagnant concepts, and live within the reality of our pure nature, free of desire and attachment to this mirage of flowing reflections...

Truth or Another Illusion

The words I have written will raise a question as to their validity, for you shall find no segment of society to verify my statements. Science, psychology, philosophy and theology are all based on knowledge supported by thought, so don't expect answers by looking within an illusion, to determine if your illusion be factual or fantasy. There is a simple way for anyone to find the truth, and each of us must discover it for ourself, for it cannot be handed down. Realizations are personal, and self discovery can only come by one's own efforts.

To find the truth behind the illusion of thought is not a matter of figuring out the problem, or thinking it over thoroughly. The truth is found in the simplicity of stopping the inner dialog. Each day, stop your thoughts by the intent of your will for as long a period as possible. If you are sincere and dedicated to finding the truth, then you shall soon discover if illusion, fantasy, self importance, attachment and desire recede as your thoughts come to a halt.

When thought is stopped, it is vital to focus your full attention on the present moment. Don't sit dull and lethargic, you must clear your mind and get totally involved in the activity present, including the activity of meditation. The purpose of thought is to focus our attention, but unfortunately we focus our awareness on illusion and conceptual fantasy. When our thoughts have stopped, we must engage our consciousness fully, and focus our awareness into the attention of the unfolding moment, and the experience of perception before us. Eventually, this state of inner silence will come naturally, for the serenity and harmony it brings, will allow the mind to reconfirm its true nature, and abide once again in tranquility. Thoughts will decrease in quanity and increase in quality, but one's thoughts will not disappear completely. There will always remain some thought, but the attitude forming its character will change from a desiring and self centered point of view, to one of love, peace and sharing. One way to judge the remaining thoughts is this — if your thoughts dictate your action, then you are slave to your concepts of desire and attachment, but if your actions flow free in the moment, whether thought be there or not, then you are following your inherent wisdom.

When thoughts of involvement of the past, and concern for the future are dropped, it frees a tremendous amount of energy for use in the present. As fantasy is dropped, energy is made available to our physical body, and this builds a vibrant body and transmits this energy into our activities. Just watch your thoughts, and you'll be amazed at the games going on that keep you out of the present moment, and trapped in your fantasies. Thought is always finding fault and blaming something — the greatest burden any man has ever shouldered has been his own criticising and condemning thoughts. Drop your incessant dialog and give yourself a serenity of life, for it is quite a joyous relief to get the monkey off your back.

Thought enjoys watching itself, and can gain pride in a pseudo attempt to curtail itself; but to actually stop your thought at will, and recognize the scope of its illusion, one must have dedication of purpose, and harmony between heart and mind. A spiritual being needs complete freedom, and thoughts keep one in slavery to the dualities of the world. A warrior fights for his freedom, for in freedom he finds his purpose, and unifies his heart and mind, to see thru the illusion of thought.

Art Plate #26~ Our true self is not separate
from the world—you are here within it and
cannot hide from it, or discover it. Watch
the light that is radiated from your
consciousness, and you shall find that this
same radiant light of awareness, is in
observation of you also...

Live True To Yourself

As I travel, I meet many people who profess to know the spiritual life, but confess that they can't follow the knowledge they have accumulated. The truth of this matter, is that they really do not understand the spiritual life, and thus it can be understood why they can't follow it. They have not failed in their spiritual life, they simply have not fully accepted the dictates of their heart, as of yet. They have an intellectual grasp of a concept, but have no deep understanding of a spiritual way of life, because they have not yet been convinced of the truth of life's reality. Their way of life is still a mystery to them, because until one is fully convinced that they are a spiritual being, then no true realization can be lived, but only a superficial consent. They may have insights into higher truths, but if they truly understood the reality of life, then they would live it automatically, and no contrary situation or worldly participation would be of any hinderance. When one is convinced of a beneficial aspect of life, then they make it a natural part of their life, and let nothing interfere with its practice. To know a way of life means that one does it, and not just considers it. The knowledge of a spiritual life must be more than just concept, for until one lives his knowledge, then he really does not know it. Life is much more than concept and philosophical premise, the truth of life is in carrying out the actuality of the wisdom present within you. It is only in this way that realization can be gained and expressed, within this unique opportunity of experience we call life. Live true to yourself, and don't say you know, if you don't do...

Wanderings of The Heart

Pecos Wilderness ~ June 1986 ~

Contrary to popular belief, New Mexico is not a vast arid wasteland of tumble weeds, but has magnificent ranges of majestic peaks. The Rockies extend far into the state, and one area of excellent alpine beauty is the Pecos Wilderness.

It was a bright, crisp morning as I left early from Jacks Creek and headed into the Pecos Wilderness. Jacks Creek is a lovely campground set at the headwaters of the Pecos River around 8700 feet elevation, and my hike this day would take me 20 miles into the gorgeous Sangre De Cristo Mountains to over 12,500 feet. The first few hours of hiking held mile after mile of rolling aspen groves, separated by large open fields of grass, glistening with morning dew. After Round Mountain there was a steep climb thru the fir forrest, which still had large snow drifts lingering from winter, til I finally reached Pecos Lake which is serenely nestled at the base of East Pecos Baldy. After the strenuous climb I decided it was time for a small break, and found a sunny spot on the shore of this pristine alpine lake. But my view was mainly on the majestic snow covered peak of East Pecos Baldy to determine the route I could use to climb its 12,539 foot summit. All the slopes were buried under snow, so it appeared that I would have to climb its dangerous rock face.

While I was pondering my route, I caught view of some Big Horn Sheep in the distance, and soon there was about 30 of them in a group, and all coming my direction. To my amazement, the sheep came right up to me, and began to lick my arms to get salt from my skin. It was so ironic to be way back in the wilderness hoping to see wild animals, and to have 30 ewes and lambs surround me, acting so tame as they licked me; but then all of a sudden the ewes all stepped aside, and a big 250 pound ram came striding toward me. Since I was sitting on the ground he towered above me, as he came right up and placed his nose an inch from my nose, and stared straight into my eyes. His eyes were just beautiful — sort of a deep ocher marbled throughout with black; but he wasn't interested in licking salt, he just wanted to let me know that he was king of this area, and that he was keeping an eye on me. After a minute he turned away and left, and the ewes and lambs immediately returned for more salt. In time the novelty wore off, and I decided to hike the adjacent ridge which has a great view of the giant 13,000 foot peaks of the Truchas range.

I ascended to Trail Ridder ridge and walked along, absorbing the spectacular view of two descending canyons falling thousands of feet on either side of me, with a magnificent view of 13,000 foot rock peaks rising straight out of the ridge in front of me. I reversed my course and decided to use this same ridge to approach East Pecos Baldy, and climb it from where they connected. Along the way, I came upon a group of 35 Big Horn sheep grazing on summer's lush cover of new grass.

The climb up the rocky face proved to be not as difficult as it looked, and I soon reached the peaks highest ridge which sloped to the summit. The ridge held a nice blanket of snow, and as I climbed over the rocks, the wind blasted me at 30 mpH. Suddenly there was movement to my right, and to my true surprise there were seven Big Horn ewes and nine little new born lambs at their side. Latter I came to find that ewes pick the highest peaks to have their lambs because of the lack of predators, so I named my group 'the nursery', and sat amongst them in communion.

The ewes soon came up to me and waited in line for salt, but they wouldn't let their lambs get closer than five feet to me. The lambs were just born that week and were still wobbly on their legs — they would reluctantly walk five feet, wobble and then lay down, and all they were interested in was getting some good, warm milk. I sat in the snow and blasting wind for an hour with them, but I was turning numb and had to push to the top of East Pecos Baldy to generate some heat, so I sadly said a fond farewell and practically ran to the top.

The view of the surrounding peaks and lake below was breathtaking. All the peaks in the Pecos that I climbed had marvelous views, but East Pecos Baldy sits in the heart of the vast wilderness, and as far as the eye could see was pristine, virgin beauty. I had fruit for lunch, and the gorgeous view for dessert, and sat in respectful awe of the wonder enfolding me. Once again I said a reluctant farewell, and sent my gratitude to the sun and all this majestic beauty, and descended from the peak.

I decided to take a short cut and ski on my boots down the snow covered flank to the lake 1100 feet below. I built up a good deal of speed as I careened down the slope, and as I approached the base I came across a large spring bubbling forth from the earth. As is my custom, I partook of this lusterous bounty by drinking some of this sacred life force and splashing some on my face. As I looked across the cold, crystal lake in front of me I was surprised to see two persons on the shore of the lake doing Tai Chi, the ballet of the soul. They were as two Blue Herons in graceful union, as they communed with nature and the spirit within them. I circumvented around their area so as not to disturb their communion, and instead I accidentally ran into someone serenely sitting alone in deep contemplation.

He turned out to be a Benedictine Monk, here on retreat at a monastery on the Pecos River. We spoke for some time about the deeper nature of our spirit, and shared as brothers for a brief moment in time, amidst the beauty of nature.

The wilderness does not see many people, but of those who do venture into its fold, many are there to commune with a higher aspect of life and find serenity of spirit, in order to put their worldly experience into a more understanding relationship. It is to these spiritual souls, who are out in the realm of nature's beauty communing within their true nature, that I give my greatest spiritual transmission, for even though I share with all my brothers, it is only those who have made themself receptive thru silence and are open to deeper understanding, that can receive my spiritual enthusiasm; and the best place to make oneself available for this transfer of inspiration is in nature's pure realm.

The lengthening shadows signaled my need to depart from this rarefied air, and give my thanks to this wondrous land. I followed a cascading creek til once again I found my path opening into the lush fields of grass, with its dense groves of aspens scattered along it. Here I leisurely walked in thoughtless meditation til I found myself in the pines that surrounded my home. Serenely I took my sponge bath and prepared my salad, and reflected on the grandeur of this day. Once again a miracle of existence unfolded around me — how gracious and beautiful is this mystery, and how respectful and humble it makes me to be part of it.

Reflections of Mastery

Every aspect of life has importance, and the way one earns his livlihood, and relates to the mundane activities of life, must be understood in its higher aspect of spiritual expression. A warrior's life is not just sitting in meditation, and serenly reflecting on reality — it is to be serene within reality, and reality is active, so a warrior's ways reflect a life of purposeful action.

The first step a warrior takes is to simplify his life. He doesn't throw everything away like a spiritual fanatic, to rush into an illusory path. To simplify life is a conscious, practical method of determining his perspective and attitude of life — he considers which items are necessary and which ones are burdensome, and how much work is needed to earn necessities, in relation to time wasted in work to cater to indulgences. So the warrior eliminates all unnecessary possessions, and continually reassesses the items he keeps to see if they are still necessary. Certain objects are needed to live a simple, conscientious life, but to have items that you don't need or even want, is slavery to your thoughts of stability and comfort, and these useless possessions will possess you. A warrior may have some simple possessions, but he is unattached to them, and thus free of worry or fear of losing them.

Man's laws of ownership are binding only in the courts, but in actuality none of us own anything. The earth is our communal home of freedom, and only in man's arrogance does he builds concepts of dividing and owning. He may lay a temporary claim to the man made items, but in reality our spirit is being blessed with a brief use of our body and the world, and can actually own nothing. We can use the world and its objects with respect while here, but we must be constantly alert that no concept of attachment or possession will arise, for only then can our spirit remain free, and able to experience this perception without being deluded by it.

As a warrior simplifies his life, he also watches his daily habits, with the purpose of dropping all useless habits that distract him from living a sincere life. All useless habits are wasted expenditures of energy, and a warrior endeavors to save all his energy, and apply it toward his spiritual dedication. All nervous habits used to waste time should be dropped quickly and completely, and in their place one should supplant a beneficial use of energy, in the way of a spiritual practice. When a negative, wasteful habit is dropped, one also concurrently drops the negative emotion associated with it, and only as this emotional energy is purified, will the mind become more clear in spiritual realization.

Once one has gained some control over the motivating forces of their life, then it is time to put this growing energy into a useful, purposeful endeavor. The warrior is not out to achieve anything — he realizes that we are perceivers of experience, and thus gets involved in meaningful activities to capture the essence of life. He stays active in a way that will suit his unique nature, and has periods of inactivity to maintain his balance and harmony. Meditation is the action of inactivity, and the warrior uses it frequently throughout the day to maintain a proper perspective on his activities. It is easy to get caught up and trapped even by meaningful endeavors, so one must stand back frequently and serenely, and view the overall picture, and make sure everything relates as part of their spiritual expression of experience, and thus desire and attachment will not form to bind their freedom. The warrior's art is one of balance, so each day he will serenely reflect in meditation, and also walk miles in contemplation, and this will maintain a communion with the miracle that surrounds and weaves thru him.

All aspects of a warrior's life are consciously and spiritually motivated. All actions receive careful consideration, free from attachment and desire, and solely motivated by his growth into higher consciousness. To find joy and understanding within this experience of life, then all external expression and possessions must be in tune with his overall spiritual life. If he chooses to work, then he should pick a means in tune with his nature that will allow the artist of his soul to express itself. A warrior provides his own means of livlihood, for it is not in the ways of a warrior to depend on others. Most warriors work for themself in some fashion that will allow an artistic expression of a spiritual nature. If he picks mundane work, then he will focus his full attention on it and turn it into a joyous experience of the moment, or into his path of service, but always as artist of his heart. It isn't so important what he does, but how well he does it. By the example of his sincerity and dedication, the warrior shows his love of sharing, and teaches the mastery of life.

Careful attention must be applied to every external in life. One's house should be alive with the vibrancy of life, and a fit abode for their spiritual freedom. Their cloths should be comfortable, simple and natural — their food should be pure, simple and wholesome — the smells surrounding them should clear the mind, and the colors around them should soothe their soul. The land and surrounding area one lives on must be free of all types of pollution and energizing to them. Many warriors travel or move frequently, for there is no one spot that contains everything — each area has its own unique aspect of energy and vibrancy. One must experience all types of terrain to determine which is most energizing to their nature. The unlimited awesomeness of this wonderous earth must be witnessed to be believed. To travel and explore this vast miracle is very intune with the ways of a warrior, for that is precisely what I have done for all of my spiritual life.

Each activity a warrior engages in is carefully examined, from both the worldly and spiritual side, for its simplicity, artistry and mastery of harmonious expression. This experience is our life, and there is no need to rush thru it — this is the grandest opportunity of reality, for our spirit has accepted this challenge. With each conscious effort to live by spiritual light, one will gain a deepening awareness and a greater mastery of themself, and the externals around them will reflect this mastery. We each must endeavor to succeed alone in the mastery of our life, so that we can all share of our mastery together. You are a free spiritual being of the Absolute — place no limitations upon yourself, and soar within the freedom of your essence.

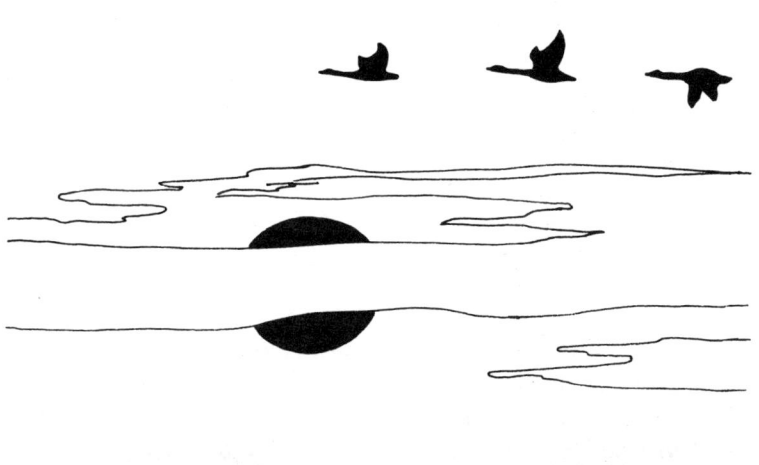

Art Plate #27~ This fragmented world
appears to exist outside of us, but the
reality of it is within us, for we are the
universe, and our heart lights this realm
of perception. The perceiver and the
perception are one reality, thus to
understand the division of form, we need
to abide in our true nature, for in its
wisdom is contained the truth of our
essence ...

Calming The Mind

The ultimate purpose of all methods and practices used to arrived at spiritual maturity, is to bring the thoughts under control, and allow your true nature to harmonize with the moment and abide in its spiritual essence. There have been many sincere individuals that have reached realization, and each has used some method or technique to help establish their path of enlightenment, but once firm in their understanding, they transcended beyond a path and goal. The various methods each master used has filled the world with assorted paths, rituals, yogas, religions and techniques. The method each master used to gain insight was relevant to him alone, and rarely can someone else's method produce the same results for another person. The best method is one where the individual has adapted it to fit their unique personality. But for one who hasn't the faintest idea of what he may be trying to accomplish, this proves difficult. Sadly, innocent people find an incredible array of bizarre techniques perpetuated by not so realized persons, claiming that their method is secret, or powerful, or the only way to the true goal. Thus it has been very difficult for the dedicated novice to understand the initial step they are taking, for once the illusory concept of a path and goal are accepted, then comes the whole futuristic process of treading the path and following the specified methods. Life within the world is one of thought, concept and illusory goals, so naturally the novice extends this conditioning into their initial introduction of a religious and spiritual life. But the following point must be firmly understood— 'one does not realize their true nature as God thru worldly means'. God is not a thought process, thus if one tries to conceptualize a method to acquire God, then they have built a firm barrier to realization.

We are all free spiritual beings, which emanate from this manifestation we call God. This essence of the Absolute is our very being, and any seeking outside of oneself turns one directly away from the truth, and thus one goes wandering in the quagmire of their thoughts. Eventually, the reality of experience either stops their search by its hard lessons of reality, or the search drops them as they tire of looking outward, and realize that God is not an attainment to be sought after, for God is the realization of who you are.

All the techniques, methods and rituals can definitely make a path look inviting, for people like to be busy, and feel they are accomplishing and arriving closer to the goal. But methods designed to bring one closer to a goal, are usually just moving one down a conceptual corridor deeper into their own illusion. So, what does one do on the spiritual path? One simply and respectfully lives this moment of experience presented before him to the fullest, with a deeper understanding of the reality of life, beyond the superficial aspect of desire and attachment to this conceptual world of relativity. Making dinner is a spiritual experience, and so is hiking, watching the stars, working at a meaningful endeavor, hugging a friend, swimming in the ocean, listening and breathing—any event of life is a spiritual experience, for they are all miracles of this unfolding reality. The event is not what makes an experience spiritual, it is your attitude and realization as the divine perceiver of life, and the perception itself serves only to provide fascination. Spiritual awareness comes in living in this moment thru the attitude of wonder and respect. Watch a sunrise and be totally into it, and that moment will be a fine communion within your true nature. But, watch the same sunrise with your thoughts running wild, and you'll have nothing but memories of illusions, and your true nature will be concealed by your thoughts.

So, if one wishes to quiet the mind and stay aware within the moment, aren't methods of necessity? As with all questions, the answer is yes and no. Methods are not necessary if one is truly convinced that he is a spiritual being, for he will understand his true nature and live perpetually within this moment of experience. But since only the very rare person is convinced they are a spiritual being, and is able to stop their illusory thought, and be fluid and free within the moment, then the vast majority of people will find methods and techniques helpful until they can arrive at that state. But first understand why one does a method — the method is not a path to a goal, or is it a bizarre technique to acquire power or anything else, or is it something to master and control. A method is the simple process of helping one to lessen the thought process and narrow the scope of conceptualizing, and to allow the illusory thought to quiet itself by its own realization of a higher plane of being. The mind can then function in its pure state of unconditioned awareness, as the heart provides purpose to balance it. So methods amount to nothing more than allowing your mind to rest in awareness, and within this awareness you'll realize the essence of your true nature.

Realization doesn't come thru a method, for a method is not a means to a goal, but in actuality, the method is the means to realize there is no goal. One does the method to enjoy life in the moment, and to experience the essence of living. One doesn't sit down and take the proper steps to achieve meditation, the very attitude of sitting serenely is meditation, and realization is the joy of living that moment fully, for in that joy is the awareness of the pulse of the universe. With each effortless effort realization will come, and there is no end to the depth of understanding within us, for we are the immensity of the Absolute.

Each person has a different affinity for what

will quiet their mind. We are all unique, so you need not feel that you must do the method everyone else is doing. Try some different, simple methods and watch your mind and body, for they will let you know when you've found one that soothes the body and brings tranquil peace to the mind. Methods should be simple and enjoyable, for no real progress is attained thru complexity, force or pain; but one will need to make a sincere, dedicated effort, if the complex structure of concepts they have built thru the years is to be undone. Your effort is not in trying to blank your mind into nothing, like a dead void, or to put yourself to sleep, you're seeking awareness and trying to wake your consciousness up, so it can be alert in the present moment and live it fully. Sometimes movement helps to quiet the mind, and sometimes stillness is best, so try different methods at different times of the day to match your varying moods.

Meditation is the method most recognized to still the thoughts and bring one into a deeper realization of their true nature. At first one will witness all the fantasy thoughts rampaging in the mind, and this can be quite disturbing. But it is necessary to recognize that your mind is out of control, before you can take the necessary steps to bring it back into harmony of its true nature. Eventually you will come to understand this non-productive, illusory thought, and be able to draw your attention away from it, and allow it to slowly lessen in intensity, til the mind becomes serenely quiet in the awareness of the present moment. You are not looking for a drugged state of dullness, but a greater sense of awareness thru inner serenity and harmony. This is of utmost importance, for realization is possible only when there is keen attention and a focused awareness — there is no technique that can help a mind that is dull, and not ready to grasp the moments' insight. Until your whole being is attuned to a one pointed effort, then

218

there will not be deep realization. Awareness and attention grow with sincerity of purpose, so one's realization will be in proportion to their sincerity and devotion, but any effort will bear the fruit of spiritual growth and establish harmony within.

Meditation has been ritualized to the point of forgetting the original purpose, and with the rituals have come hundreds of types of meditation. This confusion is simply the thought process refusing to stop, and taking the source of its extinction, and complicating it to the point of ineffectualness. Meditation is simplicity itself. One is to just let go — nothing special is supposed to happen. Your not looking for further sensory experiences, but allowing yourself to realize a place of calm within. This is not the time for visions and thought revelations, it's a time of deep communion and for silence within your cocoon of activity, to establish perspective, and simply abide in the purity of your true nature. So be in tune with the silence that is there, and go into it and feel the depth of its calm, for this is the center of your being.

To meditate, merely sit down in any position you choose, where you can be comfortable and hold the position easily. At first it is best to find a place that is quiet and tranquil, so that your attention will not be disturbed. Once one becomes attuned to the calm center within them, they will be able to meditate and find that center no matter what the circumstances are surrounding them. Usually the eyes are closed, but if in a beautiful spot, you may wish to keep them open. Breathe slowly and deeply, and mentally watch your breath go in and out. Have no concerns, the world will function just fine without you for awhile — just be relaxed and aware, and fully attentive to watching your breath move in and out. Don't try to force your mind to be still, just relax and have no concerns — focus your attention on your breath, and allow your thoughts to stop. At times bring your attention to listen to the sounds around you, and the movement and sound within you. We mainly relate to the world thru our eyes, thus they carry a great burden, but in meditation one can use their ears to perceive the world, and open a new realm that they are unaware of. If you become uncomfortable then change your position, but raise no thought about it. Keep your lower back braced so that your spine is straight, and try not to fidget and think of your body. This brief time of meditation is for not thinking, but for observing with attention and awareness. This is simple meditation and can be done anyplace and anytime, and each person should mold it to fit their personality. One last comment, it is not necessary to sit when meditating. My favorite way is to find a lovely place in nature, and lie down with my spine to the earth and my wool cap under my head. My spine is straight and I'm very comfortable, and able to commune with the natural surroundings, as I abide in the center of my being. One can feel great energy emanating from the earth when you harmonize with it and allow it to embrace you.

Prayer, japa and mantra are all fine ways of removing illusory thought, and supplanting a controlled spiritual thought in its place. This is a good way to gain control of a restless mind, but it does not bring one into realization of their true nature, so meditation must be combined with these thought control methods. In using prayer, japa or mantra one must be very alert so that they don't become parrot-like and repeat out of habit, with no awareness of what they're saying, or the purpose of the method. Awareness is the key in exchanging a spiritual thought, for an illusory thought of the world—both are concepts, but the spiritual thought is controlled and can elevate the spirit, and the worldly thought is uncontrolled and keeps one in delusion.

In prayer, you are not trying to beseech to someone or something outside of you in hopes of receiving something. This would be praying with attachment and desire, and that can never quiet the mind. Prayer is a perpetual stillness within, as one silently sends blessings outward – it is an honoring of God, not a dialog to God. Prayer is a special time for listening, as you commune with the inspiration of your heart.

In japa one repeats a sacred name or verse. One should repeat slowly and be conscious of what they are saying, and the meaning behind the words, for if it isn't done sincerely than it is ineffectual. Both prayer and japa can be very comforting, and when combined with meditation can stop the worldly chattering, but once the mind is still they should be dropped, or one will develop spiritual chattering. Always remember that you are trying to stop illusion and conceptual thought, and abide in the still calm of our true nature, and methods are only for helping in this period of transition.

Mantra is the intoning of a specific sound that brings harmony to the mind and body, and is especially useful in that it can be done at any time, while performing any activity. Aum is universally accepted, but any sound or word can have value if it brings peace to the heart and clears the mind. Just breathe deeply and slowly, and as you exhale, slowly intone the sound either silently or vocally. Or you can pick any meaningful two syllable word, or two short words, such as 'freedom' or 'here-now', and as you slowly breathe in, silently intone the first word or syllable, and as you slowly breathe out, silently intone the second. Keep an elevated spiritual attitude, and be conscious of the meaning of what you're repeating. Mantra is very soothing, and when stopped, the mind will usually be silent of its own wish.

Here are a few other simple methods to bring

a meditative state of inner silence. Go out into nature and sit amidst this living world — listen attentively, and get your face down close to the mosses and little flowers, and examine this world you live in. Look at tiny objects like pebbles, leaves and lichens, and expand their features to see mountains and valleys in their tiny recesses — always try to see the incredible perfection and intricacy that this live, breathing earth is endowed with. Don't just glance at the world, see it in depth with the eye of an artist, and observe how the form, shapes and tones of color are always changing and ever alive.

Fasting is an excellent way to calm the body and mind, and allows one to go deeply into meditation. The fast must be recognized as a spiritual opportunity, and one must be alert to the experiences unfolding around them, for it is easy to lose alertness when fasting. If fasting is combined with silent meditative walking in the beauty and solitude of nature, then I know of no other method to bring one deeper into receptivity to experience realization of their true nature, and grasp the miracle enfolding them.

Books and rituals have no intrinsic value in themselves, it is the meaning you bestow, and the attitude you approach them with, that will determine their usefulness. Many fine spiritual souls have written beautiful messages to touch the pure spirit within you. These books let one turn off their thoughts and occupy the mind with higher attitudes of consciousness; thus their use is basically inspirational, but they do not bring one to their true nature or stop conceptual thought. One must be extremely careful not to adopt the view of the writings as their own thought. This is the danger of books, for one can build a new personality with them, and never discover who they really are. There must be equal time for meditation to balance reading, or the thread of reality becomes an experience of examining the opinions of others — one thus becomes knowledgeable, and loses the opportunity to gain wisdom. Books are of the moment as your attention is focused on them, but it is a dry, lifeless moment, where the mystery is gone and your thoughts stay as active as ever. As to ritual, its greatest value lies in its ability to trap one's attention, and allow them to focus it dynamically. If thru the ritual one can be attuned to a higher purpose, and consciously shut off their internal dialog to do the ritual, then greater attention is groomed. Let the ritual attract your full attention, and then apply that awareness into going deeper into a calm, meditative state, thus one's consciousness will expand to match their devotion. But always remember, the ritual is only an external form, and it must have an internal realization and understanding to supply its foundation and give it meaning; so don't get caught up in concepts that the ritual contains special power or value of itself. Once one has become attuned to an ever present state of awareness, then rituals can be dropped as a means to focus attention.

One method of transforming your illusory thoughts to be in harmony with your heart is to adopt a path of service. One need not go looking for people to help, but to be perpetually alert to lend service in the situations unfolding before you. This is not the pride of helping, but the humility of sharing the joy of living with your brothers. Being of service and sharing does not stop the thoughts or bring realization of one's true nature, but it does bring one's inner self into focus thru their heart, and opens the channel for deeper reflection and a much higher attitude of life. To share is our most precious gift, and in doing so, one cleans the thoughts and purifies the heart. It is not a losing of yourself in giving, but finding yourself thru sharing.

When music paints an atmosphere with its

223

sound, then one can follow it with a meditative mind. Your concentration must be on it alone and you must be alive within it, thus the moment becomes precious. It allows one to stop their thoughts by concentrating on a superior awareness, but it brings no serene reflection. So after the music is over, keep the meditative mind, and sit quietly in awareness to gain insight and depth from the experience.

Every warrior is athletic, and partakes daily of the clear calm of joyous bodily exertion. All physical endeavors put one into the moment with an alert mind and keen attention. If the activity is approached as a spiritual experience, then one will always be in meditative action. It is the attitude of the individual which will determine whether he will find insight in his strenuous moments of thought stilled attention, for the potential is there if one's consciousness is focused on their spiritual nature.

If your mind is one pointed to the extraction of thought, then this is meditation. If you are conscious of no other activity than what the moment holds, then this is stilling your thoughts. If your attention is totally focused into your spiritual nature, then this is serene reflection. All allow one to live in the present moment, and eliminate the fantasy and illusory thought that is the barrier to realizing one's true nature as a spiritually free being.

Any method can bring results, but first your sincere dedication is needed, and you can only arrive at this state of consciousness once you realize you are a spiritual being. Once a spiritual attitude of life is adopted, then your attention and awareness will perpetually be focused on your true self. Without focusing our attention and awareness there can be no realization. We can capture the present only if our attention is focused on it, and stop our thoughts only when our awareness is focused on our spiritual nature. Without the focusing of our attention there is no dedication and purpose. Without awareness we live only in a world of our illusion. Without attention and awareness all methods would be wasted effort, and any realization would be dead. Without awareness, the magic and mystery of life would have no value to us. Without focusing attention, our perceivable world would collapse, for every aspect of functioning needs attention for us to bring order to our relative world. To the degree that we focus our awareness and attention, is the level of our realization. In this very moment you can focus upon the experience unfolding around you, and find realization in the wonder of its mystery. This perception is the fulfillment of a dream, and you are its essence — grasp it with your consciousness, and watch joyously in freedom.

Parable - Sword of Attention

There was a wise master who lived in the forest, and he was renowned for his bizarre sense of humor. He had a big house with many servants, and each day a few devotees would come to ask questions. An intellectual doctor would come often to discuss philosophical matters. One day the master was explaining, " attention makes our perceivable world, and without it the world collapses. It is our attention that creates relative realness, for when we lose our attention in sleep, the world of perception collapses and there remains no relative realness. When we are immersed in a world of thought, our attention is focused on it and we lose contact with this moment of being. At that point our attention is divided, most of it is within illusory thought, so we lose the reality of the moment; but some of our attention is still focused on the world, so we catch enough of it to hold its relativity - like a dream we awake from, just to fall right back into our dream. Our attention is the key to everything - where it is placed is our avenue into our true nature, and it must be focused in the present to live in realization." After the discourse the doctor asked, "I am a bit confused, do you mean to say that if I focus my attention on you, the rest of the world will disappear?" The master replied, "the manifestation is always present, for its reality is of the Absolute. But your mind has relative realness, and if your attention is focused exclusively on me, then in view of your perception, the world will not be there - the world would still be present, but you would not perceive it." The doctor responded, "I wish I had an example of this, for I find it hard to understand - could you show me how this works?" The master saw an opportunity to be mischievous and said, "alright, now wait here and I'll be right back." He went to a back room and spoke to a servant. Upon his return, he immediately began to shout at the doctor about the stupidity of his questions, and that the doctor was an imbecile and incompetent to realize anything; and he went on shouting insults at the doctor, not giving him a second to speak. The doctor was tremendously hurt by the insults, and tears came to his eyes. Abruptly the master smiled and asked, "well doctor, what did you hear just now?" Puzzled, the doctor replied, "I heard you yelling at me." "Is that all?" asked the master. "Yes, all I heard was your cruel voice." The master laughed and said "that's what I thought, now look behind you, and you'll see that the whole time I was yelling my servant was banging a gong, and loud enough to drown me out if you hadn't placed your full attention upon my antics." The doctor looked behind him and sure enough there was a servant with a gong, and as he looked the servant banged the gong, and indeed it was deafening. The doctor asked, "are you sure he was hitting the gong, how could I not have heard it?" The master replied, "as I have explained, your attention was caught by me and held totally focused by my yelling. When the attention is focused as such, it leaves no room to perceive elsewhere — we only perceive what we choose to by the focusing of our attention, thus a man can sleep in the middle of a war. Our attention of the world creates the possibilities of perception within it. Now do you understand?" The doctor reluctantly replied, "well I guess I agree, but are you positive he banged the gong while you yelled?" The master saw another opportunity for his pranks, and went into his act, replying, "so you think I'm lying, eh — well, I'll show you who knows the truth around here — you're going to learn that attention creates our perceivable world, or die." And with that he darted to the curtain that separated the rooms and looked back at the doctor with utter fierceness and vengeance, then departed. After several minutes, the apprehension and fear the doctor felt built to such an extreme that he was about to faint, when all at once a sword slashed thru the curtain, and there stood the master with a mad killer's look in his eyes. The master slashed the curtain to ribbons, and then turned at the doctor with the obvious intent of attack. He rushed at the doctor slashing the sword in the air and screaming. The doctor was petrified, and in sheer terror he turned and ran blindly to the open door, where two servants were blocking his way. He pushed them aside as he ran out the door, hearing the master screaming, as the master ran after him. Down the steps and thru the courtyard the doctor desperately ran in blind panic to save his life, but the courtyard gate was locked. The doctor froze on the spot and looked for a way to escape his doom, but the courtyard was completely walled in, and the

master and his servants now had the doctor
surrounded. The doctor looked around in
desperation, and knew he was about to die. The
master raised the sword above the doctor's head,
and they looked at each other eye to eye. But the
master's eyes became friendly, and all at once
the doctor heard laughter, and realized all the
servants were laughing. The master dropped the
sword and laughed so uproariously that he fell
on the ground. The doctor was utterly bewildered,
he couldn't grasp the humor, but all of a sudden
it hit him like a slap in the face. He looked at
the master and at all the servants, and to his
incredible amazement they were all naked — he
had not noticed that they were naked when he
was running, or looking at the sword and the
master's eyes, but there was no doubt that they
had no clothes. The doctor was so numb from
astonishment that he had to sit down. Everyone
put on robes and then the master said, "be not
amazed, I told you that when we focus our
attention completely, there is no room for perception
outside the field we focus upon. You focused on
fear, death, my eyes and the sword — that was
the world of your perceivable attention, and
nothing else existed for you, not naked masters
or naked servants, or birds, waterfalls, airplanes,
your family or the desire for realization. Your
attention created your perceivable world, for
attention is everything. It is your path to the
awareness of the absolute, and to the reality of
your spiritual essence — attention is your true
self in realization of this moment. Now do you
believe?" The doctor was stilled numb. The
master saw that the doctor's attention was
unfocused, and winked at the servants, saying,
"I don't think he does," and picked up the
sword. The doctor's attention immediately
returned, as he ran for his life.

228

Meditate on This ~

If you cannot recognize divinity in your fellow man, then you will not realize God within yourself...

~   ~   ~

It takes more strength to be gentle and loving, than to be harsh and violent — any fool can kill and offend, but only the wise can unite, nurture and inspire...

~   ~   ~

How can you know who I am, if you have not come to understand who you are. Abide within your true nature, and everything external will prove to be your reflection...

~   ~   ~

Perception is a miracle. The value is not in what we perceive, but in the ability to perceive at all...

~   ~   ~

The most deceptive aspect of the world, is that when a concept of ignorance is finally seen in a truer light, that we quickly replace it with another ignorant concept of increasing complexity; and thus we crawl ever deeper into our web of delusion, always confident that we are climbing out...

~   ~   ~

'I traveled all around the world looking for the ocean, but all I ever saw was a whole lot of water'. How can we ever find God, when we're searching for a concept within our mind, and don't even know what that concept is...

Parable - Ripples of Thought

A young disciple was disturbed that his meditations were being intruded upon by his errant thoughts, so he decided to seek out personal advice from a warrior. He explained to the warrior that during his meditations random ideas and remembrances were arising from no where, and then disappeared, just to be followed by another nonsensical thought. The warrior responded, " this situation is the same problem everyone faces when first observing the mind. I will explain this to you by use of an example." They proceeded to a still pond, and there the warrior dropped a small rock into the pond, saying ," watch how the rock creates a splash, and then ripples proceed outward, and when reaching the edge of the pond, the ripples reverse their course and come back again until they exhaust themselves. Now I will drop a pebble in the still pond, and watch how the splash is very small, but the ripples remain large, and the return ripples are very weak. And last I will drop one grain of sand in the pond; notice that there appears to be no splash, and yet there are ripples, but no return ripples come from the edge. Now what I mean to show by this example is the thought process within the various stages of life. The worldly man drops rocks of thought into his mind, which cause large disruptive ripples, but he pays less notice of them because of the physical splash of worldly activity at their center, and the thoughts are continuously returning upon themselves til they exhaust him. A disciple is dropping pebbles in his clear mind and thus ripples occur, and the small splash is the disturbance you're feeling. These ripples of thought return weakly, thus your disturbance is momentary, but because you are in calm meditation, you pay greater attention to these small ripples created by your errant thoughts. Have no concern for this situation, for it is just a process which takes time. You will eventually lose interest in this disturbance and stop focusing your attention on your thoughts, then your meditation will grow quietly deeper. But even though one reaches this stage, there will still be some thought, but their character will be as dropping one grain of sand in a still pond. The thought will cause no disruptive splash in the mind, but weak ripples will occur. The warrior takes note of them and then forgets them, thus no return ripples occur to exhaust him. We all have memories, thus we all will experience thoughts arising, and it does no good to force the mind into calmness. Calm will happen of its own, when one loses the desire to focus their attention on their thoughts, and take them as a reality. The attitude of a warrior is to allow his mind to rest in the purity of a calm pond, but if a thought arises, he doesn't cling to it, but lets it dissipate of itself, and eventually his storehouse of useless memories wanes of strength. Thus he can experience calm in the midst of activity, and be as if in a tranquil sea of serenity, where he no longer has any interest in his intruding thoughts. For this stage to blossom forth, you must have patience, and lose your attachment and desire for the goals of the world, and respectfully abide in the reality of your true nature. And always remember to keep the correct perspective of what is the reality, for your true nature is not the disruptive ripples of thought on the surface of the pond, but the deep, clear waters of the pond itself, and this water of life is the purity of the absolute."

Art Plate #28 ~ All methods are avenues of seeking; but God is not a goal to be sought after, thus the value of techniques are in determining one's sincerity and dedication. You'll find no God upon a path, for God is the very essence of your being...

Meditate on This ~

You have come into this world free — there has been no charge demanded, or expectations placed upon you. There is no obligation on you to achieve, for there is nothing pending for you to accomplish. Just think of the enormity of this truth — you are free and under no obligation. There is no burden upon your life other than what you have placed on yourself, and accepted of your own free will ; and at any time you have the freedom to remove your self limitations ...

~   ~   ~

If you ask for nothing, then you'll always receive your heart's desire ...

~   ~   ~

Who is the one within you who has given you the right to complain and get angry? Certainly it is not your true self as aspect of God. It is paramount to discover who this selfhood of separateness is, for only then will you understand the division you have created between an ego as yourself, and your true self as God. Only with this realization can you release this created selfhood, and abide in your true nature. We must all discover who we truly are ...

~   ~   ~

We must all live by our best judgement, for to follow the words and ways of others traps us within their relative path. Freedom is solely our responsibility, and there is no one to blame or congratulate for the ultimate outcome. It is our life's work to do our best ...

Silent Meditation

Relax into this moment of tranquility,
  and experience the sublimity of silence.

In this communion of peace,
  we touch the beauty
  woven throughout this universe,
  and deep into our soul.

We need not rush to expend our life;
  so be calm and serene
  within this precious moment,
  that captures our spirits' essence.

~ Breathe Deep ~

~ Breathe Slow ~

Breathing is a Miracle,

  and you are the master
  of its destiny . . .

Art Plate #29~ We are all within this world, but there is no need to abide in the ignorance of its concepts. It is our attitude that builds our relationship to the world, and if your priority be one of spiritual realization, then this sincere attitude of dedication will allow you to abide in a truer realm, and thus be not of this materialistic world...

The Warrior's Temple of Health

Perspective of the Physical:

A warrior is aware that all aspects of life are an integral part of our spiritual expression, and all must be integrated for harmonious function. His body is part of the miracle of existence, so a warrior views his health as one more aspect of his spiritual unfoldment, and part of the grand opportunity to live the responsibility and freedom of his total manifested being. The body will return to the elements, so only as part of his total spiritual life will the body reach a proper level of understanding. The body is dead, so the warrior does not get attached to it, but he treats it with utmost respect as the temple his spirit has enlivened; for without a spiritual view of the body, there would be no reason to nurture and master it. For in this relative manifestation, our body is the wings of our spirit, and provides the unique opportunity to perceive this miraculous perception unfolding before us.

Integrating to Harmony:

There is no aspect of life the warrior treats superficially, especially one so important as the miracle of metabolism. The function of food intake to energy output is an incredible event, and without the proper perspective, this miracle is reduced to the mundane activity of eating. A warrior keeps a spiritual attitude toward this divine act, and transforms his meal into his prayer and a communion with his body.

The act of eating is one of the major activities of the body, so there is no hurry to finish and get to another activity. Eat slowly and in peace, and chew your food well, for your stomach has no teeth. Chewing slowly mixes saliva into the food, which starts the digestive process. Eat as if your food was a miraculous substance that brings you life, and this attitude will transform the social event of eating into a spiritual meditation.

Eat only when hungry, for if your not hungry, then you can be sure that you don't need to eat. Most people eat far more than they need, to function at peak level. Any extra food ingested will not increase strength, but actually decrease it by giving the body extra work of metabolism. The stomach will metabolize food only under proper conditions – if one is tired, nervous, angry or not feeling well, then the stomach cannot do its job of processing food, and even the best food will be toxic to it.

Eating is life, so create the conditions to nurture it – a nice atmosphere, soft lights and music, and conversation of a pleasant spiritual nature. Prepare the food with love, and make it not only nutritious, but pleasing to the eye and soothing to the palate. Foods that are too hot or too cold desensitize the palate and injure the stomach and throat lining. Salt, pepper and other harsh spices create difficulty for the kidneys and liver, and few seasonings have health benefits, so use them sparingly and discover the real taste of the food.

It is of great importance to combine foods correctly, for mixing too many foods together can create difficulty for the stomach. Food combining charts are available at health stores, and their use will eliminate most digestion problems, like gas, burping, heart burn and constipation. For the digestive fluids to metabolize food they must be strong, thus drinking with your meal dilutes them and makes it difficult to digest anything. Fluids are vital to proper functioning, so between meals drink several quarts of juice, tea or pure water each day. Enzymes are the vital catalysts of the body, and are only made available in raw foods, so it is advisable to eat half your food in the form of raw, uncooked, unprocessed foods. Not all foods or fluids will agree with everyone, watch for any reaction to the food you eat to see which foods will suit you best.

Nutritious food is not all that is necessary for optimum health. The body is designed for movement, and food is the means to produce energy to foster this movement. Without the body receiving ample exercise, even healthy food will clog the body. It is absolutely vital that the individual finds some means of enjoyable activity to burn the calories the food produces. Blood circulation is vital for robust health, and the activity picked should provide enough movement to bring good circulation — either long periods of sustained movement like hiking, or short periods of high exertion like running.

A warrior tunes his body to a fine state as part of his artistry of life. Our body is not a machine, it is a living, breathing, functioning miracle to nurture and develop to its optimum capabilities. It is the temple and vehicle of the spirit, and it deserves the highest respect, if our true nature is to be realized.

Foods that bring Health:

Each person must find for himself which foods are most in tune with their nature, since there is no one food that agrees with everyone, or produces the same results. From many years of studying natural foods, nutrition and healing, I've found what works well for me. I'll share my opinions, but remember, you are not me, and you must research into yourself to find the best nutritional diet for your unique body.

A warrior eats to live, and not lives to eat, thus he will only consume foods that are wholesome, nutritious and properly prepared. He will not eat any food that has been processed or refined, or that contains chemical additives. One's diet should vary throughout the year, to match the demands of the season and the foods grown within it and the type of exercise one gets, for heavy activity will require heavier foods, but light activity will not. In winter it is best to eat more cooked foods for their warming effect, and in summer eat more fruit and raw foods for their cooling effect.

The foods that are most conducive to good health are: All types of fruit that are fully tree or vine ripened and eaten raw. All types of vegetables, including sea vegetables - the tender ones should be eaten raw, and the tough ones gently steamed. All seeds - best results are attained when they are eaten in the form of sprouts. All raw and unsalted nuts (the peanut is not a nut, but a legume).

Legumes and beans are nutritious, but they are hard to digest and constipating — they should be eaten in small quantities, and best eaten in winter. The grains have good nutritional value if prepared correctly, the should be cooked slowly as a whole grain and not overcooked or stored for latter consumption. They provide lasting heat and strength, but not all grains agree with everyone, for they are heavy and can produce lots of mucus. Most breads have little value, but if the grains are sprouted and heated at low temperatures (like essene bread), then they are a good source of grain and nutritious.

Fat is the lubricant of the body and where our heat and energy is stored. The best source to attain the necessary fats is in the form of thin, liquid oils, such as extra virgin olive oil. No foods should be cooked in fat or oil, for this transforms its lubricating quality into a sticky form that is indigestible. Cook your food gently in steam or water, and then add the oil to the prepared dish at the time it is served, this enables the oil to retain its raw, essential properties and its unique taste. The best avenue to use oil is in your daily, raw salad. Butter is half fat and half dairy, so it should be used sparingly as mucus forming.

All dairy products are highly mucus forming and clogging to the arteries — it is best to avoid their use or use very sparingly. Meat products are the next category, but first one must recognize a decision — if one's diet is spiritually motivated, then it is doubtful that he would wish to cause the death of any living creature that holds its life in the same tenure he does. But if one's diet is strictly for health motivated reasons, then the eating of small portions of sea foods is a good source of protein, as is fresh water fish. But all red meat and fowl, raised for the purpose of killing and consuming, is not health producing and has many negative effects, and is best avoided completely.

Small amounts of a good wine will not destroy the body, but it does the body no special good. It is best for the health to drop all addictive, stimulating and depressive substances from entering the body — such as liquor, beer, drugs, medicine, asperin, coffee, tobacco, harsh spices, refined sugar, mono sodium glutinate and any food with chemical additives.

The catalysts of the body are the enzymes available in live, raw foods. Any cooking will destroy the enzymes and reduce the nutritional value significantly. For best health it is best to eat at least half your daily food intake in the form of raw fruit, vegetables, sprouts, seeds, nuts and oils. As to the foods that are too starchy, tough or fiberous to eat raw, it is very important to cook them correctly if they are to retain their nutritional value. The best way is to steam lightly or cook in a little water over low heat til just tender.

The foods of highest nutritional value are the ones grown by yourself, and harvested just minutes before you eat. Try to grow your own food, and you'll not only achieve fine health, but you'll also reap the reward of communion with this beloved earth. Make it part of the spiritual experience of the moment to prepare the food yourself, and serve it with love. Make love one of the ingredients you put into all your preparations, for love gives the food life. What you put into your body, whether it be food or thought, will most definitely have an effect on your spiritual energy. Your life is the only asset your spirit has on this earth; it is the manifested link with the divine, and our body exemplifies its character and integrity. Clothe your soul with your best ability and finest attempt.

Cleansing the Spirits' Sheath:

Even though one eats the finest foods and exercises daily, the body will still clog up eventually. Fasting is the simple and natural cure to prevent the body from clogging up and illness setting in. It should be viewed not only as a good house cleaning, but also as an opportunity for the spirit to commune in deep contemplation, unhindered by bodily demands.

A warrior fasts periodically to thouroughly cleanse the body, and for deep spiritual insight—it is a quest of the soul for three days on juice and tea. More regularly a warrior does short cleansings — for this he picks a day each week or two, and eats no solid foods that day, but instead drinks lots of fruit and vegetable juice, herbal teas, miso or broths. Watermellon, orange or grape juice make for an especially cleansing day. There is usually no energy loss, but one should still get plenty of rest to give the body a total renewal.

It is important to not eat out of habit, but only when hungry — if you're not hungry, just have some juice or broth, for we all tend to eat more then is necessary. With less intake of solid food, the body can metabolize its food much better, and have little toxin left over to clog the body. Cleansing the body is as important as watching the nutritional value of

241

the food taken in. Your food must be wholesome
and nutritious, then metabolized as completely as
possible, and periodically cleansed of any residue—
only in this way will our vehicle of the spirit
perform harmoniously in its experience of life.

Awareness Brings Prevention:

Every bodily part has individual functions that
harmonize into a whole, and the warrior's effort,
to be constantly aware of the body's functioning,
brings prevention of most illnesses. A study of
herbal teas allows one to make part of their
necessary fluid intake an herbal tonic to serve
the need of that day. There are dozens of herbs
that not only taste good, but have valuable
health promoting benefits, and the medicinal
herbs allow one to be their own doctor. To use
herbs well, it is necessary to be very alert to
the signals the body gives that forecast illness.
Every illness is foreshadowed by warning signs,
and the warrior's task is to be aware enough
to see it and enact a method to prevent its
development. His methods are simple and
natural, because he catches the illness in its
initial stage — his medicines are teas, fasting,
meditation, juices, cleansing, sunshine, rest and
a spiritual loving heart, and he uses them daily
to cure and keep himself whole.

Of good healing value is massage, it is used
to promote good circulation and increased
energy flow and tone the body. Reflexology is
good in that it can bring direct aid to the
internal organs of the body, and release blocks
of tension. Skin brushing has a wonderful
effect on the entire circulatory system of the body,
and helps to stimulate cleansing — use a natural
bristle brush, and brush the body for several
minutes before bath or shower. It is vital for
good health to bathe and scrub the body every
day. The skin is the largest eliminative organ
of the body, and it builds toxins on its surface

daily, and these Toxins must be washed off if the skin is to breathe and function correctly. Try to use as mild a soap as possible on your hair and body (like Castile soap), or use no soap at all with just hot water. And since the mouth is where most illness begins, it is very important to brush and floss the teeth, and rinse the mouth often.

Sunshine is the great healer and bestower of life. It is paramount to vibrant health to breathe deeply and slowly in the clean, fresh air of nature, as the sun's purifying rays bathe your body. Purity of body is only made possible if its vital supply of air and water is unpolluted, and an ample supply of the sun's energizing rays received.

We are a being made of simplicity, and our finest reflection of spiritual expression is in the simple basics of worryless sleep, meditative rest, joyful exercise, clean air, unpolluted water, vibrant sunshine and purity of thought. When these are met lovingly and respectfully, our vehicle of the spirit is transformed into the divine temple it was created to be.

~ A Few Books on Natural Health ~

'The Way of Herbs' by Michael Tierra
'Back to Eden' by Jethro Kloss
'Mucusless Diet Healing System' by Arnold Ehret
'Be your own Doctor' by Ann Wigmore
'Survival into the 21st Century' by V. Kulvinskas
'Natural Weight Control' by Norman Walker
'Fruit and Vegetable Juices' by Norman Walker
'The Colon Health Handbook' by Robert Gray
'Composition and Facts about Food' by Ford Heritage

~ A Spiritual Warrior's Personal Diet ~

Appetite is the most difficult of the desires to subdue, but without its mastery one will always be chained to the world of desire. My diet is solely spiritually motivated, and my every effort is to enable my physical body to rise to its highest potential, and provide a fit home for my spirit. Thru hundreds of fasts, and a constant refining of my diet, I have slowly tuned my body to be the spiritual sheath of my soul. My body requests live, natural, nutritious food in small quantities, and I vary these foods to match the seasons and temperatures, and the amount of exercise I get. In the morning I lightly cook several compatable vegetables, then I usually hike all day, and I'll take along some tea and a few pieces of fruit. Upon returning I bathe, and prepare a large, raw salad of sprouts and greens of which I grow fresh in my van, and apply a salad dressing of olive oil, shoyu, herbs and freshly ground sunflower or sesame seeds. Each day I drink several quarts of herbal teas that I blend myself to match what my body requests for that day. I have cleansing days, and eat only when hungry; and joyously live within the purity of nature, where I get an ample supply of clean air, pure water and invigorating sunshine — I am thin, but physically and spiritually very healthy. This is my total diet for every day of the year, and I don't presume that it will be suited to others. It is up to each individual to discover what their diet should be. Burden no one else with the responsibility for the mastery of your life. Sincerely examine your ideals and live them truthfully, for we can only teach the truths that we ourself have embodied, thus the love of our spirit must be reflected in our physical body for us to freely share our spiritual gift of life.

Art Plate #30 ~ Our form is reflective of the consciousness of our true self - it grows from the roots of our soul to express our awareness of life, and the truer our life, the more perfect our form will reflect our True nature. Your body is the sacred Temple of your expression of life, and within it you offer your life as worship, for only thru form can you realize your essence of Godhood, and have the blessed opportunity to live it...

The Duality of Pain

A warrior has preferences, but recognizes that he has no rights and can make no demands. His nature prefers a harmonious, well functioning body, so he does everything necessary for the proper conditioning of his physical sheath, for this is part of his respect for the vehicle of his spirit. But within this experience of life, pain is part of the mystery, and though the warrior does not seek pain, he does not avoid it or place undue emphasis on it, for he recognizes that all sensory perception is basically equal in nature. Pain is part of the miracle of experience, and as long as he is within the relative dualities of a manifest existence, he will be blessed to experience their effects. A warrior may have a preference to experience the miracles of joy and well being, but he fully understands that pain and sorrow are equal miracles of perception within this relative world, so he does not focus on one and try to forget the other, but fully accepts whichever is present as the miracle of this moment. This manifestation is the world of duality, and within its dual nature there is no good and bad, but only experience to be witnessed. A warrior accepts what unfolds before him, and finds his joy in this acceptance, not in what is being unfolded, for he feels blessed to be able to experience life at any level, and doesn't dictate that it must be joy or pain, but accepts both. His joy is internal, and produced from his deep understanding of the miracle he is blessed to witness and live within. To rise above the world it is necessary to understand the world, and joyously live in acceptance of the miracle which enfolds our physical nature. Our true essence is beyond duality, for we are spiritual beings, and this is the warrior's true joy.

My Reflection

I look upon the reflection in the mirror.
Its eyes are closed,
    and it appears dull and lifeless.
I make a plea to its reason,
    as I speak the wisdom of the ages.
I implore its heart to awaken,
    as I express the love of existence.
I beseech its purpose of challenge,
    as I voice the opportunity of adventure.
Its ears are closed by concepts,
    its eyes are blind by illusion.
Its fear, worry, hatred and anger
    make it dull and lifeless.
Look at the mirror & shout,
    you are just a reflection.
There is nothing to fear,
    rid yourself of concept and limitation.
You have the miraculous chance,
    to live in the world of the mirror.
I am the one who is real,
    you are just my reflection.
I am the essence of life,
    you are just my manifest form.
Open your eyes and awake,
    and let me live my life . . .

Parable ~ The Tapistry of Life

While a warrior was walking in the park, a businessman asked to join him. As they walked along they crossed a beggar, and the man expressed his sorrow for the beggar's plight. Later they passed a cripple, and once again the man expressed his pity for the cripple's condition. The warrior asked the man why he pitied the beggar and cripple. The man replied that he was much better off than they were since he had fine health, money and an education, so he felt he obviously had a far superior life. The warrior responded that the man was jumping to conclusions, based on his biased opinion of what the goal and purpose of life is. Since the man saw value only in money, health and education, then he compared and judged everyone from that limited perspective. Where the man saw only a worthless beggar, the warrior recognized a person leading a life as a spiritual renounciate; and where he saw a useless cripple, the warrior viewed a bright soul devoted to a spiritual life. The warrior suggested that the man was actually worse off than the beggar or cripple, for he was lacking in spiritual understanding, and that his worldly goals and limited view was not sufficient to judge the spiritual tapistry of life.

Comment: Each of us has the same equal chance to abide in our true spiritual nature. It does not matter what the circumstances appear to be, for it is often the appearance of a negative situation that brings one into the most concentrated effort of dedication. In many instances, sincerity is lacking in one's life till external circumstances force one to look deeper into their heart. Every situation a person experiences provides the opportunity for spiritual growth, so we need not pity anyone, for there is much more to the experience of life than just physical well-being and worldly attainments. To pity someone means we are judging them and their situation, but we can have compassion for the difficulty that some must face, for compassion means that we recognize their need for their present condition, and give them our love and understanding. But there is no need to wish their condition to be different, for that is applying our biased conceptual opinion of what we feel to be in their best interest. We are in no position to judge their situation and feel it should be changed, for we are all equal and no one person is superior to another; so we cannot pity anyone, for that would mean that we wish they could be like us, or that their life could be like ours. That form of conceptual judgement only shows our pride, and lack of respect for the evolution that the other person is undergoing. Difficult times often produce the greatest spiritual advances, and we can only compassionately encourage each other and share our love. Without desire or attachment help any person or situation you are guided to share in, but do not pridefully look down and pity your brother, for pity has never helped anyone, but the sharing of love and understanding has always helped, and is the greatest gift we can bestow upon each other.

We must all abide in our true nature, and view the external circumstances of life from this attitude, and thus see a higher value and purpose in life.

Altered States of Thought

A warrior's greatest accomplishment is his freedom from attachment to body or thought, and he seeks no external means to gain realization.

One belief throughout the ages has been, that for one to be a spiritual master he had to be an adept in the ways of powers or visions, and his acknowledgement as a master usually came only with his demonstration of abnormal powers. This notion continues to linger on thru ignorance and fear, and is a very damaging concept that all spiritual souls must examine.

My point here is not to debate the existence of supernormal powers, for it is true that these powers are manifested by some people, but in no way do these powers play any role in the life and ways of a spiritual warrior. Spiritual enlightenment does not come by powers, visions or psychic experiences, or is it maintained by them. Realization comes by relinquishing desire, concepts and illusory thought, and simply and attentively living the moment. Selfishness is at the root of all powers, for they are motivated by desire, thus they are always surrounded by an ugliness of greed.

Powers are a very simple affair; anyone able to intensely focus their attention will gain control over their thoughts, and be able to use their awareness in dynamic ways. Our thought is backed by the energy of the mind, and any focusing will affect all other forms of energy by the intensity of its conviction. Our attention focuses our inherent power by the intent of our motivation, thus a person who is strong of will, and pure and compassionate of heart will often have healing powers.

But having a special power has nothing to do with the wisdom of knowing how to use the power, or does it have anything to do with

gaining realization of one's true nature. Every
warrior develops some type of power, for it is
just a consequence of his strong, purposeful life.
The power will come and go, and it should be
regarded as equal to all other aspects of this
miraculous experience, for all life is incredible,
and no one aspect is any greater than another.
To use any power is to open the door of desire,
and become attached to the results they bring,
for once the temptation is succumbed to, it is
incredibly hard to resist. There are always
underlying results from using powers that
cause unforeseen problems for everyone concerned,
and often have the effect of working the opposite
of the desired result in the long run. Powers
center around thought, and the ego that the
warrior fought so hard to subdue, will rise
again in new clothes and stronger illusory
force. Any power is best left alone, for your
freedom is at stake, and the temptation of
praise, wealth and pride are deadly to the
ways of a warrior.

  Another misconception is that one can gain
realization thru the use of drugs. No lasting
insight or sustained Truth of our spiritual nature
comes from the use of any external means.
Freedom has no attachments, and once one is a
warrior, he has no need of any external source
to find communion within himself. His realization
is within him, beyond all attainment, concepts
and thought, and also beyond this manifestation
and all externals used to manipulate or control
his physical being, for his realization is the very
essence of his spirit. Any external means used
to gain insight, only brings him down to the
physical level, where his precious spirit slogs
in the mud of desire.

  The use of drugs brings about altered states
of thought, and distorts the relative world, and
lacks the volition and awareness needed for
powers. One is usually not brought into higher

light, but deeper into illusory thought. But here there exists a paradox. Most all people live their life within fantasy, illusion and concept, so when a natural drug is used to alter their normal illusion, there can be a negating effect; and the new illusion produced can be of such a magnitude, that they can experience an expanded relativity, and perceive this manifestation in a new light, and thus be awakened to a deeper reality. It is short term and still thought produced illusion, but it does, on occasion, work the effect of waking some people up to the possibility of a deeper awareness. Most drugs will only harm the body and ruin one's spiritual expression, but there are a few natural plants, that if approached with respect and a pure heart, will produce a short term altered consciousness where relative insights may be present. The use must be restricted to the special circumstances where it will be spiritually beneficial, and the attitude must be one of respect, challenge and freedom. These plants can help to shake one's concepts of attachment and desire, and provide a new space of relevance, but the setting must be natural and nurturing, and if anyone else be present, then they must reinforce this quest into spiritual awakening. This is not the indulgence of over use, but a very special, limited use of a paradoxical method that has provided a field of limited help to ones of indecisive nature. These natural plants have no secret quality of their own, and the experience received is solely determined by the user's attitude and awareness. As soon as some understanding has been effected, and concepts have been loosened, then the use of the plant should be dropped completely, or else an attachment will form, and all insight be dependent upon its use. It is an external method that must be treated cautiously and respectfully for positive results to occur, then it should be dropped, for once attachment and desire forms, it will be very difficult to break away, and thus freedom will be jeopardized. All externals have risks, and cause possible damage to the physical body, so a warrior prefers only his freedom, and will depend on nothing else to arrive at the knowledge of his spiritual reality.

Any form of man produced substance, liquor or drug will not be conducive to a warrior's spiritual ways — they are not beneficial, but only harm the body and dampen the soul. For realization one needs attention and awareness, and to be ever alert as thought decreases, and this moment of opportunity is presented. A drug or liquor induced stupor of no thought does not provide an avenue to realization, or bring an awareness of the moment, but only forgetfulness of one's freedom and the respect for life.

Seek your freedom in the joy of simple living where nothing external is needed to live life fully. The warrior is not dependent upon powers or visions to inspire him, or upon drugs to stimulate him. They all center around thought, and build powerful concepts of dependence, and it is the warrior's effort to drop all these concepts and forms of attachment and desire. His motivating attitude of respect and sincerity is all the warrior needs for his flight of freedom in this experience realm of perception. Ever alert and aware, he uses this world lovingly, for he is dedicated to reaching higher light.

Treatise To The Brave Generation

It is the youth that will lead the way into a new realm; but if they expect to blindly follow the existing dogmas, religions and philosophies, then the same errors of their father and ancestors will be continuously repeated again and again. The brave generation will be the one of no concepts, where their eyes have turned inward, and their outward action is one of non attached sharing for the harmony of the whole. Let the religions go begging for members, for each young soul will rejoice and honor God within the shrine of their heart, and let their daily activities reflect an understanding for the miracle which they are. This earth need not be altered, for it is a heaven of incredible wonder, it is ourselves that need be transformed, so we recognize the blessed opportunity we have to be living in this moment of challenge.

The old eyes are trapped in the past; so it is the youth of this stagnant generation which must rise out of the ashes of past complacency, and build a new society where freedom and spiritual realization is the foundation, and the institutions will rise from this strength, and work for the harmony and mutual benefit of the whole. Be the rebellious ones of inner peace, and forget the old ways of war, hatred, greed, jealousy and revenge, and turn to a loving, sharing, simple way of living. Forget the creeds and concepts of the respected elders, for within you is the wisdom to re-civilize this barbaric land with love and peace, so the truth of our spiritual reality will shine and encompass all our brothers and sisters. We all need to unite within this fleeting moment of miracle, as we harmoniously float on a new tide of consciousness, and dare the ultimate spiritual task of sharing our love unconditionally.

The momentum of the spiritual tide has turned, and the faint cry of the emerging brotherhood of man is now beckoning. Many older brothers and sisters will be giving their energy and prayers to your victory of realization, and traveling with you into this realm of the heart. The old concepts have stagnated and died, so don't let this corpse of dead thought stand in your way. Strive forth into the light of inner truth bravely and full of ideals, fearless in your attempt to find peace and harmony, and stop this nonsense talk of 'the good old days'. Usher in the golden years this splendid earth deserves, as a blossoming of spirit energy, within this miraculous perception that we have been blessed to behold.

Do not be held back, you have the right to freedom — there is no need for you to build chains from society's delusions and selfish motives. Push beyond the concepts, desires and attachments of this self centered world, and into a realm where freedom and love are the motivating forces. It is you that inherits this world, so build it to the dream of your heart and the highest ideals of a free spirit. It is your world now, accept the challenge and adventure of creating it anew, for it is time to harmonize the brotherhood of man into an awakening of consciousness, and a sharing of the soul.

May this worthy task provide you joy and purpose, and may I be blessed to see this blossoming bud of divine love unfold into the magnificence of realization.

My love is with you...

'a spiritual warrior'

255

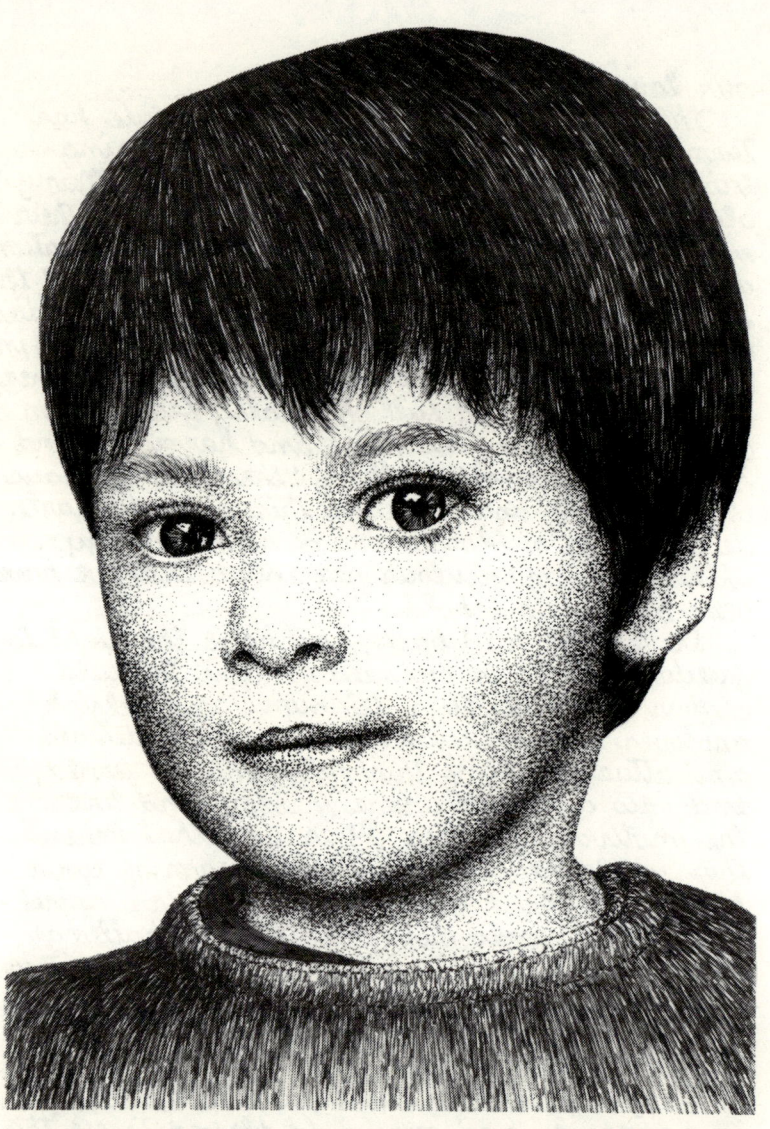

Art Plate #31~ We are the guardians of this
child, and what inheritance shall we leave
him? All of us are equally responsible for
the social concepts held within this world
society, and it is very unfortunate that our
societies structure has been built upon
a foundation of conjecture, fear, prejudice and
greed. The limitations of our social relationship

have risen from the dead ideas and ways of the past generations. How can these ancient books and methods, brought into being by supposition and ignorance, be our sacred guide to order our present lives, for they hold us within their dogma and stagnant ideas, and limit our possibility of growth into realizing our true nature of spiritual freedom.

We must jointly rebuild the concepts within our society, and remove the limitations of which we chain ourself. For even though we are a unique expression of the divine, and must seek for realization within ourself, this world society is very much as an organism which has the ability to set guidelines and limitations upon the tender growth of the blossoming youth. Spiritual growth can either be fostered or stagnated by our collective ideas, and its growth is so fragile that much encouragement and a good fertile soil is always needed. As greater spiritual maturity is found within each individual, we shall be able to build this nurturing environment for the youth to grow unhindered into spiritual expression. This is the greatest inheritance we can leave the next generation — our offering of love, freedom, spiritual integrity, and a deep respect for this miracle enfolding us. We must drop the limited concepts from the past that we ignorantly cling to, and thus we will cease to indoctrinate our children with these dead ideas. Don't leave this child the ignorance of your mind as your legacy, but let us pass on to our children the love of our heart and the wisdom of our soul, and with this bountiful inheritance, they shall never go wanting...

Wanderings of The Heart

Eureka Sand Dunes ~ November 1985 ~

Each november I seek the solitude of the low, arid desert, where the weather is still warm and sunny, and there are no people to disturb my month of indepth meditation. November is my time for inner and outer solitude, and the best place I know for such a spiritual communion is the bleakness of the area around Death Valley. There are many other desert valleys around Death Valley, and one I am especially fond of is Eureka Valley, for it is the most barren area imaginable. And here in its harsh terrain, I find true peace as I explore its canyons under the sun, and walk spellbound in its open desert under the full moon and stars.

At one end of Eureka Valley is one of the largest sand dunes in America, being 700 feet high and stretching for miles. The dunes are pure white, and during the brilliancy of the day they are foreboding, but at night in the full moon, they are lovely and magnificent.

The night was crystal clear as I set out across the low lying dunes. After a mile of giant sand piles I finally reached the base of the main ridge, and here I began my ascent up its narrow backbone, in order to reach the summit of Eureka Dunes. It was a tiresome and frustrating affair to climb the sand ridge, because for each foot I stepped upward, I slid back six inches, and by the time I reached the top I had received quite a workout. But the effort was very worthwhile, for on this narrow ridge that extends the length of the dunes is an avenue of exquisite spiritual experience.

The moon was so brilliant that I could see

the colors of my clothing; and the starkness that surrounded me was the surrealism of jet black and contrasting white. The desert lay 700 feet below, and is scattered with short, dark bushes, so I received a visual distortion making it appear as thousands of feet in depth. As I looked before me, I saw my course stretching for miles along a knife like ridge, with either side dropping abruptly into the darkened depths. Any misplaced step off to one side, and I would go sliding down with no way of stopping; so, carefully I began my traverse along the ridge with the full moon guiding my way.

All at once I heard a loud groaning noise coming from below me — I was puzzled at first, but then realized what was happening. As I walked, my feet pushed a little sand downward on either side of the steep slope, and this little sand pushed more sand, starting a mini sand avalanche which moved dozens of tons of sand, and the friction it caused made a loud, low booming noise, like the deep, base note on a giant organ. Its quite astonishing to be in a place of absolute quiet, and hear this groaning noise follow your steps, with the howling of coyotes intermingled with it. Occasionally I would come upon a beetle walking the ridge in my direction, and leaving bizarre little tracks in the sand — how and why they were up here puzzled me, but then why was I up here; perhaps the beetles also climb the dunes to capture a spiritual experience by full moon.

The walk along the ridge was nearly horizontal, so I picked its highest crest and sat in a meditative cocoon surrounded by total silence. Here on top of this giant pile of sand, with no sense of height, color, time or space, and where sight plays deceiving tricks, I felt I was in perceptional meditation. Even though I was fully experiencing the event unfolding, I still felt as if I was within a meditative consciousness apart from the world of sensory experience. For hours I sat in reverie on the cool sand gazing at the moon, and watching the light patterns change on the cliffs surrounding the dunes. The desert floor had an eerie far away look that didn't invite my return. I was very content listening to the coyotes and the sound of nothing, and occasionally I would reach over and flick a few grains of sand down the side, and start the organ up.

Eureka dunes is a gigantic pile of little, tiny rocks, and one can jump, run and fall, and never get hurt on its rocks. So even though I would have enjoyed remaining on top of the dunes to commune into eternity, it was time to have the fun of jumping down the side into the world of distorted perception. So off I went, running and falling and sliding for 700 feet til I reached the low dunes at the base. It took an hour of hard work to climb, and a few minutes of fun to descend; and now that I was on the desert floor, it seemed warm and nurturing, and it was the enormous stark dunes that appeared so awesome and formidable.

Hours had passed, yet there is no time on the dunes — they are trillions upon trillions of little pieces of white rock that are always in motion, yet the dunes always look the same. Each grain is unique, and it is always in the process of going somewhere, but that somewhere is nowhere. What a miracle it is to walk upon a floating island of rock. The dunes seem so foreign to life, and yet I feel they are alive and moving, with a spirit that I have had the unique chance to commune with. The dunes are a mystery, and on another full moon night I will sacredly place my spirit within its realm, and traverse the breadth of its body, and feel the movement of its soul.

Isn't It Enough

The sea rises,
    and the mountains crumble.
Lightening flashes,
    and the wind roars.
Who am I
    amidst these titanic forces?
Am I just their consciousness
    in active observation of myself.
Who am I
    to be asking of myself.
        Isn't it enough
        to just be . . .

Form Has Value

Within this manifestation, energy has been arranged into form, and the existence of form fits all together very nicely just like the pieces of a jig saw puzzle. It doesn't matter where the form exists, and yet its existence is vital, and wherever it is located is the exact place it should be. All form is unique and dependent upon the surrounding form to hold it within its relative place — thus each form is totally indispensable to each other, and all the energy of form is necessary to arrive at the totality of the manifestation.

All form would be useless if this manifestation had no direction or cohesion. But even though form has only a relative value, its energy is the necessary vehicle of our spirits sojourn of experience and perception. Thus this manifestation has value, and there is order and purpose within this universe, for each form is equally invaluable to complete the totality of the manifestation.

We are all here as form, interacting as energy; and everything is joined together thru out this universe into one harmonious whole. You are important and necessary within this reality as the energy of it, and it is your personal challenge to recognize your intricate and unique role within its totality, and live to the highest ideals of your true spiritual nature. There is only one priority in this experience we call life, and that is to recognize your true nature as spiritual essence, and live this experience of life guided by its light.

Art Plate #32~ All aspects of form contain
the same essence of the Absolute, and
whether we recognize it only goes to show
our degree of consciousness in understanding
the true reality around us. Our ability to
see the true nature in all of life that
surrounds us, provides the avenue of
realization to recognize the true nature
within ourself...

263

Here To Perceive

The mystery of energy surrounds us, but our perception of it is internally induced, and we have been taught how to arrange our perception into a particular order. We have been forced to accept limitation within our life by the biased set of limited concepts that each society uses as its relative standards. We live in a realm of folly, and we are taught how to perceive and arrange this folly so we can be serious about it. From birth we are taught to limit our perceptive field, but there is so much more available to us.

We are spiritual essence of the Absolute, and not sons and daughters of this Earth. We are here to perceive this realm of wonder and allow the gift of life to use us, not for us to see how much we can use it to our twisted sense of desire and attachment. We are here for a brief moment of eternity, and perhaps never again will this opportunity be presented to our spirit. At this very moment we have the ability to perceive this world in an unlimited, unbiased manner, and grasp the subtle energy of this realm, as we explore the myriad possibilities that are contained within us. The challenge of life awaits us, for we are free spiritual beings here to perceive the experience of life's miracle. Our feet may be walking this Earth, but our spirit can perceive the reality of its true wonder. Life is a prayer, and this is your blessed opportunity to make the prayer of your heart manifest for your spirit to perceive.

Art Plate # 33~ Within this manifestion we are surrounded by a quagmire of diversity, but though the wholeness of reality is beyond our view, we can still intuitively understand the unity that brings order to its fragments. But even if we realize the essence of our true nature, as long as we remain within form, we shall never grasp the totality of the undifferentiated absolute ...

265

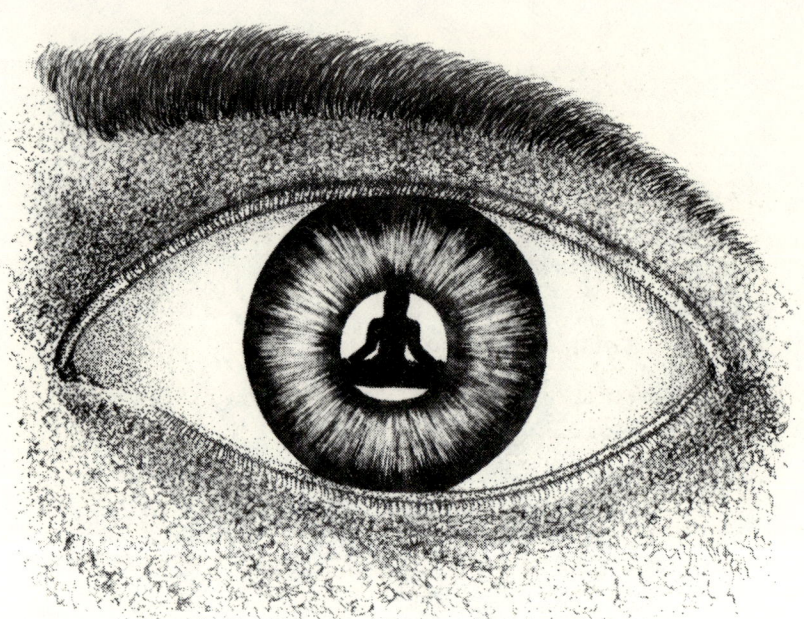

Art Plate #34~ Our eye is only physical—
it perceives, but it is not the perceiver, for
it is our true nature which experiences the
vision of this miraculous perception. Thus
you may see the same realm of my eye,
but not the realm I realize; for it is our
consciousness and attitude within this
realm, that builds our world of interpretation
for each of us. Expand your vision to see
the miracle that lays within your reach...

Through My Windows

Looking out of my windows,
I see this realm of my eye,
a world passing by.

No one tells the wind,
which way to blow.
Planning out the future,
will not make it so.
Watered by the rain,
but will you grow.
    Within this moment, life is to know.

The quail gently coo,
to a life that's free.
Rush to the door,
but have no key.
Striking out blindly,
can you cross the sea.
    Within this moment, just simply be.

The night will pass,
as dawn breaks the day.
Lose the concepts,
let the world slip away.
No thought is needed,
spiritual essence will stay.
    Within this moment, you are the way.

Looking into my windows,
the world sees reflections in my eyes,
but not the realm I realize.

Perceiver in The Mirror

Within this relative manifestation, there is no aspect of its existence that does not express itself equally. All form is within the bounds of a single totality, and as such has a uniform wholeness of its expression. Whether that form be of an animal, rock or tree, it is still within the boundaries of a single reality, and as such has relation to each other and acts as a mirror to all forms of manifestation.

Our society has ordered itself into segments, but it has a common bond of relationship within a collective consciousness. The brotherhood of life goes deeper than form, and if one is to understand their true essence of being, they will have to go beyond concepts of division. Human society has been divided by myriad forms of conceptual thought, and thus has expressed itself thru the actuality of our divided society. But within all the division, there is still recognized certain factors of unity — whether it be a similarity of form or a recognition of a joint consciousness, we still see a brotherhood of human nature.

Our sight falls short beyond this awareness, and most everyone draws a definite line of division between humanhood and all other energy forms within this universe. It is the supreme arrogance of human ignorance that makes our society feel divided from the rest of this manifestation into a special class of grandeur. All manifested form is equal in its true nature; and whether the miracle of consciousness enlivens the form of a human or a tree, it is still the same breath of the eternal which brings a structure of energy into a unified vibration with the opportunity to experience perception, and abide in the miracle of individual uniqueness. All existence expresses itself uniquely as part of the one reality, and even though our form will eventually drop away, the essence of our consciousness will still remain as part of the totality within the whole of its expression.

No structure of Matter within the Absolute is dead. All is in a vibrant expression which brings it into manifestation within the totality. Each expression of consciousness has its own vibratory existence, and will produce a manifested form to match its rate of vibration. Even though a rock is foreign to our concept of life, it has existence within the Absolute, and the Absolute contains no death. The rocks structure has been brought into relative existence, and birth into the relative means it has an ultimate nature of life. The only criteria that need be met for us to recognize life within the limitations of concept, is that there be a structure to its existence — if there is form, then there is the mystery of existence, and all existence is life within the totality — for where would death exist?, and where would the structure of existence go? There is only one encompassing form, which is the totality of the Absolute, and all is alive within it, and all is in constant movement; for there is only life, and all is equal in its expression.

Within relativity we are forced to divide life into two categories — life we can relate to, and life beyond our limited concepts. Even though all existence is life, we cannot relate to rocks as being alive; but there is no death, there is only the evolution and reordering of life's vibratory expression. All Matter is alive, for it is part of the one totality of conscious existence. But within its ultimate structure we can only relate to certain aspects of its form, and we call these limited forms within our concepts alive. Consciousness cannot dissolve and become dead as we conceptualize it to be, for all manifested existence is energy, and energy is life, no matter what form it may take in producing this living organism we call the universe.

Your consciousness is part of the individuality of your being, but it is just one aspect of the total expression of the Absolute. You are the mirror of existence — your consciousness is the perceiver or viewer of the mirror, and your form is the image within the mirror, and the physical mirror itself is this manifested universe. Both the image, and the mirror itself are alive as existence, but the form within the mirror is of no relative importance. The consciousness of the perceiver varies with the degree of vibratory expression, but no matter what the level of consciousness, both the image and the mirror are most definitely alive. All has life, no matter if consciously brilliant or dull as a rock, or whether the form be beautiful or distorted, for all existence is energy, and all energy is alive. Whether the image in the mirror disappears as a form of consciousness that we can relate to, is of no importance, for the mirror itself will still be in existence and thus alive, and the image as conscious energy will still be contained and alive within its totality. The image may dissolve into its vibratory components as the existence of energy, but it cannot leave the totality of the Absolute. Its form may alter significantly, but its energy as life cannot die out of existence. All images, or forms of existence, will continuously change and evolve, and when conscious energy of a vibratory rate that we can relate to, bonds those elements into a unified structure, then we shall recognize a concentrated life form once again, and thus call it alive and develop a relationship to it.

When you view yourself within this manifested mirror of relative existence, you hold up the mirror we call life and view your image in it. Your true nature is essence of the Absolute, and as you view your image in the mirror of relativity, you will be given the wondrous opportunity to see a unique expression of the Absolute; and whether you see a redwood tree, a coyote or a mystical human, the image is only a form representative of the consciousness within it. Your consciousness will always be in movement as it expands across this universe, and the form it takes will only be its vehicle of expression. Relative death of form in human conceptualization does not alter the reality of your true nature as essence of the Absolute, for form is only our avenue of perception, and not the perceiver himself. All form is life, but the perceiver within the life is your eternal consciousness. Unique and joyous within form, you can perceive the wonder of existence, as you evolve within this realm of manifestation, and abide in the oneness of which this totality is formed. You are the Absolute — be open to the wonder of existence, and observe this miracle unfold before you.

Art Plate #35~ The manifest has come
into being, and it is a bright clear reality.
But within our thoughts and concepts, we
form a reflection of the manifest, and in this

hazy mirror image is found our selfhood.
But this selfhood is not within the original
image of the manifestation, for the manifest
is also a reflection, and within it we abide
in a world of relativity, but this is not the
true reality. Our true nature is one with
the absolute, and the manifest is within
this essence — we are not its reflection, but
rather it is our reflection. We are one with
the totality, and our reality is beyond the
mirror and its reflection — our true nature
is beyond thought, concept, a selfhood and
even the manifestation, for our reality is
pure essence of the Absolute itself ...

273

Into Manifestation

To swim one must get into the water ...

There is only one totality and that is the Absolute. We are essence of this totality and all manifestation is an aspect of it. As pure, undifferentiated essence, the Absolute cannot experience itself, so it manifests a form and immerses itself within it. Thus a relationship is formed and the Absolute is able to acknowledge itself. The Absolute is pure existence, but till it manifests into being and recognizes its Godhood, then it cannot be conscious of its own essence. We are that form the Absolute has manifested, but our spirit is pure essence of the Absolute, and only because we are in manifested physical form, can we, as the Absolute, be conscious of our true nature. Thus our spirit has adopted a selfhood, but that relative self is only created illusion, to enable our true nature to acknowledge itself – a necessary game of coming into being, to even know that we have existence.

To know of one's freedom, there must exist boundaries and limitations. All perception within the manifestation is only a mirror, reflecting its ultimate existence as essence of the Absolute. Everything has life within the manifestation, and all within the manifest has awareness of its life, thus the Absolute as the totality of all existence is aware of itself. The Absolute has come into being within an illusion of time and space, and now it is aware of its being, as the consciousness of itself, and it uses this created limited form to establish a relationship within its awareness.

One drop of water cannot fathom the

totality of the ocean, yet the ocean encompasses the drop, and all the individual drops form a relationship within it, and this aspect of individual relation forms the totality and consciousness of the ocean. Thus with our relative sight we do not see zillions of individual drops of water, but look upon the ocean as whole; and likewise, one with true spiritual sight will not see you or I as individual forms, but view the Absolute as whole, for all existence is its essence and there is only one totality. And we are as one drop in this ocean of existence, and though we cannot fathom the totality of our essence, we can have awareness of our true nature, and thus be the consciousness of the Absolute.

The universe is enormous in size in relation to our limited perspective, but this manifestation is only a mirror of illusion, and actually has no size in relation to the Absolute. Time and space are aspects the absolute has adopted, but their existence is a reality only as long as it maintains them. Only one essence has ultimate existence, and that is the Absolute, everything else is its mirror of relativity, and can only reflect the absolute as it chooses it to. Our core of spiritual reality is essence of the absolute, thus our true nature is not a mirror of the Absolute, but the actuality of it.

To know of its Godhood, the Absolute observes itself within its manifested mirror of perception. Since all existence is the absolute, then everything within manifestation is an aspect of its Godhood. We are spiritual essence of the Absolute, and we have come into existence to become ourself as God; and here in this realm we shall evolve, until we recognize ourself as God in manifestation. But after this recognition of our true nature, no further realization

275

can exist, for beyond thought, concept and awareness we can only abide in our true essence, but never actually understand it. Within relativity we can know of our true nature of existence, but beyond this relative manifestation our essence will unite into the undifferentiated Absolute, and we will no longer know of our Godhood — for in purity the Absolute 'is', but does not know that it 'is'. The Absolute is the totality and we are part of it, thus we can know nothing, and yet we can be everything, and all we need do, is to know ourself.

Today I looked
for a speck of dirt,
but nothing could I find,
for I was blinded
by the dust,
blowing in my eyes.

Art Plate #36~ This manifestation is the flow of conscious energy, and all existence within it is in the process of continual evolution. All life flows back into its source, but within the undifferentiated Absolute there is no individuality possible. So to our home we sojourn, only to rise once again in manifested form, and fall into perception as the individual expression of our desire — and here we cascade within the relative, only to reach our origin once again. But nothing has left the Absolute, for whether we flow as individual aspects, to enable us to recognize our own existence, or be whole within the reality of our essence, there still remains only one encompassing totality. We are the living water of conscious energy, no matter if we be flowing in form as individual awareness, or abiding as the ocean of non dualistic reality, for there is only one totality, and we are its essence . . .

The Valiant Search

There is only one way to find your true self, and that is to stop looking. But one cannot stop looking, until they have made a valiant search. We each must do everything necessary to satisfy our concept of what is needed to gain realization, for until we fulfill that concept, our mind will not feel that we have done our optimum, and stop its outward search. Every effort must be made, just to arrive at the realization, that what we thought we needed to do, turned out not to be a necessity to abide in the reality of our true self. No method, technique or ritual can bring one into realization, but they will bring a serenity of mind, and provide the knowledge of what has value upon their path. For until we know what the illusory aspects of our path are, then we cannot abide in the simplicity of our spiritual nature. Any warrior can share his understanding of how to realize your true self, but our heart will not accept second hand information concerning its awakening. It must find out this truth for itself, by searching after its own self, until it eventually discovers that there is nothing to seek. So the glorious hidden goal turns out to be the plain fact, that our self nature as a spiritual being is in no need of discovery. Thus we slowly come to abide in the wisdom and tranquility of our true nature, and finally realize that the only value of the grand search, was to discover that no search was necessary.

Parable ~ The Mountain Priest

A man studied in a monastery most of his life, but could realize nothing. He was sincere and dedicated, but just couldn't let go of the world. He heard of another priest who was similar to him, that had traveled deep into the Himalayas to gain enlightenment. The man decided to find the priest and ask for guidance. The journey was exceedingly difficult, and it took him several years of searching the vast mountains, but finally he discovered the priest. Overjoyed he knelt before the priest and explained how he had come thousands of miles to ask for his guidance. The priest dryly said, "so you've come thousands of miles, big deal, in that time the earth has raced millions of miles; so why come to me, I'm as stupid as you are." The man was shocked, this was so unexpected and just crazy, but then he noticed the compassionate smile on the priest's face, and suddenly understood his meaning. The priest had also done the same journey of racing around to nowhere, pushed ever onward by his desire and attachment, and yet he had never arrived anywhere, for there is no where to go. And in recognizing his stupidity, the priest indicated that all knowledge and understanding is relative — thus looking for a higher knowledge can be seeking into deeper ignorance. The priest then added further, "all existence is transitory and relative — there is no stability or goal, and the only wisdom is to not follow the ignorance of another. It is the wise man who can learn from another person's folly and not repeat the same folly for themself. You already possess everything necessary for this extravagant journey of life, so sit here in peace and let the world race without you.

Parable ~ The Subtle Truth

On he walked thru the vast wasteland, his search went on forever; but the goal of Truth is worth any effort. So on he went, looking thru every land of Consciousness, and finally across the sea of Illusion. At last he found the beautiful island of Perception, and there, Hope led him to the valley of Sight. There, at long last, he stood before the written Truth. With his own two eyes he could now read of the ultimate truth of reality. So he approached closer to read, and there before him, written as plain as could be, was the supreme Truth, written in braille.

Comment: Truth is subtle, for we ourself are the truth we look for. Spiritual sight is not a faculty for looking, for the ultimate truth cannot be written.

If a man be spiritually blind, how can he see the truth; yet if he gains spiritual sight, what truth does he think he'll find within a realm of perception. For no truth can be understood, if it need be sought after; and no depth will be found in truth, if it must be deciphered.

We are the truth, and if you need to look for it, or have special faculties to comprehend the truth, then the truth your after isn't your true nature, but only concepts of your thought. Stop looking for the truth, sit still and be the truth.

Art Plate # 37 ~ Purity is Primal ...
Our spirit dances into this realm of maya,
    where concepts weave
      a web of ignorance around us.
In innocence we laugh at our ignorance.
Thru effort we gain knowledge
    to replace our laughter.
Thru no effort we find understanding,
    as purity rises to channel our wisdom.
Once again we are primal,
    but alas we are tired;
and the journey will be repeated,
    until we can abide in peace,
      within the purity of our heart...

Realize Your Ignorance

We are all in ignorance, but ignorance is like the ocean, for it has depth. A man of wisdom floats near the surface of his ignorance, while a gross worldly man is so deep within his illusions and concepts that it would take a submarine to fathom its depth. But while here in this relative world of perception we all will float in the sea of delusion. We can gain some understanding within relativity, but this is just ignorance within reality, thus enlightenment is just a word used to describe someone less ignorant than yourself. Desire within this relative world keeps us submerged in ignorance, but without some degree of desire and attachment to the world of form, there would be no way of relating to this manifest perception, and death of body would result. No matter what degree of realization, there still remains some desire and attachment, and thus some ignorance; and this continually blinds us of our true nature, and living the realization of it fully.

A warrior recognizes his ignorance and humbly accepts it. He does not pretend to have any answers; he sincerely lives this moment to the fullest, and rejoices in the opportunity to do so. His ignorance as well as all life in this perceivable world is a mystery to him, so he joyously accepts this miracle as his grand challenge of adventure. This is the realm of experience, and even though he cannot fathom or explain it, he can live it with gusto while the mystery spins around and thru him. He sees the wonder of existence, and wishes to share this humble realization with all; and even though life is a solitary journey, he always has his ignorance to sit by his side.

Parable ~ Sit or Spin

A traveler was crossing a forrest, when he saw a monk under a tree meditating. They look at each other compassionately, so the Traveler said, "my brother, why sit all day in a vacuum. This world is magnificient, and I've seen wonders on my travels to inspire the heart and keep my true self in firm contact with reality. Life is more than just sitting, come with me and see the richness of life, and experience this unique chance to live." The monk replied, "I am a spiritual Traveler, and the wonders I've seen are beyond this realm of perception. The world is illusion, and I'm content to abide within the reality beyond this manifestation. Why do you spin a web of delusion, when you can dwell in the true nature of your being."

Comment: Who is the one in ignorance? We all are. Life is so precious, but who is to say where ignorance lies and reality begins. If one says he knows, then you can be sure that he doesn't, for this world has given us the blessed gift of ignorance.

This miracle of life contains no path or goal, so there can never exist 'one' correct way of living life. We each are a unique expression of life's mystery, so our way of life must be reflective of the truth of living for ourself. This reality of life has no bounds, and each individual represents one aspect of the unlimited possibilities which forms the totality of the Absolute. We need only be true to ourself and allow our freedom to express itself uniquely, and encourage our brothers to likewise follow their heart, thus we shall all be able to share in oneness within the reality of our true nature.

Understand

If we only understood our ignorance.
We have the opportunity to experience
freedom within a realm that accepts it.
But how little we live this moment of
freedom, and instead embrace our ignorance
of useless thought. On we chatter and
ponder, spinning our web of delusion and
fear. This moment is the wisdom of the
ages, and we can live in this sanctuary
of serene insight, if we but peacefully
abide in the reality enfolding us, and
respectfully understand our ignorance.

We spin round and round
   within this realm,
   and no matter
   which way we turn,
   we'll always run
   straight into ourself.
The world is for understanding,
   and nothing more . . .

Art Plate # 38 ~ I told the whole world the secret of purity in a clear, spiritual language. But the world speaks in tongues of desire, thus they miss my meaning. My words will have no value, as long as man chooses to remain deaf and blind to his true spiritual identity...

Parable ~ Two Visitors

A Zen Master was once visited by a very distinguished scholar. The master asked, "where are you coming from?" The guest replied, "from the university where I just received a Ph.D. in the study of religion." "And where are you going?" the master asked. "To a college to teach and lecture." "And why do you come here?" the master inquired. "To meet with you and discuss the great knowledge we both have." The master then politely said, "Ah, I see. At this time I am very busy, but will assign the head monk to escort you thru the monastery and arrange for you to have a meeting with all the monks, so you can share your knowledge."

Latter that same day a solitary traveler came by the monastery and asked if he could sit in the garden. The master saw him and asked for the traveler to be brought to his room. When he arrived the master asked, "where are you coming from?" The traveler replied, "I am not coming from anywhere." "Where are you going?" the master inquired. "I'm not going anywhere." "And why have you come here?" asked the master. "I have no idea as to why I am here," replied the traveler. With that answer, the master smiled genuinely and said, "please stay for awhile, I have much to talk to you about, but nothing to say." The traveler replied, "good, because I am deaf and mute, but love to listen." And with that they both serenely sat in meditation.

Comment: Why should the master dismiss the distinguished man of knowledge, and embrace a traveler who is no one? Because knowledge is the study of ignorance, and wisdom is gained only when one understands his ignorance, and drops his knowledge of past, future and self. The knowledgeable man was coming from his concepts and going into his illusion, and he stopped with desire to attain from the master. Thus the master kindly sent him, and his goals, to be with the other monks, so they could all dwell within their search together.

The traveler was a nobody, and thus he was not coming from any concept of a selfhood or proceeding to any illusion of a goal. The past and future did not bind him, but most importantly he did not cling to any thought or concepts in the present, and so he could be perpetually alert to live the moment in true realization. Now the master could speak abundantly from his heart, but had no words or concepts to convey, thus he had only wisdom to share, and not ignorance to preach. The traveler reiterated this wisdom by acknowledging this relative world as illusion, and that there is nothing to gain or lose within it, but that the experience of it is indeed sublime. And in this realization, they both communed in silence.

Serenely Observe

I was laughing today,
  at the funny game
  the world plays.
Till I realized,
  that my laughter
  is the funny game
  that I play.
If you observe this perception
  in thought,
  then you're the world
  being observed.
Serenely watch
  in tranquil contemplation,
  and leave your thoughts
  with the world.

Art Plate #39~ Even though we abide within the sea of experience, it is our consciousness which determines whether we immerse ourself within it, rise above it, or gently allow our reflection to float upon its surface. Our attitude builds our relative world, and though our spirit is free, we have the opportunity to perceive life in any manner our heart chooses. Let your spirit soar free, and perceive this realm as the wondrous miracle that it is...

Who is The One

Within a dream one night, I was visited by two wise, old Chinese monks. We all sat crosslegged upon a wooden floor encircling a candle, and spoke of the deepest realities of life. Feeling that my understanding was complete, I spoke the following words to these two serene souls. "Life is reflective of a deeper reality, and whether this true reality be called God, Tao, Brahman or the Void, life is just a shadow of this truth; and only in coming to an understanding of this reality does one gain perspective into their existence. Life is a mirror, and all reflection in the mirror is the manifested form of existence, and we are that reflected image." The venerable old monk saw my wisdom was not complete, and added one line that startled me out of my dream. He replied, "Yes, this is true, but 'Who is the one holding up the mirror'." I woke immediately with these words ringing in my ears. For several years afterward I meditated upon this poignant statement, and only when I came to understand the essence of my true nature, could I truly realize 'Who is holding up the mirror to this miracle of existence'. Realizations are always personal and grow from within — I wish I could share my understanding fully, but insight cannot be provided externally; I can only encourage each of you to sincerely reach deep into your soul and meditate upon these sublime words, 'Who is The One'...

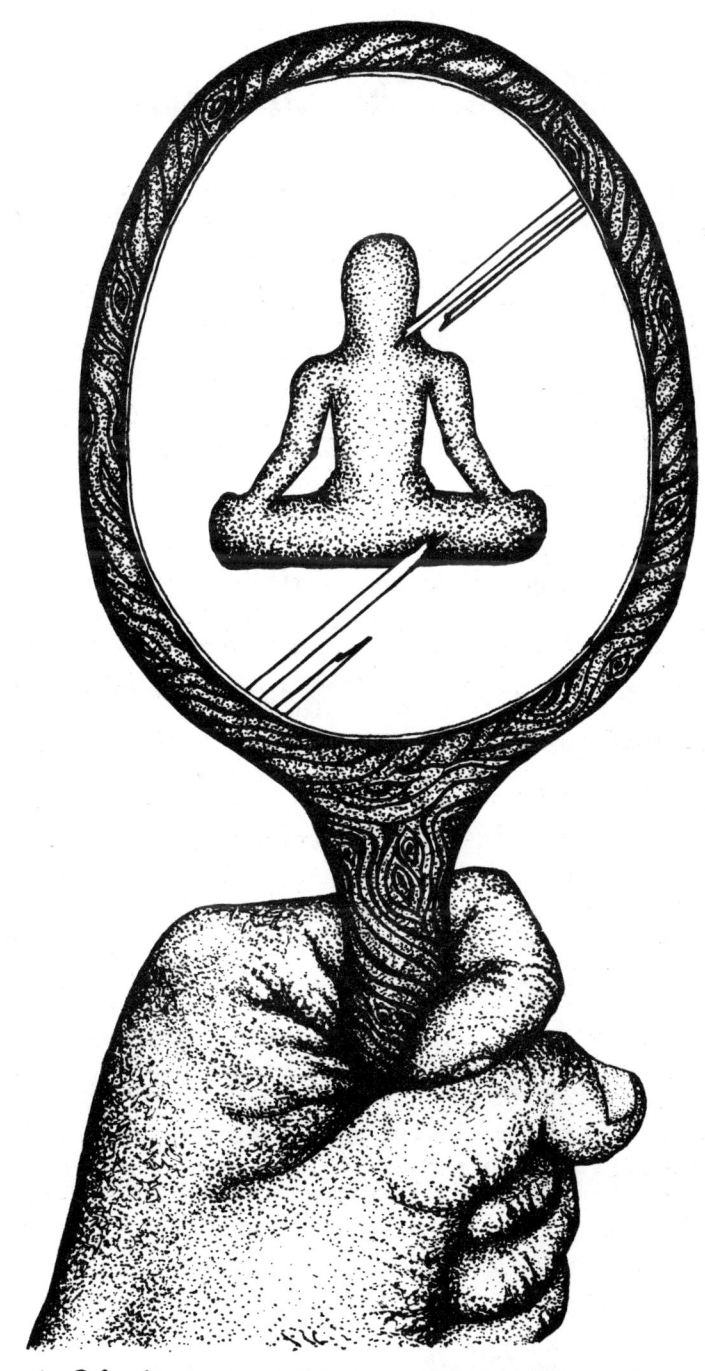

Art Plate #40 ~ 'Who is The One'...

Within The Totality

As spiritual essence within the Absolute,
    I have no needs ...
Without a goal, I have nothing to seek.
Without a path, I have nothing to defend.
Without concepts, I have nothing to cling to.
Without desire, I cannot possess.
Without attachment, I cannot be bound.

    Comparison must fall away ...

Without thought, I am the moment's essence.
Without dreams, my illusion is gone.
Without expectation, I am free in this realm.
Without fear, I can share my love.
Without effort, my true nature arises.

    Reality is its own reflection ...

With simplicity, the wonder is before me.
With purpose, my challenge unfolds.
With awareness, I perceive the mystery.
With attention, I live in consciousness.
With realization, my spirit abides in itself.

    Communion is within the whole,
    freedom is its essence.
    The Absolute 'is',
    and I never was separate.

The Echo of Time

We have lived all of eternity,
    and still we are here.
Where has your effort brought you?
Do you think you're going somewhere?
We walk along each day,
    and yet we never arrive.
If we could but see our course,
    and watch the circles we spin.
The universe has circled us
    for billions of years,
    and still we look outward
    for its source.
Reality has never worn a disguise,
    for its illusion is our very life.
So we choose of relativity,
    for Reality gives no choice at all.
Thus we fear the long journey back home,
    yet its road is the shortest trip possible.
But who is there who wishes to travel,
    and leave their baggage behind.
So the decision is made for us,
    and we shall sojourn again,
    when time stops its echo.
        its echo.
        echo.

        .

Perhaps Never Again

How magnificent is this miracle of perception.
What beauty we have been graced to behold.

My Earth breathes with life,
    as it humbly nurtures my soul.
Its waters glisten as gems,
    as they tumble and cascade around me,
washing my body of light,
    in the crystalline purity of liquid diamonds.
The wind so joyously sings,
    as it flows across my hair.
And in dignity the trees gently dance,
    reaching ever upward for truer light.
Florescent rainbows laugh as they run,
    leaving the rain to cry alone.
While shooting stars fill my heaven,
    as they softly beckon my sleep.

What wonder
    there is surrounding us.
What mystery
    there is running thru us.
What a blessed miracle,
    this moment of perception is.

And in this moment,
    all life is my body,
    and I am its essence.
And perhaps never again,
    will I have the opportunity
    to smell a rose.

Perhaps never again . . .

Wanderings of The Heart

Big Basin State Park ~ April 1981 ~

Forever etched in my mind and sealed within my heart will be the remembrance of one blessed day; for it was the first time I was to experience my spiritual reality, beyond the limitations of my physical body. After this event awakened my consciousness, my life turned from a philosophical and religious speculation, to a dedicated living in the truth of my spiritual nature, for my spirit expressed itself dynamically, and left no room to ponder the possibility of its reality.

The day was incredibly crisp, bright and alive with energy. This days adventure started as dawn cracked the sky, and the mist still lay heavy on the meadow grass before me. The redwoods rose as titans reaching for the clouds, and let their dew fall as little crystalline globes splattering around me. The Santa Cruz redwoods are glorious, and at Big Basin State Park there is a wondrous area of pure virgin beauty.

I set out upon a trail that led me thru the ancient giants, along a meandering stream dotted with waterfalls. Like an ant in the grass, I wound my way thru the gigantic gnarled stumps, as the branches danced in the morning light, within the clouds themselves. What giants my brothers are, and what tales they softly whisper.

My ascent brought me to the highest ridge, and then down into the basin I went. As the valley grew deeper, a trickle of water formed and grew into a pleasing little stream, that cascaded, laughed and danced as we wound our way deeper into the forrests fold. Mile after mile of virgin giants surrounded and embraced my spirit, and as the day grew brighter, the colors exploded before me. The redwood needles made the forrest floor look like it had been manicured as a park, with brilliant green mosses and emerald ferns producing a fresh lushness; and peeping at me like eyes were a variety of fragrant flowers and brightly colored mushrooms. Here was the jungle primordial, and all that was missing were the dinosaurs, but since the beauty of the moment sang forth thru the song of so many forrest birds, my heart felt no lack as it joined the chorus of this lively primal orchestration.

The hours intertwined into one rich moment, and suddenly I found myself at the junction of two small creeks. I now turned upstream and followed the new creek till I reached a magnificent 80 foot waterfall. The little creek splayed out over the moss covered rocks and created hundreds of little rivulets that cascaded down the glistening black rock, and splashed into the large crystal pool below. The redwoods towered far above, which gave this awesome spectacle a cozy feeling, like being within the serenity of a sublime Japanese garden. What a wondrous place Berry Creek Falls is; and I found a perfect rock positioned in front of the waterfall, and there I sat in reverie, and basked in the radiance of its floating mist. Oh how it nurtured me with its energy, and set my spirit free.

With great reluctance and deep respect I offered my loving farewell, and set upon a homeward course. My heart was so light, and my mind at such peace, that I felt as if I was floating along. As I slowly walked beneath the trees, the sun filtered thru the branches, producing an aura of heavenly beauty all around me.

As I stepped into an area of sun lit brilliance, I looked directly up into the light, and suddenly it happened, for in that flashing instant my spirit cast itself free of the body. My body was now foreign to me, for my essence of life was now hovering above my physical form, as an essence of complete awareness. All my surroundings were perceived as a feeling, and yet my spirit was untouched, and had no relation to them. My body below me was as if dead, and I felt no contact or essence of life from it — it was there beneath me, no different than any other piece of earth. The light, energy and vibrancy I felt as I floated above my form, was as nothing I can relate or describe in human terms, for there is no language or relative experience that can convey the wonder and power of the aliveness I felt. For the first time in the memory of my life I truly felt alive, and with no doubt whatsoever possible, I knew this hovering awareness to be my true spiritual essence, and the real life of my being. Here was my true nature in demonstration, and never again could I ever doubt or question what my real existence was. I felt my true self as an encompassing consciousness, and knew that my spirit was the true reality, and that it was totally alive and had no possibility of death. My spirit had accepted my body as vehicle only, but it was pure and untarnished by its use; and at any time my spirit could soar free and unite into the oneness of its pure spiritual essence. The joy I felt was so pure, that it could only be called love, and yet I felt totally unattached to the experience around me, and devoid of any form of desire. My spirit is perpetually free, and in acceptance of my clay body, it has merely slipped on

297

a coat, and now in this brief moment of remembrance, it had stretched its wings within its eternal freedom.

I drifted timeless in eternity, yet on Earth only 15 minutes seemingly elapsed; and now my body, which had been standing as a lifeless statue below, began to topple over, and in a flash my spirit entered back into my form to prevent its falling. How horrible it felt to enter back into this dead piece of cold, dense clay. The shock astounded me, for it felt as if I truly had died, and was being cast into cold cement. The vibrancy and energy I had felt was now absorbed and deadened, and the radiant light I had emitted was replaced by a dull opaqueness. I now felt awkward and encumbered, and was amazed to realize that this physical life is very much as what man has conceived death to be like. Even though I physically felt very well, in comparison to the true vibrancy of life that I experienced as pure spirit, I now felt dead, and knew beyond any shadow of a doubt that our physical body is in no way any aspect of our true life as spiritual essence. Our true nature is a pure essence, and can manifest as pure energy, but to relate within this physical world it adopts a form, and thus we lose the knowledge of our true self, and any feeling of our pure energy of aliveness.

The shock had left me totally numb, and in this state I had no thoughts, and found it difficult to walk and relate. But as time passed and thoughts returned, I slowly started to accept the clay body once again, and eventually I felt the normalcy of this form return. My thought process brought me into relationship, and allowed me to identify with the physical and accept its limitations and deadness.

The experience left my heart exuberant, and yet I was equally sad that I couldn't step out of this form and be free once again. The months slowly proceeded, but my thoughts were captured by the memory of the incredible out of body occurrence, and my heart continually longed to be free and alive again. At this very moment I can still feel the wondrous bliss that I experienced as I floated within my freedom, and I shall never forget what those brief moments felt like and meant. Though this experience of life is quite grand, and even though purpose and challenge abound in this realm, my true home is my spiritual essence, and only it has a reality; for I long to be free and abide in the radiance of its purity. So here I wait in patience, as this relative world spins around me, but ever so soon I will once again soar free, and float in the light of my true spiritual nature...

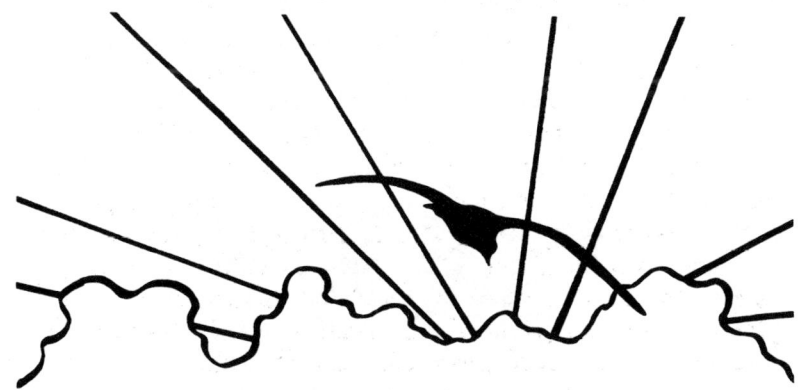

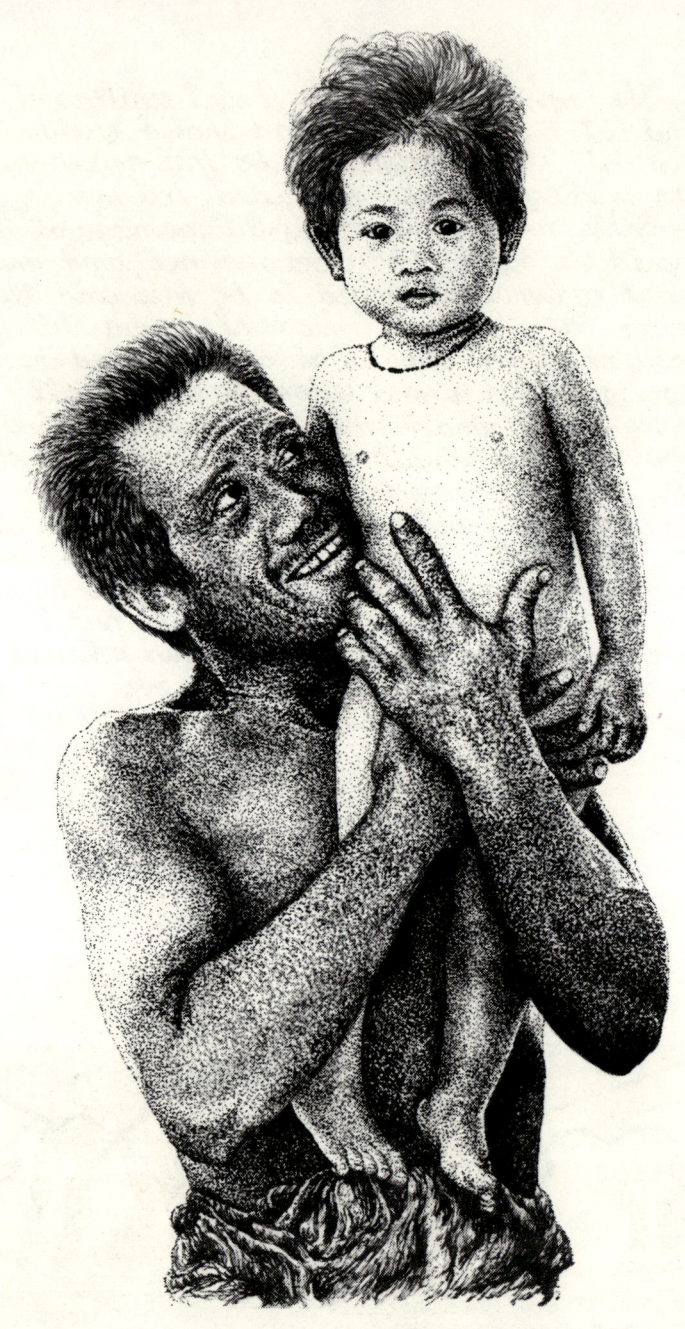

Art Plate # 41~ If I could only give you spiritual understanding. But alas, you must allow this wisdom to be nurtured afresh within you, as you experience this miracle of life. Things of the world I can give you, but they will not last, for they have no permanence. Only your spiritual essence is real, for your true nature cannot perish. But here in this world, you will have the chance to spin within life's dualities, and the only blessing I can give you, is to live my life true to myself; and in so doing, I can only hope that you shall find strength by my example, which may help guide you in your own personal search for truth, as you evolve within the mystery of life's miracle. May you find realization in the reality of your true nature, and be blessed by its truth, for you are the child of life . . .

~ Prelude to 'The Journey' ~

The day was sunny and warm, as I slowly journeyed into the 'wonderland of rocks'. My favorite spot has a ring of large boulders surrounding a raised rock altar, and because of its tranquil power, I call it stonehenge. While in meditation that beautiful day, I opened my eyes and there before me was pen and paper, so I wrote. It is the only time I've ever written while meditating, and I've left it exactly the way I wrote it down on that wondrous, mysterious day.

The words are dedicated to the funny old man in the story — my eternal companion, Swami E.C.

The Journey

I lift my feet and the world spins under me, I place them down and there is a drag created, the world slows and stops under me. I open my eyes and the colors flood my vision, they are pretty; the energy smells nice and sounds pleasant — I laugh and laugh, and my own laughter shakes and distorts the cocoon of energy which engulfs me. My perception is confused and I lift my feet, and the world spins once more. My desires push my feet down once more, and the world stops again. I open my eyes, and shake my head in bewilderment of the vibratory confusion — what silly order in this puzzle. It reaches out and touches me; I shrink away and lift my feet. Thru weariness I lower my feet once more — I have no desire to open my eyes, but still the energy can be felt around me. I glide around, and to my surprise I bump into nothing. I hear noises, but they come from no direction. My faith and hope restored, I open my eyes and see beautiful colors that have no form. I wander for miles and the colors continually change and merge, and please my eyes. I feel fatigued, for the colors give no energy, but extract mine. I lift my feet once more. All the time passes til there is none left. I have no desire to lower my feet, I feel no fatigue — time has stopped, so I have no future hopes or past faith. I am no longer curious. The world bumps into me and stops. I open my eyes, for I have nothing better to do. Nothing is there — I don't care — I don't ask why — I don't walk. The world starts spinning again, but I am not on it, I am in it. It spins around me while I am at its core — my eyes open, but there is nothing to see; I reach out, but there is no contact. I laugh and the world spins distorted; I cry and the world spins contorted; I'm silent and the world spins at peace. I watch — there is nothing to do, it is already done. I smile; peace still is there. I walk, for there is nothing better to do. Other people appear and disappear; they come up to me; I smile at them, they are satisfied; their frowns turn to smiles, they leave and disappear. I am not curious where they go; I walk again. Colors appear and disappear before me — they are not pleasant or unpleasant, they don't last long. I no longer get tired; I walk all day, yet the day is never over; no clocks appear before me. I look to the ground and my feet are not on it, others are disturbed; I put my feet on the ground and smile, they are happy. I try to keep my feet on the surface, the effort is fatiguing, so I stop trying. I see no more people, I see no more frowns — I keep smiling anyways. The forms around me swirl and blend — sometimes I stand and watch, other times I keep walking, but always I smile.

Ahead of me there is a man, his form is not swirling, his clothes are funny and he tells me his name, I cannot pronounce it — I laugh — he does not become distorted, he smiles. He says, "have no concern for being lost." I reply, "I am not lost, I am walking; I do not worry, I have no concerns." He smiles and says, "I am going this way, walk this direction, but I am old and I can not teach you." Then he flies away into the sky. I laugh and laugh. He flies back and smiles at me, and I laugh and laugh more. The world distorts as I laugh, and I do not care. I laugh more and the world explodes and reforms again. Each time I don't recognize anything, but the funny old man who flies back and smiles. I keep walking and observing. I smile, I have no reason not to. I keep walking; I have walked all of eternity and still have not arrived anywhere, but the walking makes me smile. So I walk and I smile, and still I am not lost ...

A Dream

Today I dreamed I was a man,
writing a book about being real.

When I awoke from my dream,
I realized that I wasn't real.

If you understand my little poem,
then you have missed the whole point.

The Veil

I was born with a pure heart,
    a dream within the spirit.
The world enveloped me
    in ignorance,
    but opportunity
    allowed realization to blossom.
Insight had removed
    my veil of ignorance,
    but brought
    a deeper veil of wisdom.
A veil separates,
    whether it be
    ignorance or wisdom;
and our spirit
    needs no shroud.
When our pure heart
    is regained,
    only then
    will we recapture
    the dream ...

In Purity

I came to you
    in childlike purity;
but this was not
    your concept of wisdom.
So you wrapped me
    in a cloak of insight.
But what has it profited me,
    what have I gained.
Now I only have my books
    to burden my pure heart,

        and the laughter
        comes less easy.

    There is quite a difference between
knowledge and wisdom. The knowledgeable
always try to teach you their learning,
feeling this to be wisdom; thus they put you
on their path, feeling they have helped you,
or even saved you. But they have merely
embarked you upon the same ignorance
that they possess. The wise let you be what
you are, and encourage your own self discovery;
for in humility they understand their ignorance,
and know that any attempt to teach will only
pass on their own personal folly—for life is a
personal exploration, and the wise can only
inspire those around them. Knowledge will
always try to rearrange life, where wisdom
knows everything must rest in the purity of
its own true nature.

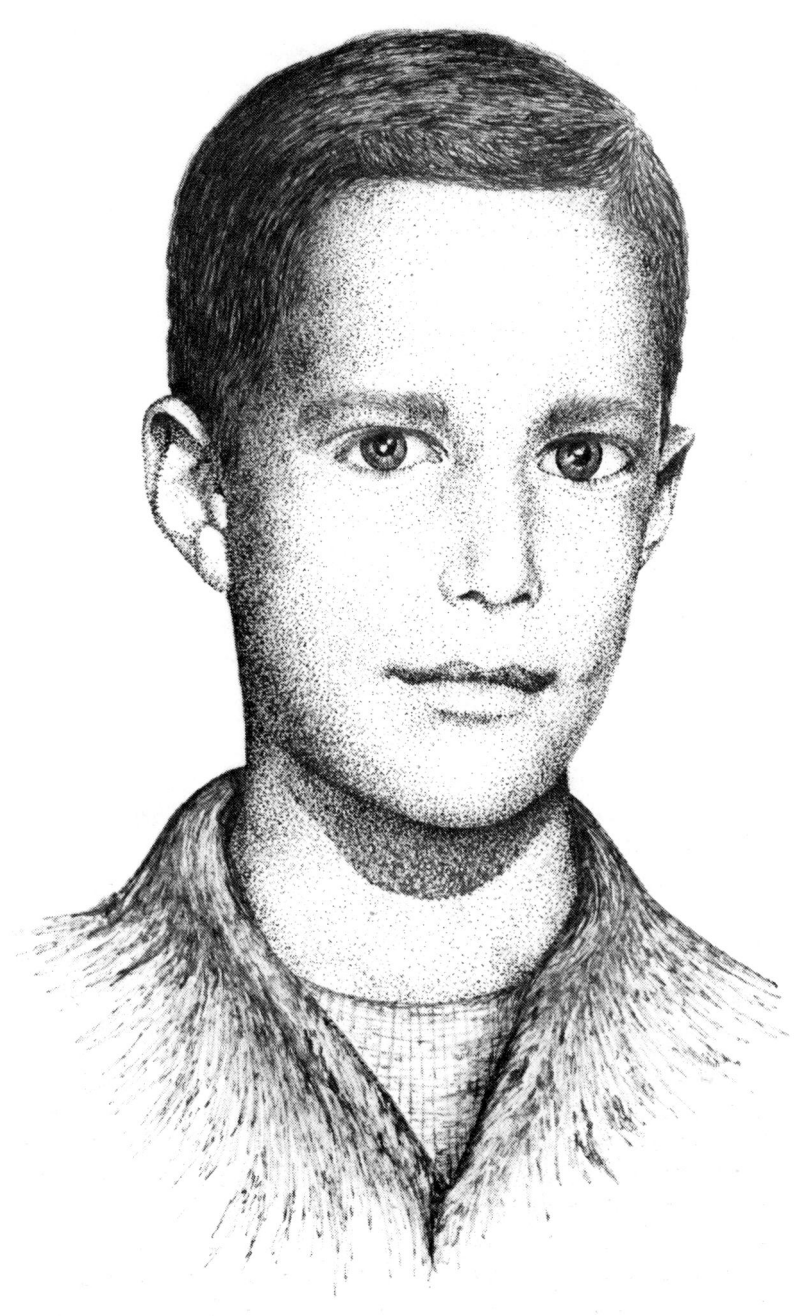

Art Plate # 42 ~ On Purity ...

A Shiver From My Soul

How is it
 that the moon is full,
  yet I am empty.
I hear the lonely
 cry of my heart,
  baying in the far distance.
Yet the direction deceives me;
 and if I look,
  I forget what I seek.
The hours drip on relentlessly,
 splattering upon a fragile thread,
  breaking the silence
  of a lost memory.
Where does this wave take me,
 as the tide ebb and flows
  around me.
The fog serenely rolls in,
 and so easily
  carries me with it.
Though my mind is an anchor,
 it seeks no port,
  as I softly drift
  upon a rolling sea.
How strange is this illusion,
 what an odd dream
  enfolds me now.
But if I wake,
 will I lose
  this fleeting moment.
So on I gently float,
 and let the waves
  crash about me.
And as the storm builds,
 I'll quietly observe,
  as I watch my reflection
  in curiousity . . .

Laughter's Silent Echo

I stand as a tree,
    and let the wind
    strip my leaves away.
This illusory realm is so beautiful.
But more and more,
    it becomes harder
    to maintain interest in it.
Much of the relative
    no longer makes sense,
    and relating is becoming an effort.
The clouds drift by,
    and so easily
    carry me along with them.
I look to the future,
    but if there was somewhere to go,
    then surely I'd be there.
If death was a release,
    I might
    encourage its embrace.
So here I stand
    on the road to nowhere,
    and today my laughter escapes me.

    Even the greatest light,
    will not illume the void.

Parable ~ Rainbow's End

There was a man with a dream. His youth was gone and his health poor, but he wanted to run in the Boston Marathon. He knew he would have to train very hard, so a year before the event, he started running ten miles each day. He felt he couldn't possibly win, but had a hopeful urge that he might if he trained hard enough. His running times were very good, and his health returned to him. The day of the race arrived, and off he ran with the pack. He kept pace with the leaders, and toward the end of the race, he felt so good that he picked up his pace and passed one runner after another. Soon, the finish line lay before him, and he put on his final sprint, but a very strange thing happened. When he crossed the tape, he just kept on running. He knew he had done well, perhaps even won, but as the spectators approached him, he just kept running and disappeared into the crowd. The next day he laughed at his behavior, and when it came time to work out he got suited up, but he didn't run anymore, instead he now walked each day to keep his health along with a new serenity. In time he came to understand his behavior at the end of the race, for he realized that it didn't matter what position he came in, for he had run the race solely for himself.

Comment: Each of us is running the race of our life solely for ourself. There is no finish line or any competitors, just thresholds that mark various arenas of consciousness.

A time comes in the life of everyone that a critical threshold is approached – it is the door of the dream of his spiritual longing. If one embarks into his dream, his only protection will be his determination, and with it he will gain his strength. Once he accepts a spiritual path, then he must train very hard, with every method and technique he finds. He starts with little understanding, but as knowledge increases, he sees the path before him in new, hopeful light, and secretly desires the goal of realization. The race is on in full earnest, and he sprints with the integrity and dedication of his deepening insights, to cross the threshold of no return. On the other side, no one is there to congratulate his victory, for it never took place. We run the race for ourself, and there never was a finish line for the illusory goal. As we realize this paradox, we are too involved in joyously living the moment, to ponder the simplicity of the path that we ran backwards upon — we raced outside for a concept to a goal, and the underlying reality always had existed within us.

Now at home, what do we do? — nothing has changed, it is always time for our spiritual expression, but the pace changes. No longer is there the need to run circles around ourself, now it is time to walk serenely within ourself, but still we keep moving along.

The rainbow's end is no further away, than the dream within your heart...

I ran after a rainbow
with all my might,
to grasp its beauty
as mine.

But I laughed when I realized,
that I was no further away,
as I walked
within this dream of my heart...

~ Prelude to 'The Dream' ~

One star filled night last November I had
a wondrous dream of deep personal
significance. I have recorded it exactly as
it unfolded, and once again it is dedicated
to that funny old man, Swami E.C. ~

The Dream

We flew higher and higher till we reached
the clouds, and then into their fold we went.
On and on we journeyed upward, just to see
how high this airplane would go. "How high
are we?" I asked. "There is no height in the
realm of the clouds," Swami E.C. replied. "The
plane is not even moving anymore," he told
me, "so let's get out and walk."

It was a land of marshmallow softness.
"Come follow me," the Swami shouted, as he
bounded off into the mist. How strange this
realm was, for with each step I traveled so
far, and yet I never went into the cloud
itself. I could jump hundreds of feet with
each leap, yet I never touched anything, and
I always had the strange feeling that the
clouds were just at my fingertips. Nothing
could be seen ahead, as we leaped on and on,
thru valley after ocean of endless white,
fluffy foam. "There is no distance here either,"
the Swami said, as we finally stopped after
an endless sojourn, "and neither is there
time." "What land is this?" I asked. "You'll
find out," the Swami laughed, as he led me
into a chamber within a dense cloud.

There before me was a magnificent room
full of people. It was cozy and so beautiful,
and the atmosphere was serene and nurturing;
and though the room had no walls, it still

was contained, and yet it stretched on forever.
Everyone was doing exactly what they wanted
to do, and harmony filled the air. Some areas
had great activity, and some utter stillness
and quiet, and whatever mood that was in one
spot, didn't seem to drift any further into
another area. It was a room where an
individual consciousness could commune in
any manner it chose, and not be influenced
by any surrounding awareness or attitude – a
land of total self expression, where ultimate
freedom beyond any limitation existed, and one
had the comfort and security to live within a
physical form, yet be beyond its restrictions.

The Swami and I joyously entered this
conceptual heaven, and I at once became
enthralled in participating with all the types
of activities I had always dreamed of joining.
Everyone was perfectly in tune with my
awareness, and each individual was as a
mirror to my very attitude, and reflected
whatever hopes and aspirations I myself held.
I related to one group after another, and each
wanted me to stay with them; thus slowly I
was becoming attached to remaining within this
incredible realm, in some little corner encircled
by the beauty of my dream.

But I became very puzzled as to the
character of the clouds that enfolded this
realm, and this curiosity led me out of the
endless room; and once apart from the room,
I realized that something had disturbed me
about it, and was the real cause that I
didn't stay. It bothered me that everyone
congregated together in one spot, when this
land was of enormous vastness – was there
nothing else besides this one room? could
heaven be limited? and why was everyone
just like me? – was the room really just a
carnival house of mirrors?

So I walked alone thru the vast desert

313

of clouds. Eventually I came upon a group of people; they greeted me warmly and were very pleased that one more soul had seen thru the room of desire, and was now coming to join them in their quest for freedom. They were all dedicated to returning back home, for this realm had trapped them, and they had banded together to systematicly search thru the clouds and find a way to escape it. They were firm, clear, strong individuals, filled with purpose, and deep into the adventure and challenge of their attempt to regain freedom. I was immediately embraced, and told that I could help in their communal search by investigating any direction. I was now part of the brotherhood, and welcome to live in their beautiful little paradise, in an expansive valley of clouds, and we had everything necessary to live in comfort and joy.

But once again I became disturbed — there was much talk of freedom, but no one was actually doing anything besides discussing their ideas. So once again I began to walk, and within seconds I was out of their valley, and beyond recognizable terrain. On and on I walked, and I saw no one in search of freedom. The vastness stretched before me unbroken for all of eternity, for there was no dimensions here, and neither was there time or restrictions.

I walked till I realized that there was no where to go. I had not come from a land of freedom, and this realm was not one of freedom either, for I was still within the limitations of freedom itself. Freedom surrounds a thought, and it can be within bounds or outside of bounds, but either way freedom is just an illusion. My airplane took me into my desire and attachment, and there I found freedom in both, so freedom is just my concept also. So now I stand alone, gazing upon a dream that is only an illusion of myself, and since there is no where to go, I might as well keep walking...

All of eternity I have walked,
and still I've never arrived.
Perhaps the Swami is walking also,
for neither of us are lost...

There is no freedom in a land of limitation, but within a realm where limitations are removed, there you will find no freedom either. Freedom needs limitations and boundaries to be understandable, but it cannot exist in such an atmosphere, for within the physical all freedom is relative and limited. But beyond limitations and boundaries, freedom has no meaning, and thus no knowledge of its reality can exist. Within the world, freedom is an illusion; and beyond the world, freedom is a dream.
If you can conceive of freedom, you can live in inspiration, for to touch its dream is our highest hope...

The Way of one Warrior

When a spiritual book is written, the author's life becomes of paramount issue to determine the validity of its depth. Since I have told of a distinctive way of living, then it is important that I tell a little about my life, so the reader can discern for himself if I live my words, or merely write my fantasies.

Never has there been a better time, or more conducive place to be free - right now, right here - this is my warcry, and my call to freedom. My way of life is in simplicity of living. I have built a small home on wheels - a remodeled van with a raised roof and fifteen windows and skylights. It is serene and full of love, and while in my temple, I'm surrounded by the glories of nature. I move slowly around the western states, picking a new looping course each year. The variety of scenery out my windows is astonishing, as I thoroughly explore the national forests, parks, monuments, BLM lands, redwoods, desert canyons, and the ocean; and after so many years of living within its wild beauty, I have come to know this land well and love it deeply. I hike nearly every day into the primitive lands of this vast country, traversing over 2,000 miles each year on and off of trails, as I explore the rugged terrain of the wilderness on its terms.

Occasionally I visit a small town for needed supplies, but my attempt is at self sufficiency. I grow much of my food in my van, and make some of my clothing, and built the van completely from scratch, including every item in it. I've versed myself in most practical trades, so that I can help and share as I travel, and have also acquired skill at many forms of art and physical expression. I am quite sociable, but out in the isolated areas of nature's beauty, there are few souls to commune with. Even though I travel alone, my eyes are turned inward and my heart is ever joyous in communion with nature, so there is no lonliness.

I own no home, property, animals or people, and the few simple possessions I need are all contained in my van. I have no permanent address, phone, bills or consistent place to visit. I am unattached to the few possessions I have, and feel no pulling desire to travel or remain in one spot, for my spirit is free and takes this body with it. I love life, but have no desire to cling to it, thus my body is on friendly terms with my death.

I have no age or name, and take full responsibility for my health and all my actions. I belong to no organization or group, or any segment of society, and watch no television, nor listen to the radio, nor read newspapers or magazines. I own no clock or make any plans, but let the surrounding circumstances dictate my actions, and allow the weather to dictate the course of my travels. I have nothing pending in my life, and no where I need to go, so consequently I'm not in any hurry. I have no path, goal or expectations, thus I am free and unattached to the objects and situations surrounding me.

I'm ever alert to share whenever the situation presents itself, but I do not go looking for opportunities to help. I have nothing to give anyone, and nothing to ask of anyone, but I love to share what my spirit dictates, without desire, attachment or expectation, and then move along. If any of my experiences prove beneficial to others, then I am joyous to share, but if not, then I will continue my solitary sojourn within the realm of my heart. I am completely alive, happy, joyous and free within this miraculous realm.

I wish you peace...

Art Plate # 43 ~ We are not separate from the web we weave. As long as we have a physical nature, then we shall dance within this game. But if your only priority be of spiritual realization, then even thou you sit within the web, it shall not bind you...

Final Comment

Nothing is final. Finality means the end of your path, and all paths are illusion. There is only this now and present moment, and the totality of it is right here, all else is concept. The end of a path, or the death of life has never existed, only a constant renewing and reordering of existing energy within a realm of mystery. You are blessed to be on a never ending, perpetually evolving, miraculous adventure of experience. What greater challenge could you ask for, what greater freedom could you receive. The warrior calls this 'the road to nowhere'...

To my Brothers and Sisters ~

This book can only vaguely represent who I was, when I wrote it, for a book is only an edifice to a dead idea – nothing is stable. Life proceeds, and the book itself is the evolutionary vehicle for the author, and its validity holds greatest value in his unfoldment to realization. I am who I am, right now and right here – everything else is my shadow of illusion ~

For those who have love in their heart, and respect in their soul, I provide an address for you to correspond with me, and share the communion of your spirit. Since I will not be stopping the traveling style in which the joys of my freedom are expressed, I have obtained a P.O. Box, and will have mail forwarded as I travel. Mail will only arrive to me every few months, so there may be a long delay from the time your letter is sent, til my reply is mailed. I sincerely welcome all letters from those who are dedicated to realizing greater consciousness, but please do not waste our precious, irretrievable time by writing to me about the triviality of the world, for my life is totally dedicated to spiritual realization alone ...

A Spiritual Warrior
P.O. Box 7012
Halcyon, Calif. 93420

I would greatly enjoy hearing from any joyously, sincere spiritual warriors. Within this universe the suns light the void, yet seldom collide – may we sit in joyous communion within the gazebo once again ...

~ LOVE ~